Buying a Home
in
Bulgaria

A Survival Handbook

by
Dougal Robertson

SURVIVAL BOOKS • LONDON • ENGLAND

First Edition 2006

Copyright © Survival Books 2006
Illustrations and maps © Jim Watson

Survival Books Limited
26 York Street, London W1U 6PZ, United Kingdom
☎ +44 (0)20-7788 7644, 🖷 +44 (0)870-762 3212
✉ info@survivalbooks.net
💻 www.survivalbooks.net
To order books, please refer to page 307.

British Library Cataloguing in Publication Data.
A CIP record for this book is available
from the British Library.
ISBN 1 905303 02 5

Printed and bound in Finland by WS Bookwell Ltd

ACKNOWLEDGEMENTS

I would like to thank everyone who assisted me in the writing of this book, both in Bulgaria and in the UK: the staff of Barrasford & Bird for information on the Bulgarian property market; Georgiev, Todorov & Co for information on the legal aspects of buying and Bulgarian tax law; Bulgarian Dreams for guidance on what to buy and where; and of course the people of Bulgaria for sharing their wonderful food, wine and culture. Thanks also to Joe Laredo for his precision editing and ability to spot an inappropriate turn of phrase, Kerry Laredo for laying out the text and producing the index, and (last but not least) Jim Watson for his excellent illustrations, cartoons, maps and cover design.

TITLES BY SURVIVAL BOOKS

Alien's Guides
Britain; France

The Best Places To Buy A Home
France; Spain

Buying a Home
Abroad; Australia & New Zealand;
Bulgaria, Cyprus; Florida; France;
Greece; Ireland; Italy; Portugal;
South Africa; Spain;
Buying, Selling & Letting Property (UK)

Buying and Renting a Home
London; New York

**Foreigners Abroad: Triumphs
& Disasters**
France; Spain

Lifeline Regional Guides
Brittany; Costa Blanca;
Costa del Sol; Dordogne/Lot;
Normandy; Poitou-Charentes;
Provence/Côte d'Azur

Living and Working
Abroad; America;
Australia; Britain; Canada;
The European Union;
The Far East; France; Germany;
The Gulf States & Saudi Arabia; Holland,
Belgium & Luxembourg; Ireland;
Italy; London; New Zealand;
Spain; Switzerland

Earning Money from Your Home
France; Spain

Making a Living
France; Spain

Other Titles
Renovating & Maintaining
Your French Home; Retiring Abroad;
Retiring in Spain;
Rural Living in France;
Shooting Caterpillars in Spain;
Surprised by France

Order forms are on page 307.

WHAT READERS & REVIEWERS

When you buy a model plane for your child, a video recorder, or some new computer gizmo, you get with it a leaflet or booklet pleading 'Read Me First', or bearing large friendly letters or bold type saying 'IMPORTANT – follow the instructions carefully'. This book should be similarly supplied to all those entering France with anything more durable than a 5-day return ticket. It is worth reading even if you are just visiting briefly, or if you have lived here for years and feel totally knowledgeable and secure. But if you need to find out how France works then it is indispensable. Native French people probably have a less thorough understanding of how their country functions. – Where it is most essential, the book is most up to the minute.

LIVING FRANCE

Rarely has a 'survival guide' contained such useful advice. This book dispels doubts for first-time travellers, yet is also useful for seasoned globetrotters – In a word, if you're planning to move to the USA or go there for a long-term stay, then buy this book both for general reading and as a ready-reference.

AMERICAN CITIZENS ABROAD

It is everything you always wanted to ask but didn't for fear of the contemptuous put down – The best English-language guide – Its pages are stuffed with practical information on everyday subjects and are designed to complement the traditional guidebook.

SWISS NEWS

A complete revelation to me – I found it both enlightening and interesting, not to mention amusing.

CAROLE CLARK

Let's say it at once. David Hampshire's *Living and Working in France* is the best handbook ever produced for visitors and foreign residents in this country; indeed, my discussion with locals showed that it has much to teach even those born and bred in l'Hexagone. – It is Hampshire's meticulous detail which lifts his work way beyond the range of other books with similar titles. Often you think of a supplementary question and search for the answer in vain. With Hampshire this is rarely the case. – He writes with great clarity (and gives French equivalents of all key terms), a touch of humour and a ready eye for the odd (and often illuminating) fact. – This book is absolutely indispensable.

THE RIVIERA REPORTER

A mine of information – I may have avoided some embarrassments and frights if I had read it prior to my first Swiss encounters – Deserves an honoured place on any newcomer's bookshelf.

ENGLISH TEACHERS ASSOCIATION, SWITZERLAND

HAVE SAID ABOUT SURVIVAL BOOKS

What a great work, wealth of useful information, well-balanced wording and accuracy in details. My compliments!

THOMAS MÜLLER

This handbook has all the practical information one needs to set up home in the UK – The sheer volume of information is almost daunting – Highly recommended for anyone moving to the UK.

AMERICAN CITIZENS ABROAD

A very good book which has answered so many questions and even some I hadn't thought of – I would certainly recommend it.

BRIAN FAIRMAN

We would like to congratulate you on this work: it is really super! We hand it out to our expatriates and they read it with great interest and pleasure.

ICI (SWITZERLAND) AG

Covers just about all the things you want to know on the subject – In answer to the desert island question about the one how-to book on France, this book would be it – Almost 500 pages of solid accurate reading – This book is about enjoyment as much as survival.

THE RECORDER

It's so funny – I love it and definitely need a copy of my own – Thanks very much for having written such a humorous and helpful book.

HEIDI GUILIANI

A must for all foreigners coming to Switzerland.

ANTOINETTE O'DONOGHUE

A comprehensive guide to all things French, written in a highly readable and amusing style, for anyone planning to live, work or retire in France.

THE TIMES

A concise, thorough account of the DOs and DON'Ts for a foreigner in Switzerland – Crammed with useful information and lightened with humorous quips which make the facts more readable.

AMERICAN CITIZENS ABROAD

Covers every conceivable question that may be asked concerning everyday life – I know of no other book that could take the place of this one.

FRANCE IN PRINT

Hats off to *Living and Working in Switzerland*!

RONNIE ALMEIDA

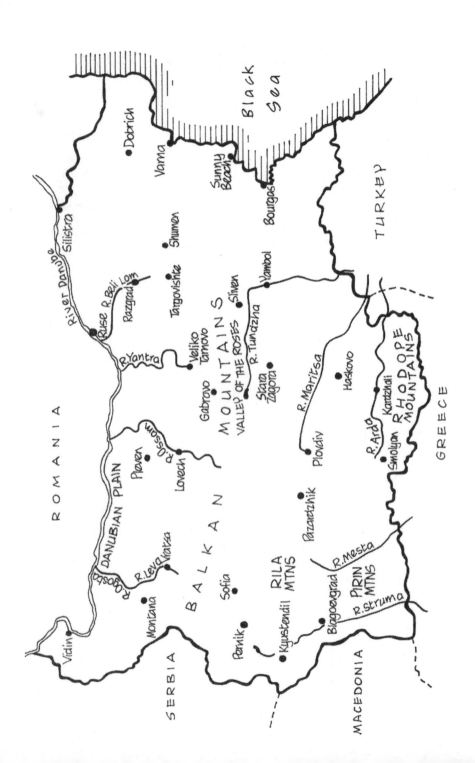

CONTENTS

APPENDICES   275

INDEX   297

ORDER FORMS   307

IMPORTANT NOTE

Bulgarian laws and regulations regarding buying and letting property are liable to change periodically – especially with Bulgaria's impending accession to the European Union (scheduled for 2007). We cannot recommend too strongly that you check with an official and reliable source (not always the same) and take expert legal advice before paying any money or signing any legal documents. Don't, however, believe everything you're told or read – even, dare I say it, herein!

To help you obtain further information and verify data with official sources, useful addresses and references to other sources of information have been included in all chapters and in Appendices A to C. Important points have been emphasised throughout the book in bold print, some of which it would be expensive or foolish to disregard; ignore them at your peril or cost. Unless specifically stated, the reference to any company, organisation, product or publication in this book doesn't constitute an endorsement or recommendation.

THE AUTHOR

Dougal Robertson was born in the United Kingdom but at the age of two moved to Australia, after a brief stint in Oman. After graduating with a degree in journalism and a postgraduate diploma in international relations, he worked as a writer, music journalist and publicist for several years in Melbourne. After working in London for four years, he travelled extensively throughout eastern Europe. He now lives in Sydney, where he works as a freelance journalist.

AUTHOR'S NOTES

- Frequent references are made in this book to the European Union (EU), which comprises Austria, Belgium, Cyprus, the Czech Republic, Denmark, Estonia, Finland, France, Germany, Greece, Hungary, Ireland, Italy, Latvia, Lithuania, Luxembourg, Malta, the Netherlands, Poland, Portugal, Slovakia, Slovenia, Spain, Sweden and the United Kingdom, and to the European Economic Area (EEA), which includes the EU countries plus Iceland, Liechtenstein and Norway.

- Times are shown using the 24-hour clock, which is the usual way of expressing the time in Bulgaria.

- Prices are normally given in Bulgarian currency and euros. The unit of Bulgarian currency is the lev, which is fixed to the euro, one euro equalling 1.95583 lev. One lev is therefore worth around €0.50 or £0.35 or $0.60. For the sake of convenience, euro equivalents in this book are given at the rate of €1 = 2 lev. To avoid confusion with Bulgaria's former currency, the leva, which was abandoned in 1999, the word lev is used for all amounts and not the plural, leva.

- Prices quoted should be taken only as estimates, although they were correct at the time of publication and usually don't change greatly overnight. Prices are quoted inclusive of tax (which is the method generally used in Bulgaria) unless otherwise stated.

- His/he/him/man/men (etc.) also mean her/she/her/woman/ women. This is done simply to make life easier for the reader and, in particular, the author, and isn't intended to be sexist.

- British English is used throughout, but American English equivalents are given where appropriate.

- Bulgarian words (which are mainly confined to place names) have been converted to their English-sounding equivalent from Bulgarian, which is written in Cyrillic (a process known as transliteration). As this is an inexact science, you will find other versions of these words and place names in other books and websites, etc. For example, the region and town of Ruse is often written 'Rousse'.

- Warnings and important points are shown in bold type.

- The following symbols are used in this book: ☎ (telephone), 🖷 (fax), 💻 (internet) and ✉ (email).

INTRODUCTION

If you're planning to buy a home in Bulgaria or even just thinking about it, this is the book for you! Whether you want a villa, farmhouse, townhouse or apartment, a holiday or a permanent home, this book will help make your dreams come true. The purpose of **Buying a Home in Bulgaria** is to provide you with the information necessary to help you choose the most favourable location and the most appropriate home to satisfy your particular requirements. Most importantly, it will help you avoid the pitfalls and risks associated with buying a home in Bulgaria, although these are no greater than in most other countries.

You may already own property in your home country; however, buying a home in Bulgaria is a different matter altogether. One of the most common mistakes many people make when buying a home abroad is to assume that the laws and purchase procedures are the same as in their home country. This is almost certainly not the case! Buying property in Bulgaria is generally safe, but there are different rules to be followed when purchasing different types of property and there are many things to consider when it comes to taxation, the buying process and obtaining a residence permit.

Before buying a home in Bulgaria you need to ask yourself exactly why you want to buy a home there? Do you 'simply' want a holiday home, is your primary concern a long-term investment, or do you wish to work or retire there? Where and what can you afford to buy? Do you plan to let your home to offset the running costs? How will local taxes affect your investment? **Buying a Home in Bulgaria** will help you answer these and many other questions. It won't, however, tell you where to live, what to buy, or, having made your decision, whether you will be happy – that part is up to you!

Until recently, buying a home in Bulgaria was for many people a case of pot luck. However, with a copy of **Buying a Home in Bulgaria** to hand you will have a wealth of priceless information at your fingertips – information derived from a variety of sources, both official and unofficial. Furthermore, this book will reduce the risk of making an expensive mistake that you may regret later and will help you make informed decisions and calculated judgements instead of uneducated guesses (forewarned is forearmed!). Most important of all, it will help you save money and will repay your investment many times over.

Property remains one of the best long-term investments and it's certainly one of the most pleasurable. Buying a home in Bulgaria may not make you rich, but it's a wonderful way to make new friends, broaden your horizons and revitalise your life – and it will provide a welcome bolt-hole to recuperate from the stresses and strains of modern life. I trust this book will help you avoid pitfalls and smooth your way to many happy years in your new home, secure in the knowledge that you've made the right decision.

Good luck!

Dougal Robertson
July 2006

1.

MAJOR CONSIDERATIONS

Buying a home abroad is not only a major financial commitment but also a decision that can have a huge influence on other aspects of your life, including your health, security and safety, your family relationships and friendships, your lifestyle, your opinions and your view of the world. You need to take into consideration any restrictions that might affect your choice of location and type of property, such as whether you will need (or be able) to learn another language, whether you will be able (or permitted) to find work, whether you can adapt to and enjoy the climate, whether you will be able to take your pets with you, and not least, whether you will be able to afford the kind of home (and lifestyle) that you want. To ensure you make the right move, it's best to think about these and other major considerations before making any irrevocable decisions.

WHY BULGARIA?

Bulgaria (officially the Republic of Bulgaria) has started to grow rapidly as a tourist destination and it's easy to see why. A warm climate and beautiful beaches along the Black Sea coast, stunning mountain scenery and popular ski resorts inland, picturesque villages and the opportunity for a quiet rural life across the country. Bulgaria is less than half the size of the UK, so it's easy to travel across the country, and its population is a mere 7.5m (see **Population** on page 52). When the Communist system collapsed in 1990, Bulgaria turned its attention to western Europe and has now embraced democracy and opened its arms to tourists and foreign investors. Already a member of NATO, Bulgaria is modernising fast and is due to join the European Union (EU) in 2007 to become part of the euro zone in 2009 (Bulgaria's currency is currently the lev, which is tied to the euro – see page 147).

Much of Bulgaria's heavy industry disappeared with Communism, and the country began to concentrate on exporting food and natural products. As a result, food and wine in Bulgaria is excellent, with a huge range of seasonal produce and of wines, which are made in almost all parts of the country – reds in the south, north and centre, whites in the north and east (see http://bulgarianwines.com). Bulgarian food centres around salads, which resemble Greek salads, and specialities include pastries, pancakes, yoghurt and honey.

At the crossroads of 'east' and 'west' and bordering Europe's longest river, Bulgaria has a rich and colourful history. Its many architectural splendours include the remains of Roman amphitheatres, Thracian tombs and Turkish fortresses, and over 150 monasteries.

Perhaps Bulgaria's biggest attraction is the low cost of living (see page 32) and property, which is the cheapest in Europe. This is beginning to change, however. Property values in Bulgaria have been increasingly rapidly in many areas – up to 35 per cent in 2004/05 – and are expected to rise by around 25 per cent per year leading up to EU membership. The highest rises tend to be in the coastal areas, where there's increasing development for tourism.

 You shouldn't expect to make a quick profit when buying a property in Bulgaria and you should look upon it as an investment in your family's future happiness, not merely in financial terms.

It's important to ask yourself **exactly** why you want to buy a home in Bulgaria. Are you looking for an investment property or do you plan to work or start a business there? Are you seeking a retirement or holiday home? If you're after a second home, will it be used mainly for long weekends or for extended stays? Do you plan to let it to offset the mortgage and running costs? If so, how important is the property income? You need to answer these and many other questions before deciding on the best location and the most appropriate type of property to buy.

Many people buy a holiday home with a view to living there permanently or semi-permanently when they retire. If this sounds like you, there are many more factors to consider than if you're 'simply' buying a holiday home that you will occupy for just a few weeks a year (in which case it's usually wiser not to buy at all!). If, on the other hand, you plan to work or start a business in Bulgaria, you will be faced with a completely different set of criteria.

Can you really afford to buy a home in Bulgaria? What will happen in the future? Is your income secure and protected from inflation and currency fluctuations? In the '80s many people purchased second homes overseas by taking out second mortgages on their family homes, stretching their financial resources to the limit. When the recession struck in the '90s many people had their homes repossessed or had to sell at a huge loss when they couldn't meet the mortgage payments.

SURVIVAL TIP
Before making any irrevocable decisions about buying
a home in Bulgaria, you should do as much research as
possible (see page 21), study the possible pitfalls (see
Avoiding Problems on page 22), and be prepared to rent
for a while before buying (see page 98).

Advantages & Disadvantages

As in any country, there are advantages and disadvantages to buying a home in Bulgaria, although the benefits for most people outweigh any drawbacks. The country enjoys a mild climate for most of the year, with hot summers on the coast and sun and snow in the mountains. Access is getting easier and cheaper as more tourist operators fly to regional airports. Most charter companies fly direct to coastal and mountain resorts during the tourist season, and it's likely that budget airlines will begin flights to the country after it joins the EU.

Part of Bulgaria's attraction is its status as a relatively unknown country, offering much to discover for those willing to spend the time: quaint rustic villages, elaborate churches and monasteries and spectacular natural scenery. In fact, Bulgaria offers a huge range of leisure and cultural activities. Although Bulgarians have a reputation for being surly, this owes more to James Bond films than reality. Most Bulgarians will go out of their way to help you and, if you make an effort to learn some Bulgarian, you will be welcomed wherever you choose to buy your home.

All of life's essentials (and most of the extras) are cheap and, although property prices are rising rapidly, they remain good value by western European (and particularly British) standards. Even if you plan to retire to Bulgaria and live off a foreign pension, you will be able to live well.

Other advantages to buying a home in Bulgaria include strong demand for rental accommodation in the resort towns, low maintenance and building costs, quality fresh food and impressive wines, a relaxed, traditional pace of life in rural areas, great hiking and scenery in the interior, and beautiful, clean white sand beaches along the coast.

There are a few disadvantages as well, including communication problems if you don't speak Bulgarian (and can't read the Cyrillic alphabet), restrictions on land ownership, lack of flights in the 'off' season, poor roads and infrastructure in some areas, overcrowding in popular tourist areas during the summer, and the expense of getting to Bulgaria if you own a holiday home there and don't live in a nearby country with good air connections.

While much of Bulgaria is pristine forest and mountains, there are pockets of heavy industry, although this largely collapsed in the years following the demise of communism. For example, coal mining is still carried out on a small scale in the Pernik region, which has a legacy of pollution from the mining industry. You should be especially careful if you're considering buying property on the Black Sea coast south of Varna or south of Bourgas. Bourgas is home to a large commercial port and an oil refinery, while Varna has a huge port and naval base and the remains of Bulgaria's shipbuilding industry, both of which can cause pollution.

RESEARCH

A successful purchase is more likely if you thoroughly investigate the various regions, the types of property available, prices and relative values, and the procedure for buying property in Bulgaria.

SURVIVAL TIP
The secret of successfully buying a home in Bulgaria is research, research and more research.

It's easy to be overwhelmed by the natural beauty of Bulgaria and the low property prices and rush into signing a contract without giving it sufficient time and thought. If you're at all uncertain, don't allow yourself to be rushed into making a decision by fears of an imminent price rise or because someone else is supposedly interested in buying the property you want. Although many people dream of buying a holiday home or retiring overseas, it's vital to do your homework thoroughly and avoid the dream-sellers who will quite happily take advantage of your ignorance and tell you anything to sell you a property. There are many people who make expensive (and occasionally catastrophic) mistakes when buying a home in Bulgaria, usually because they do insufficient research and are in too much of a hurry, often setting ridiculous deadlines such as buying a home during a long weekend or a week's holiday.

 It isn't uncommon for buyers to regret their decision after a few months or years and wish they'd purchased a different kind of property (or even purchased in a different country!).

Where it's possible, you should try to obtain advice from people who already own a property in Bulgaria. They will usually give you valuable information (often based on their own mistakes) and you will **really** believe it if you hear it 'from the horse's mouth'! It also helps to read specialist property magazines such as *Homes Overseas* and *A Place in the Sun* (see **Appendix B** for a list) and to visit property exhibitions such as those organised by Outbound Publishing and Homes Overseas magazine (see **Appendix A**). There are also many websites where you can find information and advice from other expatriates (see **Appendix C**).

SURVIVAL TIP
The cost of investing in a few books or magazines (and other research) is tiny compared with the expense of making a big mistake. Nevertheless, don't believe everything you read!

AVOIDING PROBLEMS

The problems associated with buying property abroad have been highlighted in the past decade or so, when the property market in many countries went from boom to bust and back again. Buying a property in Bulgaria can be a straightforward and relatively pain-free procedure, but it can also be complicated and painful – especially if you aren't prepared for or realistic about potential problems. Make sure you're aware of the buying procedure (see **Chapter 5**) and take the usual precautions regarding offers, agreements, contracts, deposits and obtaining proper title to a property.

The most common problems experienced by buyers in Bulgaria include:

● **Buying in the wrong place** – Do your homework (see **Regions** on page 53, **Location** on page 77 and **Research** above) and rent first (see **Renting Before Buying** on page 98).

 The wrong decision regarding location is one of the main causes of disenfranchisement among people who purchase property outside their home country.

● **Buying a home that's difficult or impossible to sell** – If you think you might need to sell (and recoup your investment) in the short to medium term, it's important to buy a home that will be easy to sell. A modest, reasonably priced home is likely to be much easier to sell than a large, expensive home, particularly one with high maintenance costs. A quality property in a popular area with a good location (usually close to the beach or with sea views) will usually attract buyers. The most popular areas are around the coastal and mountain resorts, but supply can exceed demand in some areas. Your dream home may not be to everyone's liking and you must be realistic about what's likely to sell.

● **Paying too much** – Foreign buyers, particularly the British, are often asked for more than the market value of a property and many pay the asking price without question because it's so low compared to prices in their home country and they're reluctant to negotiate for fear of losing the property. This is unlikely to happen when buying through an agent but you should be wary of paying too much when buying direct from the vendor. See **Cost of Property** on page 31, **Property Prices** on page 107 and **Negotiating the Price** on page 110.

- **Underestimating restoration and modernisation costs** – That run-down village house for €20,000 might look like a bargain, but renovation can cost as much as new building, as well as taking time and causing innumerable headaches (see **Renovation & Restoration** on page 133).

- **Buying a property for investment, e.g. to let out in the summer, and being too optimistic about the income** – Competition is fierce in the tourism industry and you will need to do your research well. The letting season in some areas can be as short as four months, making it difficult or impossible to cover the cost of maintaining a home, let alone making a living (see **Chapter 9**).

- **Not having a survey done on an old property** – Surveys aren't common in Bulgaria but for property over five years old a survey should be seen as a necessity, not as an afterthought. For a small fee you can avoid potentially disastrous consequences (see **Inspections & Surveys** on page 126).

- **Not taking legal advice** – Many people have successfully bought property without legal advice but you must ask yourself whether it's worth the risk (see **Legal Advice** below).

- **Taking on too large a mortgage** – If a bank offers you money at a competitive rate, it can be hard not to take on a large mortgage. But you must consider what will happen if there's an economic downturn in Bulgaria or in your home country, if mortgage rates go up, or if the cost of living rises? (See **Chapter 4**.)

If you're looking for a holiday home, you may be better off not buying a house or apartment outright and instead think about investing in a scheme that restricts your occupancy of a property to a number of weeks each year, such as co-ownership, leaseback or timesharing (see page 124).

 Don't rush into any of these schemes without fully researching the market, and before you're absolutely clear about what you want and what you will get for your money.

Legal Advice

Many people who buy homes in Bulgaria don't obtain legal advice, and most of those who experience problems have taken no precautions at all. Of those who do take legal advice, many do so only **after** having paid a deposit and signed a contract or, more commonly, after they've run into problems.

SURVIVAL TIP
The most important thing to do before buying property in Bulgaria is to obtain expert, independent legal advice from someone who's familiar with Bulgarian law.

You should never pay any money or sign anything without first taking legal advice in a language you understand from an experienced lawyer. You will find the small cost (in comparison with the price of a home) of obtaining independent legal advice is excellent value, if only for the peace of mind it affords. Trying to cut corners to save a few euros on legal costs is foolhardy in the extreme when such a large sum of money is at stake.

You may be able to obtain a list of lawyers who speak your language and are experienced in handling Bulgarian property sales, either in Bulgaria or in your home country. For example, British buyers can obtain a list from the Law Society in the UK. An internet search will reveal a list of lawyers. Specialist lawyers advertise in overseas property magazines (see **Appendix B**).

There are professionals who speak English and other languages in Sofia and a growing number in the popular coastal areas, as well as a small number of expatriate professionals. But it's wise to check the credentials of all professionals you employ, whether Bulgarian or foreign.

SURVIVAL TIP
It's never wise to rely solely on advice offered by those with a financial interest in selling you a property, such as a builder or estate agent, although their advice may be excellent and totally unbiased.

Finance

You should have your finance in place before you start looking for a property and, if you need a mortgage, obtain a mortgage guarantee certificate from a

Investing in Property Abroad

People invest for two reasons: capital growth and rental return. The investor must first decide on the type of investment; be it residential, office, commercial or land.

Certain areas must be researched, such as; mortgage market, outside investment in the real estate market, political/economic environment, foreign investment laws and currency risk.

Finances are also important. Usually a specialist lawyer will be able to provide you with generic advice or be able to put you in touch with the right expert.

Independent legal advice **must** be sought. Be aware of lawyers working for the agent or recommended by the agent; they might not be as independent as you perceive.

The buying process usually goes through these stages; reservation, preliminary sale agreement and final contract. Your independent lawyer will advise you of suitable ownership form, taxes and any risks associated with your investment.

Always seek professional advice from the start, do your home research and question information from agents and sales people.

Finally, **every potential investment carries some risk.**

Miroslava Pervazova, Head of Bulgarian Law
Tel: 0870 800 4593. Email: miroslavap@maxgold.com
The International Property Law Centre

lender; this guarantees you a mortgage at a certain rate, although it's usually subject to a valuation. Because Bulgaria is considered an emerging market, with an associated degree of risk, most foreign (i.e. non-Bulgarian) banks will be unlikely to offer you a home loan to purchase property in Bulgaria and you may need to take out a personal loan or investigate other financing options if you cannot buy the property outright. Mortgages are available from Bulgarian banks, but interest rates tend to be high (see **Mortgages** on page 155).

After signing a preliminary contract, you will need to pay a cash deposit to the seller of 10 per cent of the agreed purchase price. Because this can be quite a large amount, it's common to negotiate a smaller, 'goodwill' payment, with the balance of the deposit paid within a week or ten days.

BUYING FOR INVESTMENT

Bulgaria is growing in popularity as a holiday destination and many people believe that property values, which are as yet low compared with those in other western European countries, will rise as rapidly as they have done in Spain over the past two or three decades (up to 25 per cent per year for several years in some areas), making Bulgarian property a canny investment. As a result, many people are buying to invest, particularly along the coastal areas and near the mountain resorts.

Before buying for investment, however, you must be clear as to what exactly you expect to obtain in terms of 'return' as well as of the risks involved. There are various kinds of property investment. Your family home itself is an investment, because it provides you with rent-free accommodation and can also yield a return in terms of increased value (a capital gain), although it can be difficult to profit from this unless you trade down or move to an area or country where property is cheaper. In addition, there are the following types of investment property which might give you a more tangible return:

- A holiday home, which can provide your family and friends with rent-free accommodation while (hopefully) maintaining or increasing its value; you may be able to let it when you aren't using it to generate supplementary income.

- A home for your children or relatives, which may increase in value and could also be let when not in use to provide an income.

- A business property, which could be anything from a private home with bed and breakfast or guest accommodation to a shop or office.

● A property purchased purely for investment, which could be a capital investment or provide a regular income from letting, or both. In recent years, many people have invested in property to provide an income after they retire.

A property investment should be considered over the medium to long term, i.e. a minimum of five years and, realistically in the case of Bulgaria, 10 to 20 years. In some areas, property has increased in value substantially while in others it has remained static. You also need to take into account income tax if a property is let (see **Taxation of Property Income** on page 196) and capital gains tax (see page 198) when you sell a second home. **Bear in mind that property isn't always 'as safe as houses' and property investments can be risky over the short to medium term**.

When buying to let, you must ensure that the rent will cover the mortgage (if applicable), running costs and periods when the property isn't let. Keep in mind that rental rates and 'lettability' vary according to the region and town, some areas having far more properties than demand, leading to low prices and/or occupancy, while 'in-demand' areas have higher rates, although property costs are also higher. Gross rental yields (the annual rent as a percentage of a property's value) of around 12 per cent are possible in ski resort areas, while on the coast 6 to 8 per cent is more usual; net yields (after expenses have been deducted) are 2 to 3 per cent lower.

Before deciding to invest in property, you should ask yourself the following questions:

● Can I afford to tie up capital for at least five years?

● How likely is it that the value of the property will rise during this period, and will it outstrip inflation?

● Can I rely on a regular income from my investment? If so, how easy will it be to generate that income, i.e. to find tenants? Will I be able to pay the mortgage and running costs if the property is empty and, if so, for how long?

● Am I aware of all the risks involved and how comfortable am I with taking those risks?

● Do I have enough information to make an objective decision?

See also **Location** on page 77, **Mortgages** on page 155 and **Chapter 9 (Letting)**.

CLIMATE

Despite being a small country, Bulgaria has a varied climate due to the mountains and valleys crossing the country. There are essentially two climatic zones. The northern part of the country has a continental climate, with cold winters and warm summers, while the south-west and the Black Sea coast in the east have more of a Mediterranean climate, with hot summers and mild winters. The two zones intersect along the Balkan Range, which runs through the middle of Bulgaria from east to west.

There are four distinct seasons in most areas. Summers tend to be dry and not too hot, with temperatures rarely rising above 30°C (86°F) and low humidity. While there can be long, hot spells, these are often interrupted by storms, with hail and heavy rain. Away from the coast it can become oppressively hot at the height of summer, i.e. in July and August. Further inland the weather is cooler, with warm summers in Sofia. Along the coast there can be occasional cold snaps owing to north-easterly winds. If you're after the maximum amount of sun, the Black Sea coast and south-western valleys of the Rhodopes mountains should be on your shortlist.

Winters across the country can be cold, with an average temperature for this period of 7°C (45°F) and strong winds and storms. Snow is frequent in winter and even occasionally in spring, often remaining until June in the higher mountains.

Average annual sunshine hours and days' rainfall in selected towns and cities are shown below:

Town/City	Region	Sunshine Hours	Days' Rainfall
Bourgas	Black Sea Coast	2,300	102
Kardzhali	Rhodopes Mts	2,080	100
Plovdiv	South	2,100	100
Sliven	South-east	2,280	98
Sofia	West	2,230	125
Varna	Black Sea Coast	2,300	115

Average maximum/minimum temperatures for selected cities in Centigrade and Fahrenheit (in brackets) are:

City	Spring	Summer	Autumn	Winter
Bourgas	19/10 (66/50)	26/17 (79/63)	17/10 (63/50)	9/1 (43/34)
Kardzhali	20/8 (68/46)	28/14 (82/57)	17/7 (63/45)	9/-2 (43/28)
Plovdiv	20/7 (68/45)	29/14 (84/57)	16/5 (61/41)	7/-1 (45/30)
Sliven	20/9 (68/43)	27/16 (81/61)	17/8 (63/46)	8/0 (46/32)
Sofia	18/7 (64/45)	25/13 (77/55)	14/6 (57/43)	6/-3 (43/27)
Varna	18/10 (64/50)	26/17 (79/63)	17/9 (63/43)	9/1 (43/34)

A quick way to make a rough conversion from Centigrade to Fahrenheit is to multiply by two and add 30 (see also **Appendix D**). Weather forecasts are broadcast on television and radio and published in daily newspapers.

If you're planning to live in Bulgaria and don't know whether the climate in a particular region will suit you (and in particular how you will get around when it snows), it's wise to rent accommodation for a period, preferably including winter and summer (see **Renting Before Buying** on page 98).

Earthquakes & Flooding

Be aware that large areas of Bulgaria can experience earthquakes. The two most earthquake-prone areas are the borders of the 'North Bulgarian Swell', a geological feature with the town of Gorna Oryahovitsa in the Veliko Tarnovo region at its centre, and the 'West Rhodopes Fault', running from the Rila and Pirin mountains to Plovdiv. Strong tremors also occur in the north-east along a fault line in the Razgrad region and in the southern region of Plovdiv. Areas of known seismic activity are known as 'red zones' – for obvious reasons!

There were 16 major earthquakes in Bulgaria in the 20th century. The two most recent were in 1986 and happened along the fault line between Razgrad and Skopje in the Former Yugoslav Republic of Macedonia. The two quakes damaged over 16,000 buildings and some villages were almost completely flattened.

While this may sound daunting, you're far more likely to be killed or injured driving to the airport on your way to Bulgaria! Bulgaria has been inhabited for centuries and older stone buildings are constructed to withstand all but the worst earthquake, while modern buildings have to meet 'anti-earthquake' construction standards. Cheaply-built Communist-era buildings may not, however, be so safe.

In 2005 and 2006, low-lying areas along the River Danube were affected by flooding, including the towns of Lom (in Montana), Nikopol (in Pleven), Pleven, Ruse and Vidin. As well as the Danube, the rivers Iskar, Vit, Osam and Struma all breached their banks. The floods were caused by a combination of a mild winter and an extremely wet spring. Unfortunately the areas most affected are some of the poorest parts of the country, with poor quality, marshy land.

ECONOMY

The financial implications of purchasing a property abroad are obviously one of your main considerations. Factors to be taken into account include not only whether or not you will be able to obtain a mortgage and on what terms but also the state of the Bulgarian economy and that of your home country (or the country where you earn your income). The economy in your home country may determine how much you can afford to spend on a purchase, whether you can maintain your mortgage or finance payments and the upkeep of a property, and how often you can afford to visit Bulgaria.

Bulgaria is the second-poorest country in Europe (after Romania). Gross domestic product (GDP) per head is around US$3,100 (€2,500) compared with over ten times that figure in leading western countries. Inflation is currently running at around 4 per cent.

Like many socialist command economies, Bulgaria's traditional agricultural sector was backed by a large and mostly inefficient industrial sector. The organisation of manufacturing into branches, including steel, chemicals, electronics, computers and armaments meant that when protected domestic markets were opened to competition, in 1990, local industry couldn't compete. An economic crisis in 1996 and 1997 led to the collapse of most of the country's heavy industry, already on the brink following the demise of Bulgaria's main market in the USSR, resulting in high levels of unemployment.

Since then, recovery in all sectors has been slow. Manufacturing still plays a large role in Bulgaria's economy, with exports of clothing and footwear, textiles, crude oil and natural gas and iron and steel the main foreign exchange earners. Most of Bulgaria's exports go to its main European neighbours, Italy, Germany, Turkey and Greece.

The service industry – especially tourism-related services – is playing an increasingly important role in Bulgaria's economy, however, and it now accounts for nearly 60 per cent of GDP, while manufacturing has declined to around 30 per cent, although the proportion for services includes a high proportion of government purchasing.

Economic growth is expected to continue at around 4 to 5 per cent per year for the next few years and, if Bulgaria is accepted into the EU in 2007, the country plans to adopt the euro in 2009.

COST OF PROPERTY

Although Bulgaria's currency is the lev (see page 147), prices for most Bulgarian properties are quoted in euros, although in some areas popular with UK buyers prices are quoted in sterling. For a rough conversion of euros to sterling, multiply by 0.7; for US dollars, multiply by 1.25.

The low cost of property in Bulgaria is one of the main reasons for its increasing popularity among foreign buyers. Just over 15 years ago Bulgaria was firmly under Communist rule and it is only in the past decade that the country has fully opened itself to outside investment and encouraged private industry and business. Coupled with the economic crash of 1996/97, this has meant that property prices have had little time to rise from their traditional low level.

There has recently been a phenomenal increase in values in popular areas, some developments having seen their value double in the space of 12 months, while capital growth across Bulgaria has averaged around 35 per cent for the past few years. Nevertheless, with a growing range of homes available, property is excellent value compared to the UK and Spain and there are still bargains to be found in many areas.

As in most countries, property is cheapest in rural areas, where the number of people leaving the land in search of a 'better' life (particularly since 1996/97) has left the countryside with plenty of empty properties.

Prices are being driven up by foreign buyers in the resort areas along the Black Sea coast and the mountain resorts around Pamporovo, Bansko and Borovets. Demand is strongest on the southern Black Sea coast and around Pamporovo, where restrictions on available land and a huge influx of tourists and locals working in the tourist industry have seen demand outstrip supply. Any property with a sea view will command a substantial premium, although it should be easier to resell. Coastal and city properties can cost anything from 3 to 20 times more than similar-size rural properties, although the standard and infrastructure of rural properties can be quite low (some have no mains water or electricity and most an outside toilet). New villa developments along the Black Sea coast are usually around €100,000 to

€150,000, with prices rising to €300,000 for the most luxurious properties. There's also a growing number of people buying in rural areas, either for investment or for a permanent move to Bulgaria.

Most economic forecasters are predicting a continued rise in tourist numbers to Bulgaria over the next few years, so properties on the coastal fringe and around the mountain resorts will no doubt continue to rise steadily in value. Anywhere within striking distance of the international airports at Burgas, Sofia and Varna will probably jump dramatically in value, particularly if low-cost flight operators commence scheduled flights to these destinations. There are also less well known areas of Bulgaria that could prove good value in the long term, particularly those close to historical towns or in areas of spectacular natural beauty. Towns such Plovdiv (Bulgaria's second city), Vidin and Ruse offer historical interest, while Melnik, Balchik and Batak (near Plovdiv) have the advantage of beautiful views and quiet locations.

With a budget of up to around €25,000, you should be able to find a large wooden or stone house with open fireplaces, large rooms, picturesque views and plenty of land attached, but needing renovation to bring it up to standard. A rural property in need of major renovation can often be purchased for less than €5,000, while rural properties in better condition needing only minor repair seldom cost much more than €20,000. Most unmodernised rural houses have an outside toilet, and bathrooms tend to be fairly rudimentary.

A budget of between €25,000 and €50,000 will buy you a generous property of reasonable quality in a pleasant rural or less popular coastal location, possibly in need of improvement only.

As little as €50,000 will buy you a house or villa close to one of the main towns, usually with lake or mountain views, big rooms and plenty of land, or a small to medium-size new apartment in one of the coastal towns or in the capital Sofia. For €150,000 you can be the proud owner of a large two-storey house in one of the coastal towns, a family home in Sofia or a luxury apartment in one of the popular tourist resorts. At the top end of the market (over €250,000), large, modern, renovated homes, new houses with sea views, luxury apartments in Sofia and even hotels are available.

For details of property prices in different areas, see **Property Prices** on page 107.

COST OF LIVING

As in much of Eastern Europe, the cost of living in Bulgaria is extremely low. The cost of essential items is minimal compared with prices in western

Europe, and even luxuries such as good wine and restaurant meals come relatively cheaply. Inflation, currently at around 4 per cent, is higher than in western Europe, but this will make little difference in the short term.

Anyone planning to live in Bulgaria on a western European or North American income will find that their money stretches a long way. Even retirees will be able to live comfortably (in comparison, the state pension in Bulgaria is around €50 per person a month!). In the Black Sea tourist areas around Varna and Burgas and in the mountain resort towns prices are inflated, but if you shop in small rural towns and don't eat out too often, your money will go a long way. Even major items such as new cars are much cheaper in Bulgaria than elsewhere in Europe.

On the other hand, salaries are low in Bulgaria and GDP per head (a reliable indicator of purchasing power) is less than half that of Slovakia and 20 per cent lower than neighbouring Turkey, although personal and corporate tax rates are low and will remain so at least for the medium term (the top personal tax rate is 24 per cent). Therefore, if you plan to earn a living in Bulgaria, you should calculate carefully the sort of property you will be able to afford.

It's impossible to calculate an average cost of living in Bulgaria, as it varies enormously according to lifestyle. Your food bill, for example, will depend on what you eat. In general, food and drink costs around a half to a quarter as much as in the UK, alcohol is between a half and one-fifth of the cost in the UK and cigarettes are around 20 times cheaper (not so good if you're trying to quit smoking!). Dairy products in Bulgaria are around half the price of the UK and meat around one-fifth the price. Fruit and vegetables, on the other hand, are only slightly cheaper in Bulgaria. (Most of the fruit and vegetables sold are grown locally, and therefore seasonal, and imported produce is considerably more expensive.) Coffee is around half the price of the UK; Bulgarians aren't big tea drinkers, so you're unlikely to find your usual brand and may want to bring supplies with you from home.

Prices for electric and electronic goods, cameras, computers and household appliances aren't much lower than in the UK so you may be better buying them abroad, particularly in nearby Turkey. However, clothing is much cheaper and, if you're a fan of cultural pursuits, Bulgaria's state-subsidised opera, orchestras and theatres can be enjoyed for around 10 per cent of typical ticket prices in the UK. Transport is generally cheaper than in the UK, although car hire is expensive.

Below is a summary of common items, with the average cost in the UK compared to the average cost in Bulgaria. The cost of utilities is based on a small two-bedroom house or larger two-bedroom apartment.

> **SURVIVAL TIP**
> When calculating your cost of living, remember to
> deduct the cost of social security or national insurance
> contributions if you're still resident in your home
> country and the appropriate percentage for income tax
> (see page 194) from your gross salary.

Item	Average Cost	
	UK	Bulgaria
Food		
Bread (loaf)	€1.60	€0.75
Milk (1ltr)	€0.75	€0.65
Orange juice (1ltr)	€0.95	€0.80
Cornflakes (standard packet)	€0.80	€1.60
Rump steak (1kg)	€11.40	€2.70
Chicken breast (1kg)	€11.00	€2.50
Eggs (10)	€2.40	€0.65
Alcohol & Tobacco		
Local wine (75cl)	€9.50	€5.50
Local beer (33cl)	€1.00	€0.25
Imported beer (33cl)	€2.50	€1.00
Local brandy (75cl)	€14.00	€2.50
Local cigarettes (20)	€6.00	€0.40
Eating Out		
Three-course meal with wine	€60.00	€18.00
Take-away pizza	€6.00	€3.00
Clothing		
Men's business shirt	€65.00	€30.00

Pair of men's business shoes	€140.00	€38.00
Pair of trainers	€95.00	€40.00
Denim jeans	€62.00	€24.00
Pair of women's shoes	€90.00	€30.00
Household Appliances		
Television (21-inch)	€300.00	€285.00
Microwave	€325.00	€200.00
Washing machine	€500.00	€420.00
Fridge	€365.00	€365.00
Leisure		
Cinema ticket	€9.60	€1.25
Opera ticket	€75.00	€2.25
Newspaper – local	€0.60	€0.15
Newspaper – UK	€1.50	€2.00
Cable TV rental (per month)	€42.00	€4.00
Internet connection (per month)	€22.00	€16.50
Utilities		
Electricity (per month)	€40.00	€18.00
Gas (per month)	€40.00	€8.00
Water (per month)	€30.00	€3.00
Transport		
Taxi (per km)	€4.00	€1.00
Train ticket (per 100km)	€15.00	€3.50
Petrol (unleaded – 1 litre)	€1.30	€1.00
Bus fare	€3.00	€0.20
Car rental – per day (small saloon)	€60.00	€80.00

PERMITS & VISAS

Before making any plans to visit Bulgaria or live and work there, you must ensure that you have the necessary identity card or passport (with a visa if necessary) and, if you're planning to stay long-term, the appropriate documentation to obtain a residence and/or work permit. There are different requirements for different nationalities and circumstances, as detailed below.

```
SURVIVAL TIP
Immigration is a complex and ever-changing subject,
and the information in this chapter is intended only as a
general guide. You shouldn't base any decisions or
actions on the information contained herein without
confirming and checking it with the relevant Bulgarian
embassy or consulate.
```

Bear in mind in particular that visa and permit regulations will change when Bulgaria joins the EU (scheduled for 2007) and the information in this section many already have changed in preparation for that event. To ensure you have the most recent information, check regularly with the relevant Bulgarian embassy or consulate (see **Appendix A**).

Visitors

Citizens of the following countries can visit Bulgaria for up to 90 days within each six-month period without a visa: Austria, Belgium, Chile, Croatia, Cyprus, Czech Republic, Denmark, Estonia, Finland, France, Germany, Greece, Hungary, Iceland, Italy, Japan, Latvia, Lithuania, Liechtenstein, Luxembourg, Macedonia (officially the 'Former Yugoslav Republic of Macedonia'), Malaysia, Malta, Netherlands, Norway, Poland, Portugal, Republic of Korea, Romania, San Marino, Slovak Republic, Slovenia, Spain, Sweden, Switzerland, Tunisia and Yugoslavia.

Citizens of Andorra, Australia, Canada, Estonia, the Republic of Ireland, Israel, Macedonia, Monaco, New Zealand, Poland, Romania, Slovak Republic, Serbia and Montenegro, the UK, US and Vatican can all enter Bulgaria without a visa for a maximum of 30 days in any six-month period.

Those of all other nationalities require a visa for any visit to Bulgaria.

All foreign visitors to Bulgaria must register with the local police station within five days of arrival.

If you're staying in a hotel or guest house, police registration will normally be carried out automatically for you, but you must remember to register yourself if you're renting privately or staying with friends. Most border guards won't take issue if you've stayed only a few days without registering, but if you've stayed for several weeks without registering you may be liable for a large fine (or considerable hassle). Additionally, all foreigners must complete an address registration form on arrival in Bulgaria, stating the aim of their visit and the address where they will be staying.

Visas

Depending on your nationality, you will require a visa if you plan to stay for longer than 30 or 90 days (see **Visitors** above). UK citizens planning to stay for more than 30 days in a six-month period will need a Type C visa, which is valid for between 3 and 12 months. In fact, there are five varieties of Type C visa, as follows:

Entry	Validity	Cost
Single	3 months	€50
Single (urgent processing)	3 months	€64
Multiple	3 months	€60
Multiple	6 months	€88
Multiple	12 months	€118

You may be limited in your choice of the above by your nationality (see above).

For long-term stays (e.g. for business or residence) you must apply for a Type D visa, which must be done at the Bulgarian embassy or consulate in your home country. A Type D visa is for single entry only and is valid for 12 months from the date of issue for a stay of up to 90 days in succession. The Type D visa is generally issued to people who are applying for a long-term or permanent residence permit in Bulgaria.

If a visa application isn't completed properly or the appropriate documentation isn't provided, it's usually rejected and you must go through the process again.

Some companies are starting to offer visa services if you don't have time to visit a Bulgarian embassy or want to ensure that all the documentation is correctly prepared. For example, in the UK, Bulgarian Visas (☎ 020-7538 5205, 💻 http://www.bulgarianvisas.com) charges £47 (on top of the visa fee) for a Bulgarian visa. Note, however, that such services are usually limited to form-filling and waiting in queues, and you should consult a lawyer if you're in any doubt as to the most appropriate visa or permit to apply for.

Applications

For a short-stay Type C visa, you must provide a current passport (valid for three months from the date of entry), a passport-size photograph, confirmation of a booking at a hotel in Bulgaria (or the address of a private residence where you will be staying) and either a ticket for return or onward travel or proof that you have enough funds to support your stay in Bulgaria.

The multi-entry short-stay visa requires all of the above, plus a photocopy of the personal information pages of your passport, proof of possession of enough money to cover accommodation and subsistence costs (equivalent to €100 euros per day) and, if you don't have onward travel or return airfares arranged, proof of having €300 euros to cover the cost of leaving Bulgaria.

An application for a long-stay (Type D) visa requires a number of documents, including the following:

● the application form and two passport-size photographs;

● a current passport;

● evidence of having formed a limited company (if applicable – see **Forming a Company** on page 162), a certified copy of the company's tax registration document and a court certificate that the company is solvent, and evidence that you've hired Bulgarian citizens;

● a certificate from the National Social Security Institute that you're contributing to social security and have no outstanding tax payments;

● a certificate from the tax office showing the amount of taxes paid (if applicable);

- a recent bank statement and a bank certificate that you're solvent;
- evidence of accommodation in Bulgaria and the address.

SURVIVAL TIP
The visa application process in Bulgaria can be difficult and time-consuming. You may need professional assistance or at least a Bulgarian-speaking friend.

RESIDENCE PERMITS

All foreigners staying in Bulgaria for longer than 30 or 90 days (depending on their nationality – see **Visitors** above) in succession, for any reason, require a residence permit. A residence permit holder's dependants are normally also granted a permit. Different types of residence permit are issued according to your status, including pensioner, employee and freelance professional. There's also a permit category for those investing in Bulgaria, but as the minimum investment is US$500,000, it won't suit everyone!

If you wish to purchase land in Bulgaria, you must form a limited company there (see **Forming a Company** on page 162), which is considered commercial activity, so you must obtain a permit for foreigners 'carrying out or involved in commercial activities'. Most foreigners purchasing property in Bulgaria apply for this type of permit.

If you're a pensioner, you will need to produce evidence that you're entitled to retirement income and have a bank account in Bulgaria and a Bulgarian address.

To apply for a residence permit, you must first obtain a Type D visa (see above) in your home country and then travel to Bulgaria. Once you arrive in Bulgaria, you should apply for the appropriate residence permit as soon as possible. The decision takes around seven days and, if you're successful, your passport will be stamped to show that you've been granted a residence permit, so you will be able to leave the country and return when you need to. Note that the requirements for a Type D visa are the same as those for a residence permit – so if you're successful in obtaining a Type D visa from a Bulgarian embassy or consulate, you should have no trouble obtaining a residence permit in Bulgaria.

Residence permits are valid for 12 months and can be renewed towards the end of this period. It's usually a formality to have a permit renewed, although you will need to have spent at least six months and one day of the 12-month period in Bulgaria. You will be able to apply for a permanent residence permit (valid indefinitely) after five years' residence in Bulgaria.

The full 'Law For The Foreigners In The Republic Of Bulgaria' is available on the Bulgarian Ministry of Interior website (💻 http://www.mvr.bg/en – click on 'Legal Framework'/Laws and Rules'). Because there are a number of grey areas in Bulgarian immigration law and EU membership will again change the requirements, it's recommended you talk with a lawyer who is familiar with Bulgarian and EU law about the most appropriate permit to apply for.

WORKING

If there's a possibility that you or any family members will work in Bulgaria, you must ensure that it will be possible before buying a home. If you decide to move to Bulgaria to work, you should think seriously about your motives and credentials and ask yourself the following questions:

- What kind of work can I realistically expect to do?

- Are my qualifications and experience recognised in Bulgaria?

- How well do I speak Bulgarian? (While there are many jobs in Sofia and a few in the tourist areas that don't require fluent Bulgarian, you will find it difficult to find work outside these areas.)

- Are there any jobs in my profession or trade where I wish to live?

- Will I be able to earn enough to live on (see below)?

- Could I be self-employed or start a business?

You may not like the answers to these questions, but it's better to ask them before moving to Bulgaria than afterwards.

Very few foreigners are employed in Bulgaria as salaried workers, as the wages are very low (10 to 15 lev per day on average). While there are some jobs available in Bulgaria teaching English or working in the tourist industry, you're unlikely to earn enough to live well. If you're thinking about earning a living in Bulgaria (as opposed to making 'pocket money') in most situations you'd be better off researching the market and setting up your own business, although this can be fraught with difficulty and risk. The exception is Sofia, where there's a large expatriate community and a range of jobs available for professionally qualified English speakers. A good source of job advertisements in Bulgaria is at 🖳 http://www.jobs.bg.

SURVIVAL TIP
While hoping for the best, you should also plan for the worst and have a backup plan and sufficient funds to last until you're established (this also applies to employees).

To work in Bulgaria, you will need a work permit, issued by the Bulgarian Ministry of Labour and Social Policy, which will allow you to apply for Type D visa allowing you to stay for 12 months (see above). If you plan to work in Bulgaria for a salary, your potential employer will organise a work permit, which will usually be dependent on the job being one that cannot be filled by a Bulgarian (e.g. teaching English).

RETIREMENT

If you're thinking about retiring to Bulgaria or moving to Bulgaria with a view to retiring there, you need to take additional considerations into account, including those listed below.

SURVIVAL TIP
If you do plan to retire to Bulgaria, you should ensure that your income is (and will remain) sufficient to live on, keeping in mind devaluation in the future if your pension isn't paid in euros (and if Bulgaria adopts the euro in 2009), rises in the cost of living (see page 32), and unforseen circumstances such as medical bills or anything else that may reduce your income, e.g stock market crashes. e.g. stock market crashes.

You should also think carefully about whether you want to be living in a 'foreign' country in your final years and what would happen if your spouse or partner died before you.

Many people who retire overseas return home after deciding they would rather spend their last years in more familiar surroundings.

Visas & Permits

If you've retired and plan to move to Bulgaria permanently, you can apply for a Type D visa. You will need to prove that you're entitled to retirement income in your home country, produce evidence that you have a valid Bulgarian bank account and that you have accommodation and an address in Bulgaria. Once you've obtained a Type D visa, you have 12 months to apply for a residence permit (see page 39).

Financial Resources

If you're drawing a pension from the UK, this is usually enough to cover your cost of living in Bulgaria. Note that Bulgaria is one of the few countries where a UK pension isn't indexed if you're a permanent resident; in other words, your pension payments will remain the same amount as when you left the UK permanently, irrespective of inflation in either country, although it's possible that this situation will change.

Pensions & Social Security Benefits

Unless you've worked in Bulgaria for a long time, you're unlikely to be eligible for a Bulgarian pension – and in any case it's hardly worth claiming (currently less than €50 per month). If you plan to work for a while in Bulgaria and then retire there, you may be able to make contributions to your pension in your home country instead. In the UK, contact the Centre for Non-Residents at HM Revenue and Customs (formerly the Inland Revenue) – Director's Office, Room 102, St John's House, Merton Road, Bootle, Merseyside (☎ 0845-070 0040, 🖥 http://www.hmrc.gov.uk/cnr). When Bulgaria joins the EU in 2007, reciprocal agreements with other EU countries will apply.

Health Insurance

If you won't be spending more than a month at a time in Bulgaria, it's advisable to purchase annual, multi-trip travel insurance, which will cover you for any urgent hospital or medical expenses and fly you back to your home country for specialist treatment. The UK has a reciprocal healthcare arrangement with Bulgaria, but the Department of Health strongly recommends that people take out private medical insurance or ensure they have adequate travel insurance, as the state healthcare sector is limited.

If you retire permanently to Bulgaria you will pay a small amount of your pension (around 6 lev per month) towards the Bulgarian state health system, the NOI. However it's strongly recommended to take out some form of private health insurance. Private healthcare plans are available in the UK which are accepted at private hospitals in Bulgaria; these are offered by a number of companies or through an independent broker such as Medibroker (☎ 0191-297 2411, 🖥 http://www.medibroker.com).

Taxes

If you spend more than 183 days (six months) in Bulgaria, you're regarded as being resident for tax purposes. You will then have to pay Bulgarian tax on your worldwide income (see **Liability** on page 194) but may still be liable for inheritance tax in your home country. If you plan to retire to Bulgaria, you will probably be able to substantially reduce your tax liability compared to your home country. This is a complex topic and you should seek professional advice before making any decisions.

Mobility

If you're considering buying a property in a rural or less developed area, consider how you will get to the nearest amenities and services, such as shops, doctor and dentist (see **Location** on page 77).

SURVIVAL TIP
There's little point in choosing an isolated spot or somewhere with a limited public transport system when in a few years' time you may have to rely on local bus, taxi or train services to get about.

You should also consider the terrain of your chosen home, as a location with steep slopes or steps could become a literally insurmountable problem if you develop mobility problems or become disabled. A home in a town is usually a much better idea for retirees than a home in a rural area or a village. It's particularly important for retirees to thoroughly research an area and rent for a period before buying (see **Research** on page 21) and **Renting Before Buying** on page 98).

LANGUAGE

If you want to get the most out of living in Bulgaria and enjoy the lifestyle as much as possible, you should to start learning Bulgarian as soon as you can. If you're living in Sofia or one of the other main towns, you will be able to get by with a minimum of Bulgarian – many people live in Bulgaria for years with only a basic knowledge of Bulgarian – but even then your business and social enjoyment will be directly related to how well you speak the language. Although English is spoken in the main tourist areas and many young people speak or are learning English, Russian and German are still the more widely spoken second languages. Elsewhere, a knowledge of Bulgarian is essential.

> **SURVIVAL TIP**
> **Bulgarians shake their head from side to side when they mean 'yes' and nod when they mean 'no'. But sometimes they may do the opposite when they realise you're a foreigner!**

The Bulgarian alphabet is based on the Cyrillic script, which bears no resemblance to the Roman alphabet. It's wise to carry a small translation guide for the Bulgarian alphabet with you wherever you go to try to get used to the different letters. At a minimum you should try to master a few basic words and phrases, as this will make everyday life easier – and Bulgarian people will appreciate your efforts.

Learning Bulgarian

To learn even basic Bulgarian, you will need a little hard work, perseverance and some help, particularly if you only have English-speaking friends. Don't expect to learn Bulgarian quickly. If your expectations are unrealistic, you will become frustrated, which can affect your confidence. **It takes a long time to reach the level of fluency needed to be able to work in Bulgarian.** If you don't speak Bulgarian fluently, you should begin lessons before your arrival in Bulgaria and continue them once you're there.

Language Schools & Courses

Most people can teach themselves a great deal through the use of books, tapes, videos and even computer-based courses. But even the best students require some help. Language teaching is starting to pick up in Bulgaria as more foreigners move there permanently or purchase property. As yet, however, there are few language schools teaching Bulgarian to foreigners, as most language schools focus on teaching English to Bulgarians.

Private Lessons

With the growing number of foreigners moving to Bulgaria permanently, many Bulgarians are offering private lessons, either one-on-one or in small groups. Private lessons are an ideal (although relatively expensive) way to learn a language. Private lessons generally cost from €5 to €15 per hour depending on how many lessons you take. The main advantage of private lessons is that you learn at your own speed and aren't held back by slow learners or left floundering in the wake of the class genius.

A good listing of Bulgarian language teachers can be found on the Language School Teachers website (🖥 http://www.language-school-teachers.com). Look for advertisements locally and in the English-language press (see **Appendix B**) as well as on expatriate websites (see **Appendix C**). Don't forget to ask friends, neighbours and colleagues if they can recommend a private teacher.

Self-help

There are several self-study Bulgarian courses available, including those offered by Berlitz (🖥 http://www.berlitz.bg), Eurotalk (🖥 http://www.eurotalk.com) and McGraw Hill (🖥 http://www.teachyourself.co.uk). It's usually worth purchasing a good English-Bulgarian dictionary, such as those published by Langenscheidt or Hippocrene. In Sofia and in the main tourist towns you should be able to buy phrasebooks and dictionaries from English-language bookshops much more cheaply than in your home country.

There are several other things you can do to speed up your language learning, including watching television regularly (particularly quiz shows, where the words appear on screen as they're spoken) and DVDs (where you can programme Bulgarian or English subtitles), reading (especially children's books and catalogues, where the words are accompanied by pictures), joining a club or association, and (most enjoyable) making Bulgarian friends!

HEALTH

One of your most important considerations in staying or living in Bulgaria is maintaining good health. Bulgaria's state healthcare system has suffered from years of under-investment and the quality of care varies significantly. The private system, on the other hand, is well funded and of a universally high standard.

Like the inhabitants of many former Communist countries, Bulgarians generally don't have a high standard of health. Life expectancy is lower than elsewhere in eastern Europe and the Balkans (averaging 75.9 years for women and 68.4 years for men), and almost one in five babies won't reach the age of 60.

Tobacco and alcohol are major causes of death, owing to the high number of Bulgarians who smoke, consume large amounts of alcohol and have a poor diet. Even though the traditional Bulgarian diet is extremely healthy (bread, fruit, vegetables, beans and dairy products), Bulgarians tend to eat a good deal of 'junk' food, full of sugar, salt and fat.

While Bulgaria is making efforts to increase funding for its health system, the collapse of communism and the economic crash of the late '90s led to a huge drop in health spending. Bulgaria spends less than 4 per cent of GDP on health and spending per capita is around €50 per person – compared to around €1,350 per person in the UK and €3,400 in the US.

For minor ailments and complaints the local pharmacy should be able to help you, although English-speaking staff tend to be found only in tourist areas. Pharmacies don't usually have as wide a range of medicines and other goods, such as razor blades and contraceptives, as other western countries, so it's advisable to bring these with you if you have a preferred brand.

Under Bulgaria's national health system, a visit to a doctor is free, as is emergency hospital treatment. If you need a doctor, you should visit a health clinic, where staff may speak English. Bulgaria has reciprocal healthcare arrangements with a number of countries (including the UK), which means that their citizens can receive non-urgent treatment in public (state-run) hospitals free of charge. However, it's recommended that you take out some form of private health insurance to ensure that you will be treated privately (see **Health Insurance** on page 42). If you don't have insurance, a visit to a doctor will cost around €25 (whereas Bulgarians pay less than €1!) and to a specialist more than double this amount.

The quality of private healthcare is generally high, although as in many Western countries the more you pay the better the standard of healthcare you receive. There are a number of modern private hospitals in Sofia catering to expatriates and wealthy Bulgarians, and private clinics are starting to appear in the larger resort towns. Bulgaria also has a strong tradition of herbal medicine, with knowledge of healing herbs valued greatly in rural villages.

If you're planning to take up residence, even if only for part of the year, it's wise to have a health check before your arrival (see page 181), especially if you have a history of poor health or are elderly. There are no vaccinations or inoculations required for entry to Bulgaria, but most governments advise their citizens to have jabs for diphtheria, tetanus, typhoid and hepatitis A. If you plan to spend a lot of time hiking in woodland areas or in the mountains, it's recommended you have a vaccination for tick-borne encephalitis.

PETS

If you plan to take a pet to Bulgaria, it's important that you check the latest regulations. Make sure you have the correct papers, not just for Bulgaria but for all the countries you will pass through to get to Bulgaria. If you plan on returning home with your pet at any time, make sure you are aware of quarantine regulations, particularly for returning to the EU. There are currently no quarantine requirements for entry to Bulgaria, but your pet will need a health certificate with evidence of rabies vaccination (see **Vaccinations** below).

If you're exporting a cat, dog, rabbit, guinea pig, mouse, rat or ferret to Bulgaria from the UK, you must decide **in advance** whether you might ever bring your pet back to the UK. If the answer is yes, or if you're unsure, you should have your pet microchipped, vaccinated against rabies and blood tested at least a month after the rabies vaccination to check that it has sufficient protection against the disease. Your pet will need to stay a minimum of 30 days in Bulgaria after the blood test to make sure it hasn't contracted rabies. If you're returning with your pet from Bulgaria to an EU country you will need to obtain a 'pet passport', details of which are available from the Department for Environment, Food and Rural Affairs (DEFRA – see **Further Information** below).

If you don't plan to bring your pet back to the UK, you need only an export certificate from DEFRA and a health certificate issued by an approved vet less than 15 days before departure. Regulations will probably change once Bulgaria joins the EU, but rabies is likely to be prevalent in Bulgaria for many more years.

Pets can be transported by air and sometimes carried with you (in an approved container) for an extra charge. There are companies that will accommodate your pets for you while you move, take care of all export requirements and ship them to you when you've settled in, e.g. Pinehawk Kennels (☎ 01223-290249, 🖳 http://www.pinehawkkennels.co.uk) in the UK.

Vaccinations

Rabies is endemic in Bulgaria, particularly in rural areas and your pet will need evidence of rabies vaccination to enter Bulgaria. Resident dogs will need an annual rabies booster and it's recommended they're also vaccinated against the following diseases:

- **Adenovirus or canine hepatiti**s – an acute viral disease which attacks the liver;

- **Distemper** – a potentially fatal viral infection;

- **Leptospirosis** – a bacterial disease which can be transmitted to humans and can be fatal;

- **Lyme disease** – a parasitic disease carried by ticks which can also be transmitted to humans;

- **Parvovirus or Parvo** – an intestinal virus;

- **Tracheobronchitis** – known as kennel cough and one of the most common canine diseases, which can lead to fatal complications.

Some infections will be more or less likely depending on where you live. Your local veterinarian should be able to advise which vaccines your dog will require. Vaccines are often available in combinations but separate vaccines are sometimes needed. First vaccinations are usually in two stages, with a 'booster' administered three or four weeks after the initial injection. A single annual renewal is required.

Cats aren't required to have regular rabies vaccinations, although if you let your cat roam free outside your home it's advisable to have it vaccinated annually. Cats do, however, need to be vaccinated against feline gastro-enteritis and flu.

Details of all vaccinations must be entered on a pet passport or veterinary certificate.

Sterilisation

Bulgaria has a major stray dog problem and Sofia in particular is infamous for its packs of wild dogs (it's estimated that there are four stray dogs for every human inhabitant in the capital), although the city council has put a number of measures in place to alleviate the problem.

Sterilisation of female cats and dogs not only prevents them from becoming pregnant, but can also protect against the equivalent of breast cancer if the operation is carried out before the first heat period. Sterilisation offers some protection if carried out after the first heat, but none after the second.

Castration of male dogs and cats is about half the cost of sterilising females and can be beneficial in situations where animals often run away or are aggressive or to reduce the smell of their urine.

Identification

Dogs and cats don't wear identification discs or tags in Bulgaria and there's currently no system of licensing. If you plan to bring a dog back to an EU country at any time, however, it must be microchipped, which costs around €35, although many local councils in the UK provide the service for less.

Kennels & Catteries

There are currently no kennels or catteries in Bulgaria. As more foreigners (particularly from the UK) move to Bulgaria with their pets, kennels and catteries will no doubt begin to appear. It could even be a business opportunity for those with the time to research the market!

Further Information

If you're thinking about moving to an area, try to find a local vet, who should be able to advise you about likely problems and possible solutions. Ask other foreigners you see with pets – if nothing else, you will probably make new acquaintances!

Details of the British pet passport scheme can be obtained from the Department for Environment, Food and Rural Affairs (DEFRA), Area 201, 1a Page Street, London SW1P 4PQ (☎ 0870-241 1710, 💻 http://www.defra.gov.uk/animalh/quarantine/pets/index.htm, ✉ pets.helpline@defra.gsi.gov.uk). General information can be obtained in the UK from Dogs Away (☎ 020-8441 9311, 💻 http://www.dogsaway.co.uk, ✉ contact@dogsaway.co.uk) and Animal Airlines (☎ 01625-827414, 💻 http://www.animalairlines.co.uk, ✉ enquiries@animalairlines.co.uk).

A useful book is *Travel Tips for Dogs and Cats* by David Prydie (Interpet Books).

2.

THE BEST PLACE TO LIVE

Once you've decided to buy a home in Bulgaria, your first decision will be to choose the region and what sort of home will best meet your needs. Even in the most popular areas for buying a home it can be difficult to decide on a location, and the choice is often overwhelming.

SURVIVAL TIP
If you're unsure about where and what to buy, the best
option is to rent for a while (see page 98).

The secret to buying a home in Bulgaria successfully is research, research and more research, preferably before you even arrive (see page 21). You might be lucky and buy the first property you see without doing any homework and live happily ever after. But a successful purchase is much more likely if you take your time, thoroughly investigating the towns and communities in your chosen area, comparing the types and prices of properties and their relative values. It's a rare and lucky person who finds the ideal home by accident and you have a much better chance of finding your dream home if you do your homework thoroughly. It's easy to be caught up in the excitement surrounding the property boom in Bulgaria and fail to research the market properly. You may hear and read about people who visit Bulgaria on a three-day holiday and put a deposit on a property before they go home – a recipe for disaster!

Bulgaria is about half the size of the United Kingdom and only slightly larger than Portugal. Nevertheless, it contains a huge diversity of landscapes, including low-lying areas in the north and south-east, mountains across the centre and south-west, alpine forests, farmland and river valleys (see **Geography** below). It has two distinct climatic zones (see **Climate** on page 28), giving you a wide range of choices.

POPULATION

The population of Bulgaria is around 7.5m, the majority (85 per cent) being ethnic Bulgarians. There's a large Turkish minority (9 per cent) and Roma (gipsies) constitute 4.5 per cent of the population. Bulgaria's population density of around 75 people per km^2 (200 per mi^2) is one of the lowest in Europe, and the country remains largely undeveloped, rural areas making up 80 per cent and containing over 40 per cent of the population. More than half the population lives in villages and towns with fewer than 50,000 inhabitants, so it isn't difficult to find an isolated spot if you want to get away from it all. However, country dwellers are moving to the cities in search of a 'better' life and more opportunities and an increasing number of young people are moving overseas, with the result that Bulgaria's population has been in decline for a number of years. Sofia, with a population of over 1.2m, is the only large city. Bulgaria's second and third cities are Plovdiv (325,000) and Varna (305,000). Only four other cities have populations over 100,000 (Bourgas, Pleven, Ruse and Stara Zagora) – see map in **Appendix E**.

Bulgaria's main religion is Bulgarian Orthodox, which is practised by almost 90 per cent of the population, most of the rest being Muslims, with just a few Catholics and other Christians.

GEOGRAPHY

Bulgaria covers an area of just over 110,000km² (42,000mi²) and is roughly rectangular. Its border extends for 1,800km (1,100mi) and includes around 350km (215mi) of coastline along the Black Sea. Bulgaria is bordered by Greece, Macedonia (officially the 'Former Yugoslav Republic of Macedonia'), Romania, Serbia and Turkey. Bulgaria is divided into 28 regions, each region named after its capital (see below). The city of Sofia comprises its own region.

Around half of Bulgaria is mountainous, the Rhodopes mountains in the south-west containing the highest peak on the Balkan Peninsula, Mt Musala (2,925m/9,590ft). To the south are the Rhodopes mountains, which form a natural border with Greece. North of the Rhodopes mountains is the 'Valley of the Roses', a rose-growing area producing 70 per cent of the world's rose oil. The roses are harvested in May and June. The main town in the valley is Kazanlak, an important historical site for Thracian remains and ruins. The area around Kazanlak is picturesque farmland and popular for finding a rural idyll, but in the late summer the valley can be dry and dusty. The Balkan mountains (known to Bulgarians as the Stara Planina) is the largest mountain range, running east-west through the centre of the country from the Serbian border almost to the Black Sea coast. Several smaller mountain ranges run along the western border of Bulgaria.

In the north of the country, the Balkan mountains slope down to the northern Bulgarian plateau or Danubian Plain, ending at the River Danube, which forms the border with Romania. The eastern part of the country is relatively low lying. A geographical map of Bulgaria is shown on page 6.

REGIONS

Bulgaria has 28 official regions, of which the most popular with foreign property buyers are Varna and Bourgas on the Black Sea coast, Sofia (consisting of the capital city itself) in the west, Veliko Tarnovo in the north, and Blagoevgrad in the extreme south-west (especially the ski resort of Bansko and surrounding area).

This section contains a description of each region, in alphabetical order. A map of the regions and capital cities is included in **Appendix E**. A geographical map can be found on page 6. For more information about Bulgaria's regions, cities, towns, resorts and tourist attractions, refer to one of the many tourist guides, such as those in the *Blue Guides*, *Lonely Planet* and *Rough Guides* series.

Blagoevgrad

Blagoevgrad (population 340,000) lies in the extreme south-west of the country on the border with Greece and Macedonia. The Struma River runs from north to south through the province and forms a natural link between Greece and Bulgaria.

The capital, Blagoevgrad (population 76,000), is around 100km (60mi) south of Sofia. The town has a well preserved pedestrianised town centre with a good selection of restaurants, bars, cafes and shops. There are two universities here, Southwestern University and the private American University in Bulgaria, founded in 1991.

The region's main attraction is the resort town of Bansko, at the foot of the Pirin mountains. Bansko, which is the newest but smallest of Bulgaria's ski resorts, which is developing rapidly. Bansko is being marketed heavily as the country's prime skiing destination and it has opportunities for outdoor recreation throughout the year, with extensive pine forests, lakes, walking tracks and even a golf course. Bansko also has plenty of cultural facilities and is the home of the annual Bankso Jazz Festival.

There are many good-value properties to be found in the region, ranging from larger houses to village properties, and its proximity to Sofia and the Pirin mountains makes it a popular choice. Travelling to Sofia from the regional capital takes around 2.5 hours by train and around 2 hours by car. There are also international road and rail links from Blagoevgrad to Athens and Thessaloniki in Greece.

Bourgas

Bourgas (population 426,000) – sometimes written Burgas – is one of the most popular regions for buying property. Situated in the extreme south-east of the country on the Black Sea coast, the region offers a combination of warm climate and beautiful mountain scenery. It's also home to one of the biggest resorts in Bulgaria, Sunny Beach. Bourgas is one of the most developed regions in Bulgaria and has the second-largest population (after Sofia). Much of its development is a result of the region's strategic location on the Black Sea and the availability of raw materials for export, although it has long been a popular tourist destination.

A stopping point on the ancient trading routes between East and West, Bourgas has numerous remains of buildings constructed by the Thracians, Romans and Byzantines. There are also a number of well preserved historic towns, such as Nesebar and Sozopol (see below).

The regional capital, Bourgas (population 212,000), is home to a number of oil and chemical companies and therefore has an industrial feel, although the town centre has been vastly improved recently and the city has a good range of shops, bars, restaurants and nightlife. Unfortunately, while there are pristine white beaches to the south of Bourgas, the city's port and the Gulf of Bourgas are the most polluted in Bulgaria.

North of Bourgas is Sunny Beach (*Slanchev Bryag*), the largest holiday complex on the Black Sea coast, with an 8km (5mi) stretch of clean, safe beach, plentiful sunshine and an average summer temperature of 27°C (80°F). One- and two-bedroom apartments here cost as little as €50,000. However, with more than 120 hotels and raucous nightlife, however, it isn't everyone's idea of an ideal holiday resort, and it's 'closed' between September and April, so letting is possible only during the peak holiday season.

Four kilometres north of Sunny Beach is the year-round resort of Sveti Vlas (sometimes written St Vlas) – smaller, less developed (although apartment complexes are springing up fast) and quieter but with easy access to Sunny Beach's facilities for those who want the best of both worlds. Another nearby resort is Dinevi, where a marina is scheduled for completion in 2006.

Just south of Sunny Beach is the historic town of Nesebar (or Nessebar), founded by the Greeks in the sixth century BC. Nesebar was originally built on an island but today a narrow peninsula connects the town to the mainland. Narrow cobblestone streets wind past 19th century wooden houses and there are numerous churches dating from the Middle Ages. Nesebar was designated a UNESCO World Heritage site in 1983 and attracts nearly a million visitors a year.

Like Nesebar, Sozopol (south of Bourgas) is crowded in summer with tourists attracted by its beautiful location and wealth of historic buildings. Sozopol is around 35km (22mi) south of Bourgas and located on a narrow, rocky peninsula. Also founded in the sixth century BC, it was the first Black Sea settlement established by the Greeks. Sozopol is renowned for its twin beaches, distinctive 19th century stone and wood houses and relaxed atmosphere. Popular with Bulgaria's writers and artists, the town hosts the

Apollonia Arts Festival during the first ten days of September. South of Sozopol the crowds diminish and beaches become almost deserted. Most of the resorts here are frequented only by Bulgarians, so those looking for the company of other expatriates would be better staying closer to Bourgas.

Away from the coastal resort areas, the Bourgas region offers the best of both worlds, with quiet villages and picturesque mountain scenery within a short drive of the coast. Inland, the infrastructure isn't as good as in the coastal areas, and public transport can be patchy at best.

Bourgas is linked with Sofia by air, rail and road, with journey times between six and eight hours by train, four to six hours by car and less than an hour by plane.

Property prices in the region have been rising substantially in the beach resort areas – up to 50 per cent per year in some places. Prices for rural property inland have risen slightly but are still very low by western European standards.

Dobrich

Dobrich (population 261,000) in the extreme north-east is Bulgaria's third-largest region, comprising around 6 per cent of the country's territory. The region includes parts of the Rila, Pirin and Rhodopes mountains as well as the northern stretch of the Black Sea coast. Bordering Romania to the north, Dobrich is a relatively undeveloped area, certainly far less so than areas to the south near Varna and around Sunny Beach. The region produces most of Bulgaria's grain and its position on the Danubian Plain, fed by the rivers Struma and Mesta, make it an important source of fruit and vegetables (as well as the ubiquitous tobacco).

Its location on the coast, abutted by mountain ranges, has given the region a wide range of plant and animal life, much of it protected by national parks. Birdwatchers visit the reserves around Durankulak and Shabla lakes, where several rare species can be spotted; Dobrich also has Bulgaria's only coastal national park, at Kaliakra.

Dobrich experiences cold winters, cool springs and mild summers. The region is also quite windy, with only about one in five still days. Snow cover can last for more than two months per year as a result of cold winds blowing from the north-east.

The regional capital, Dobrich (population 109,800), has begun positioning itself as the economic hub for the north-east and there are a range of national and international exhibitions held throughout the year. Part of the old town has been preserved and stands in pleasant contrast to the concrete uniformity of modern Dobrich.

To the north, the port town of Balchik is a favourite of Bulgarian artists for its dramatic seaside position and pleasant surrounds; there's a nearby golf course development. Further up the coast along the E87 towards the border with Romania, the landscape become more rocky and wild and there are fewer beaches, although plenty of nature reserves and birdwatching opportunities.

Main roads in Dobrich are of a reasonable standard and the region is served by the international airport at Varna (only 50km from Dobrich city). Travel time to Sofia is between seven and eight hours by road and nine to ten hours by train.

Gabrovo

Gabrovo (population 145,000) is just north of the centre of Bulgaria. Its location in the north of the Balkan mountains means that the climate is cold in winter, with snow on the higher peaks for more than 100 days each year, although summers tend to be comfortably warm and dry. The region is easily accessible from the main road running between Sofia and Varna, but the closest international airport is at Sofia, 220km (150mi) to the east.

Much of the region's heavy industry disintegrated after the collapse of communism and there's a legacy of empty, rusting factories and old industrial equipment. Despite this, Gabrovo is still in an important manufacturing centre, with machine- and tool-making plants, textile, furniture and plastics manufacturing as well as food, wine and tobacco production. But for most people, the region's natural beauty more than compensates for its industrial scenery. Gabrovo has a rich diversity of plant and animal life and large game reserves for hunting bear and deer.

The capital, Gabrovo (population 137,500), was once renowned for producing leatherwork and textiles (it was known as 'the Manchester of Bulgaria') and is known by most Bulgarians as the home of the biennial International Festival of Humour and Satire in the Arts, held in May, and the House of Humour and Satire, a unique museum at 68 Bryanska Street (it has a suitably off-beat website at 🖳 www.humorhouse.bg). The residents of Gabrovo have a reputation throughout Bulgaria as being tight-fisted, and jokes abound on this subject (e.g. one *Gabrovets* says to another, "Where's your wedding ring?" His friend replies, "My wife's wearing it this week.").

Despite its humorous reputation, the capital has a large number of abandoned factories and many people moving to the region prefer to live in the picturesque villages (often with mountain views), while still making use of the shops and facilities in Gabrovo.

Infrastructure in the region is often poor, although much of it is being repaired with EU funding. Many villages don't have mains water and houses often draw their water supply from a well (in fact, this is common in most rural areas in Bulgaria), which in some cases is of poor quality.

The region is not well served by trains and so you will have to rely on road transport – travel times to Sofia and Varna are between three and four hours, depending on road conditions.

Haskovo

Haskovo (population 310,000) is in the south of the country, on the border with Greece and Turkey. There is a sizeable Turkish population and this is reflected in the number of ancient mosques found in many towns. The landscape is quite flat and featureless in many places, and Haskovo is visited by few tourists, many people seeing it only as they travel pass through on the way to somewhere else. There are few important sights, but many smaller ones. For example, there are mineral springs in the regional capital, Haskovo, renowned for their healing power, remains of ancient Roman fortresses and baths dotted across the region, and, at Kenane, a magnificent oak forest and park.

Thanks to a gentle climate and fertile soil, the main industry is agriculture, almost half of the land in the region being given over to farming and food or drink production. Haskovo is a major winemaking region, with large vineyards around the villages of Elena, Mandra and Dolno Voyvodino. Fruit (including watermelons), vegetables and cereals are all grown in Haskovo, but the main crop is tobacco and Haskovo is home to Bulgaria's largest cigarette factory.

The regional capital, Haskovo (population 96,000), is one of the oldest settlements in Bulgaria – over 1,000 years old. There's an interesting History Museum and a number of old churches and mosques. The town centre has been improved markedly over the past few years and life centres around the main square, where there's a range of cafes, bars and restaurants. The area surrounding the town is quite picturesque, as there are numerous lakes and rivers.

The E80 motorway-standard road from Sofia to Turkey, which bisects the region, runs just to the north of Haskovo town and allows easy access to the northern part of the region. The roads in the south of the region are less reliable, however, and it can be difficult to travel by car in winter.

Travel by train in the region is limited as there's only one local line serving Haskovo town. There are no direct trains between Haskovo town and the major cities – to get to Haskovo from Sofia, Bourgas or Varna involves changing trains several times. Travel times are between nine and ten hours from Haskovo town to Sofia, around six hours to Bourgas. Travelling by road is much quicker, the journey from Haskovo town to Sofia taking around four to five hours. Property prices in the region are low even by Bulgarian standards.

Kardzhali

Kardzhali (population 61,200) is the most southerly of Bulgaria's regions, on the border with Greece, and lies in the eastern Rhodopes mountains. It has traditionally had a high number of inhabitants of Turkish origin and was for a long time one of the poorest and least-developed regions of Bulgaria. Although the economy picked up a little with the construction of dams and mines, the collapse of heavy industry has left the area reliant on tourism. Kardzhali has a huge number of small villages and only a few towns.

The regional capital, Kardzhali (population 44,000), was the last town held by the Ottoman Empire to fall to the Bulgarian Army, in 1912. It's useful for transport connections throughout the eastern Rhodopes and has an interesting History Museum. The nearby Kardzhali dam is popular for fishing and outdoor recreation, with restaurants and cafes open throughout the year and a number of villa developments being built nearby. Around Kardzhali are numerous strange rock formations, similar to the 'fairy chimneys' of Cappadocia in Turkey, created when volcanic rock solidified and slowly eroded over millions of years.

To the east, the town of Ardino and its surroundings has numerous historical sites and monuments, as well as areas set aside for ecological tourism. The Madzharovo nature reserve on the river Arda draws birdwatchers from all over Europe and is the habitat of vultures, falcons and woodpeckers.

While the eastern Rhodopes are excellent for walking, birdwatching and other outdoor pursuits, roads in the area tend to be of poor quality and public transport limited. You will need a car to visit most of the sights and should check whether roads in the area you're interested in buying are passable in winter.

 In some of the more isolated villages around Ivailovgrad and Kumovgrad local people are openly hostile to outsiders – many Bulgarian villagers prefer to be left alone and have minimal contact with the outside world.

But the very remoteness of this area makes it attractive to many people, as it's largely unspoilt by development and tourism. Travel time by road is around five to six hours to Sofia and up to two hours to the nearest airport, at Plovdiv.

The main train station at Kardzhali has regular trains to Plovdiv and Sofia and three to four departures a week for the Black Sea coast, taking about four hours to reach Plovdiv and seven to eight hours to reach Bourgas.

Kyustendil

Kyustendil (population 193,000) in the extreme west borders Serbia and Macedonia. Referred to as the 'Orchard of Bulgaria', Kyustendil is situated on a flat plain surrounded by mountains, providing a warm, semi-Mediterranean climate conducive to growing fruit and tobacco.

As well as agricultural products, Kyustendil is renowned for its mineral springs and the regional capital, Kyustendil (population 54,000), is renowned as a spa resort. Founded by the Thracians, the town boasts over 40 mineral springs; it was the Romans who first built bathhouses there and the Turks later built dozens of hamams (Turkish baths). There are plenty of historical sights, including medieval churches and an impressive mosque (now the History Museum).

Near Kyustendil town is the small town of Rila, close to the Rila Monastery, now a UNESCO World Cultural Heritage site. The nearby mountains provide a spectacular backdrop to the monastery, perched on the side of a steep valley, and make it the most popular tourist destination in Bulgaria. Around Kyustendil the spectacular scenery and mountain trails are a favourite with walkers and cyclists.

Transport links with the rest of Bulgaria are good, due to the proximity to Sofia, which is easily reached by road. Kyustendil town is around 90km (55mi) south-west of Sofia – around two hours by car. There are regular train and bus links and Kyustendil is on the main road between Sofia and the Macedonian capital, Skopje.

Lovech

Lovech (population 104,500) is in the north of Bulgaria between the Danubian Plain and the Balkan mountains. Attractive scenery, countless rural villages, several interesting towns and reasonable transport links make it a good choice if you're keen on mountain views and outdoor pursuits. Lovech has been settled for thousands of years, and remains and artefacts from Stone Age, Bronze Age and Iron age settlements have been found in caves at the edge of the Danubian Plain.

The regional capital, Lovech (population 50,600), is one of Bulgaria's oldest towns and is situated on the banks of the river Ossam. The town is surrounded by hills on three sides and has numerous parks – it's referred to as the Town of the Lilacs. Its icon is the Covered Bridge (*Pokritya Most*), the only one of its kind in the Balkans. Originally built in 1874, the bridge has been rebuilt and restored several times; the current incarnation is a surprisingly authentic recreation in concrete, with a range of shops and cafes.

The villages surrounding Lovech town are a popular choice as the roads in the area are of reasonable standard and quite close to Sofia and Pleven. Troyan, to the south-west, has easy access to the Troyan Monastery and is home to the Vinprom-Troyan plum brandy factory. It's a popular base for walking and exploring the nearby Balkan National Park. Tetevan, the only reasonable-size town in Lovech, is situated higher up in the Balkan mountains, with superb mountain views and plenty of forest to walk and cycle in. It's also a good spot for mountain climbing and there are opportunities for cross-country skiing in the winter.

Travelling to Sofia from Lovech by road takes around three to four hours. There are no direct trains to Sofia from Lovech town and you must usually change at Pleven (1.5 hours away) for a total journey time of four to six hours.

Montana

Montana (population 166,000) is in the north-west of Bulgaria and borders Romania and Serbia. It's a popular area for holiday homes among wealthy Bulgarians living in Sofia owing to its relative lack of development, low population density, and proximity to both the capital and the Balkan mountains. The region has recently seen a trickle of foreign property buyers but remains largely 'undiscovered'.

The capital, Montana (population 44,500), is fairly undistinguished, although it has an interesting History Museum with over 50,000 exhibits from Roman, Thracian and more recent times.

Towns further up in the foothills of the Balkan mountains are attractive choices for those seeking a rural life without too much isolation. Varshetz in the south-east of the region is an attractive spa resort with hot mineral springs and a comfortable climate. On the slopes of the Balkan mountains, winters are mild with plenty of sun, and snow cover tends to last for around two months. Spring and autumn are warm and summers are temperate. Around Varshetz and other towns such as Chiprovtzi and Berkovitza there's an emphasis on environmental tourism and activities such as walking, skiing and swimming are popular.

Transport links are reasonable, with Sofia around 110km (70mi) to the south of Montana town. There's no direct train link from Montana as it's on a railway spur but there are regular trains from nearby Boichinovtsi, which take around two to three hours to reach Sofia.

Pazardzhik

The region of Pazardzhik (population 300,500) in the south-west of Bulgaria was hit hard by the economic collapse of the '90s and is one of the poorest parts of the country, with high unemployment and an average income 20 per cent lower than the national average.

Most of Pazardzhik is situated on the Thracian Plain, making it predominantly flat and low (200m below sea level). Industry is centred on agricultural production and food processing, with a small amount of light manufacturing.

The regional capital, Pazardzhik (population 75,700), has a large population of Roma, who were resettled in the 1960s to balance the high proportion of ethnic Turks. The town is of little interest and has a reputation for petty crime, so you'd be better off looking further west towards the Rhodopes mountains and Maritsa river valley, where prices are extremely low.

Towns such as Batak and Velingrad to the west have pleasant alpine settings, mild climates and plenty of opportunities for winter and summer sports. Near Batak is the UNESCO-listed Dupkata National Park, and Velingrad is the largest mineral spa resort in Bulgaria.

There are regular trains and buses from the town of Pazardzhik to nearby Plovdiv (30 to 45 minutes by train, 40 minutes by bus) and onward links to the rest of Bulgaria. Away from Pazardzhik transport links are patchy and the roads in the south and west of the region are unreliable, especially in winter.

Pernik

Pernik (population 144,300) was until recently Bulgaria's principal coal mining region. Today, the mining industry has more or less collapsed and the region is reliant on food and tobacco production, light industry and, to a larger extent, tourism and financial and property services. Situated west of Sofia on the border with Serbia, Pernik is another region that is as yet 'undiscovered', with low property prices, but benefits from its proximity to Sofia.

The region has been inhabited for thousands of years as a result of its fertile soil and mild climate; at between 700 and 850m (2,300–2,700ft) above sea level the province sits in a natural hollow, surrounded by mountains to the south, east and north-east. Its mountain pastures give the area natural beauty but its climate is temperate-continental, with late springs and early autumns. Summers are cool, with average temperatures around 20°C (68°F), while autumn tends to be warmer than spring. Because of Pernik's location, around 30 days of the year are foggy.

The regional capital, Pernik (population 93,000), is typical of former coal mining towns and has little to recommend it. The town comes alive for the annual Surva International Festival of Masquerade Games (🖳 http://www.surva.org), held in January every even-numbered year. The festival showcases Bulgarian folklore and traditions and has grown in recent years, with over 5,000 people from 90 countries taking part in the carnival over the two days. Pernik has made attempts to improve its municipal landscape in recent years and there are a number of museums and historic sites to visit, but the most attractive areas to live are in the hills and mountains of the region.

Away from Pernik, towns such as Breznik and Vratza in the north-west are attractive places with beautiful mountain scenery, few tourists and plenty of scope for outdoor activities.

Pernik town is only 30km (17mi) from Sofia and so journey times by car are short. Direct trains (taking 40 to 60 minutes) and buses (30 to 40 minutes) leave regularly from Sofia's Central Station and the nearby Central Bus Station respectively.

Pleven

Pleven (population 333,800), in central northern Bulgaria, is located on the edge of the Danubian Plain in the foothills of the Balkan mountains. Few foreigners have purchased property in this area and there are many rural properties for sale, most in need of renovation, for less than €10,000.

The capital, Pleven (population 128,000), is often referred to as the 'City of Museums' and the city's History Museum is particularly extensive. Pleven city sits at the heart of a productive agricultural region, surrounded by low limestone hills. It's famous in Bulgaria as the site of a decisive victory by Russian forces over the Ottoman Turks dug into the town. The siege of Plevna (as it was then called) resulted in victory in the War of Liberation of 1877–78, which ended 500 years of Ottoman rule over Bulgaria. In nearby Skobelev Park, a huge memorial commemorates the victory. Pleven is also the home of a number of art galleries and the nationally renowned Pleven Philharmonic Orchestra.

Outside Pleven, three reservoirs are included in the Kailuka Nature Reserve, an attractive 'green zone' popular for swimming, watersports and walking. In fact, there are a number of national parks and nature reserves in the region, whose features include the spectacular karst (typical limestone scenery) around Chernelka and the mineral springs and waterfalls around the spa resorts of Krushuna and Steneto.

Most towns in the region are easily accessed by local bus services and Pleven town is on the main railway line between Varna and Sofia. Travel times from Sofia are between three and five hours by train and two to three hours by road.

Plovdiv

The popular Plovdiv region (population 693,000) in the central part of southern Bulgaria is bounded to the north by the Balkan mountains and to the south by the Rhodopes mountains. It's home to Bulgaria's second-largest city and near to one of the country's most popular ski resorts, Pamporovo (see **Smolyan** on page 68). The centre of the region consists of the Plovdiv Plain, part of the Thracian Valley, a fertile region of fruit and tobacco farms.

The regional capital, Plovdiv (population 340,000), is Bulgaria's second-largest city and a pleasant mix of old and new. It's one of the oldest cities in Europe and has a rich cultural and architectural history. It features Roman ruins, Thracian fortifications, Byzantine churches, Ottoman mosques and bathhouses and the splendid wooden houses of the Old Town (*Stariyat Grad*), which is built on three hills to the east of the city; the new town was built on the plain below. The Old Town is a favoured location for Bulgarian artists with its winding, cobbled streets, attractive old houses and even, soft light. There's a wide range of restaurants, cafes, bars and hotels in Plovdiv – some would say a better selection than in Sofia. Plovdiv has a huge variety of museums and galleries and is often referred to as the cultural capital of Bulgaria. It was also the centre of the democratic movement in Bulgaria, which led to the overthrow of the communist regime in 1989. Plovdiv is home to the twice-yearly International Fair, which causes a huge influx of visitors and businesspeople.

Plovdiv city is one of the main transport hubs for Bulgaria and has links with the rest of the country and to Europe. Regular trains to Sofia cover the journey in two to four hours and the trip can be made by road in around two hours. The E80 linking Sofia with Istanbul, which is one of the best roads in the country (although traffic can be abysmal), runs just outside Plovdiv. Plovdiv's airport is currently used only for charter flights during the skiing season (from December to April).

Razgrad

Situated in the valley of the Beli Lom river in the north-east of Bulgaria, the region of Razgrad (population 128,600) sits at the edge of the Danubian

Plain. To the south of the province the Ludogorie hills mark the beginning of the Balkan mountains. Away from the main towns of Isperih and Razgrad the population density is less than 60 people per square kilometre, compared with the average for Bulgaria of 72 inhabitants per square kilometre. Tourism is yet to make much of an impact in Razgrad, where the main industries are agriculture and pharmaceuticals.

Nevertheless, there are a large number of ancient sites in the region, including the largest Thracian tomb in Bulgaria (the UNSECO-listed 'Royal Tomb'), near the village of Sveshtari. Not far from the tomb is the Demi Baba Tekke, a 16th century Muslim shrine. The other tourist attraction is the hunting reserve at Voden, a large park with attached lodges for hunting wild boar, deer and mouflon.

The regional capital, Razgrad (population 33,000), was originally the Roman town Abritus. These days Razgrad's main attractions are the 17th century Ibrahim Pasha Mosque, located in the Old Quarter (*Varosh*) to the north of the town, and in June the festival of local traditional culture and yogurt fair (!). Twenty-six kilometres (15mi) from Razgrad is Isperih, a pleasant agricultural and industrial centre with a bustling Friday market and an interesting museum. Isperih's main attraction is its proximity to the historical sites around Sveshtari.

Roads are adequate in the area and the first railway to be opened in Bulgaria, in the late 19th century, connecting Ruse on the Danube and Varna on the Black Sea, passes through Razgrad town. Travel time to Varna is around two to three hours by train and around two hours by road.

Ruse

The region of Ruse (population 267,000) in the north-east of Bulgaria sits on the border with Romania. Situated on part of the central Danubian Plain, the area has been farmed and settled for centuries. It's another relatively undiscovered part of Bulgaria, with much potential for foreign buyers.

The provincial capital, Ruse (population 150,000), is renowned in Bulgaria as an attractive, cosmopolitan city and played a significant role in the collapse of communism, when local people protested against pollution caused by an enormous chemical plant across the river in Romania. Ruse is also served by the oldest railway in Bulgaria, built by the British for the Ottomans in the 1880s (local wags say the service hasn't changed since then). The city is often compared with western European cities such as Paris and Vienna on account of its attractive location on the Danube and the large areas of well preserved historic buildings.

South of Ruse city is the impressive Rusenski Lom National Park, site of the Rock Monastery of Ivanovo and the ruined citadel of Cherven. The monastery at Ivanovo is built on the side of a steep, rocky gorge and is surrounded by churches and galleries built into caves on the sides of the cliff. Further south, the remains of what was once referred to as the 'City of Churches' can still be seen. Cherven was the region's administrative centre before it was moved to the more favourable of the city of Ruse.

There are many good bargains to be had in the villages surrounding the city of Ruse and further afield, although poor roads and transport infrastructure can be a problem. Quality apartments are available in the centre of Ruse, but most foreign buyers are attracted by the houses and villas in the countryside, costing just a few thousand euros and ripe for renovation or rebuilding.

Transport links with the rest of Bulgaria are generally good, with travel times by road to Sofia around five hours and to Varna around three to four hours. Trains from Ruse city take around seven hours to reach Sofia and three to four hours to Varna.

SURVIVAL TIP
With the easing of visa restrictions in Romania, some people are finding it easier to fly direct to Bucharest and then catch a train, bus or taxi the 60km (37mi) south to Ruse.

Most EU passport holders can now stay in Romania for up to 90 days without a visa – for more information check with your local Romanian embassy, e.g. in London (☎ 020-7376 0683, 🖥 http://www.roemb.co.uk).

Shumen

Shumen (population 197,000) is a region rich in cultural artefacts and natural beauty, enjoying a warm climate and varied terrain. Situated in the north-east of Bulgaria, the province is close enough to Varna to make access easy, yet far enough from the Black Sea to be inexpensive, even by Bulgarian standards. Houses and villas for renovation in mountain villages can be purchased for less than €15,000, while properties requiring less work can be picked up for under €30,000.

The most famous tourist site in Shumen is the UNESCO-listed Madara Horseman, carved into the rock face near the village of Madara. Its origins are obscure, some historians dating the eroded carving to around the eighth century BC, while others believe it may date back to the time of the Thracians. Around Madara are dozens of cliffs and unusual rock formations.

The regional capital, Shumen (population 84,000) is surrounded by hills and bordered on two sides by the huge Shumensko Plato National Park. The town is relaxed and pleasant and there are ample opportunities for walking in the park. Shumen's main attraction is the Tombul Dzamiya, until recently the largest mosque on the Balkan Peninsula.

To the south of Shumen town are the remains of the two capitals of the Bulgarian First Kingdom. The first capital was built at Veliki Pliska and was populated from 681 to 1018AD; the second was 2km (1.2mi) away at Veliki Preslav, the capital of Bulgaria from 893 to 969AD. There isn't much left of either ancient city, although a museum at Veliki Pliska gives an idea of its former glory.

Shumen is criss-crossed by three major roads and the capital is on the main Sofia-Varna road. Travel times by road are around two hours to Varna and around six hours to Sofia. Trains take between 1.5 and 2.5 hours to reach Varna and six to seven hours to Sofia.

Silistra

Also in the north-east of Bulgaria, on the border with Romania and beside the Danube river, Silistra (population 132,700) is a predominantly agricultural region. Its position at around 200m (650ft) above sea level on the Dobrudzha plain is well suited to the growing of apricots and cherries and means the region enjoys hot summers and cold, snowy winters.

The regional capital, Silistra (population 38,900), is one of the oldest towns in Bulgaria, dating back to Roman times. Although situated on the banks of the river Danube, the town has little of interest apart from a Roman tomb and a few museums.

To the west of Silistra is the UNESCO-listed Srebarna Nature Reserve, one of only 17 sites in the world to be given the status of 'Biosphere Reserve Class A' by UNESCO. The lake at Srebarna is a haven for all types of migratory birds and is a temporary home for over 200 different species. The lake is the only place in Bulgaria where the curl-headed penguin can be seen (in spring).

Silistra town is a major cargo port for grain from the area and as a result the main roads are of good quality. Travel times by road are around three hours to Varna and seven hours to Sofia, while the train takes six to seven hours to Varna (with a change at Samuil) and 10 to 11 hours to Sofia.

Sliven

Another predominantly agricultural region, Sliven (population 132,700), south-east of the centre of Bulgaria, is an interesting mix of attractive forests and mountain scenery and rolling farmland. The region is one of the largest in the country and around 40 per cent of it is forested (around half is farmed). Sliven is also one of the poorest areas in Bulgaria and has a large number of Roma, but it's seen as having some of the best potential for developing a strong tourist industry. Property prices are low compared to the rest of Bulgaria and the region is bordered to the east by Bourgas, with its port, international airport and the huge resort at Sunny Beach (see page 55). Sliven is a major wine producing region – and the local Cabernet Sauvignon is highly regarded!

The provincial capital, Sliven (population 94,000), nestles at the foot of the steep Blue Rocks – so called on account of the bluish tinge these mountains acquire at sunset. The area was once home to so many outlaws that Sliven was known as the 'Town of the Hundred Bandits', although it's a slightly more law-abiding place these days. Sliven is renowned for its clean air and water, mild winters and cool summers and is the only town in Bulgaria not to have changed its original Slavonic name.

The nearby Blue Rocks National Park is the third-largest in Bulgaria and is easily reached from Sliven town. The park features rugged landscapes and ancient beech forests and shelters a huge variety of plants and animals, including wild boar and deer. A chairlift operates throughout the year to the highest peak, giving spectacular views over the town and the surrounding valleys.

Around Sliven town are dozens of ancient villages, where the pattern of life has remained essentially unchanged for centuries. Towns such as Kotel and Zheravna, tucked away in the hills to the north-east, still have many wooden houses and quiet town centres, while cultural and historic monuments and mineral springs dot the entire region.

The main Sofia-Plovdiv-Bourgas road passes close by Sliven town and the region is relatively well served by public transport. Travel time to from Sliven town to Bourgas city is around three hours by road and two hours by train.

Smolyan

Smolyan (population 135,000) in the far south of the country is a small, rugged region in the Rhodopes mountains, bordering Greece. Around 65 per cent of the region is covered with ancient conifer forests and there are several ski resorts, including the popular resort at Pamporovo. Smolyan has cool summers and snow on the mountains from mid-December to April.

The provincial capital, Smolyan (population 31,600), in fact consists of three villages (Raikovo, Smolyan and Ustovo). It's situated at an altitude of around 900m (3,000ft) above sea level and is surrounded by ancient forests and green meadows. Many of the buildings are traditional wooden structures and there's much less of the monumental Soviet architecture than is found in other Bulgarian towns and cities. Near Smolyan are a series of emerald green lakes, known as the 'Emerald Eyes of the Rhodopes'.

The resort of Pamporovo is busiest (perhaps overcrowded) in winter and claims to be the sunniest of the Bulgarian winter resorts (it's Europe's most southerly ski resort), with over 120 days of sunshine. Snow cover from December to April is excellent and there's a huge range of downhill and cross-country runs. In summer there are walks and mountain biking tracks through the mountains. There are pleasant walks to the peak of nearby Mount Rozhen, the Smolyan lakes, surrounding villages and the Bachkovo Monastery. The monastery, founded in 1083, is UNESCO-listed and the second-largest in Bulgaria.

Throughout the Smolyan region there are numerous villages with attractive mountain scenery and often with a local mineral spring. There's little heavy industry in the region so your choice of place to live will depend on how far from 'civilisation' you want to be – and how reliable the roads are during the winter months.

Smolyan's rugged terrain and the steep mountains of the Rhodopes mean that transport can be slow. There are no trains, and from Smolyan town the nearest city with public transport links is Plovdiv, around four hours by road over the Rozhen Pass. Pamporovo is around 30 minutes by road from Smolyan town and two to three hours from Plovdiv.

Sofia

The capital of Bulgaria, Sofia (population 1.1m), which itself constitutes one of the 28 regions, is Bulgaria's largest city and the second-oldest capital city in Europe (after Athens). Located in the west of the country, Sofia is an interesting combination of impressive monuments, attractive churches and monolithic Soviet architecture. The city's bustle and pollution can be too much for some people, and property prices are higher than anywhere else in the country.

The city is one of the few places in Bulgaria where the population is increasing, as many young Bulgarians come to Sofia for work and a 'better' life. There's a substantial expatriate community and the highest number of job opportunities for qualified professionals. Low labour costs in Bulgaria have led many American and western European companies to subcontract IT and financial processing work to Sofia. However, the presence of so many expatriates and Bulgarians looking for work in Sofia means that the average price of property is higher than elsewhere in Bulgaria, although better possibilities exist for buy-to-let properties, particularly in the corporate market.

Sofia is served by a comprehensive transport system, including trams, buses and trolley buses. Taxis are cheap (less than 0.50 lev/€0.25 per kilometre), although it's recommended to use metered taxis unless you know in advance how much you should pay to get where you're going, and the airport is connected to the city centre by regular buses.

Central Sofia is where the main cultural and historical sites are concentrated and it has wide, tree-lined boulevards, giving it the feeling of a western European capital. However, the unique character of Sofia is to be found in the small, winding side streets, with their interesting mix of old and new buildings and busy markets. There's a huge range of cafes, restaurants, bars and nightlife, as well as numerous venues where you can see high-quality performances of ballet, classical music and theatre. Most cafes and restaurants in central Sofia are open until midnight, and bars and clubs usually stay open until early in the morning.

Apartments in Sofia can be good value but are often dark and small, although two- and three-bedroom apartments are springing up in many parts of the capital, and many of them are being finished to 'Western' rather than Bulgarian standards (see page 119). Average prices in prime residential areas are between around €1,000 and €1,500 per square metre.

Sofia isn't without its problems: rubbish is often piled up in the streets, many of the roads are potholed or in a state of disrepair and in the suburbs there's a huge number of stray dogs. But the city has several large, attractive parks and the Mount Vitosha National Park, less than an hour's drive from the city centre, is easily accessed from the affluent suburbs of Boyana, Dragalevtsi and Simeonovo.

Mount Vitosha itself (just 20km/12mi from the centre of Sofia) is popular for walking and picnics in summer and, with good snow cove, for skiing in winter. The main resort on Mount Vitosha is Aleko, a small town just below the summit, where a two-bedroom apartment can be had for around €110,000.

Sofia District

The Sofia District region (population 263,000) surrounds the city of Sofia to the north, east and south (but doesn't include the city itself). Like much of this part of Bulgaria, it's a region of rugged mountains, rich in cultural and historical artefacts and buildings. The main attraction is the popular ski resort of Borovets (see below) and the region includes dozens of picturesque villages, all within two hours of Sofia, offering rural peace and quiet and outdoor pursuits throughout the year.

Borotvets is the oldest and largest winter sports resort in Bulgaria and continues to grow in popularity. Situated amongst 100-year-old pine forests at 1,350m (4,400ft), Borovets provides good conditions for snow sports, including downhill skiing (by day and night), snowboarding, cross-country skiing, ski jumping and biathlon (cross-country skiing and rifle-shooting). The runs aren't particularly long or difficult, but the resort has a lively après-ski scene (thanks mainly to the low price of alcohol!) and is exceptional value. The season lasts from November to May and in the summer there are numerous walking tracks and trails for mountain biking. Property prices in Borovets are high, particularly in the resort itself (around €100,000 for a two-bedroom apartment), although there are opportunities for buying in nearby villages at much lower prices. Borovets is popular mostly with package tourists, so there's less opportunity for buy-to-let properties and holiday rentals than in other resorts.

A popular location for buying property near the Rila mountains (part of the Balkan range) is the town of Samokov, which is close to several mountain resorts. The town itself has an interesting museum and the remains of ancient Thracian buildings can be found nearby. (The area around Samokov is also the largest producer of potatoes in Bulgaria!)

To the east, in the Sredna Gora mountains (also part of the Balkan range), the town of Koprivshtitsa is a superb example of classical Bulgarian architecture. Nestled at over 1,000m (3,280ft) above sea level, it's considered the spiritual home of the Bulgarian April Rising, the revolution against the occupying Ottoman Turks. The town can be overrun in summer with holidaying Bulgarians and foreigners, although it makes an excellent base for walking and biking in the surrounding hills.

Transport becomes less reliable the further into the mountains you go, and Koprivshtitsa is the only regional town on the main train line between Sofia and Bourgas. Journey times from Koprivshtitsa to Sofia are around two to three hours by train and around two hours by road.

Stara Zagora

The productive agricultural region of Stara Zagora (population 390,000) in the centre of the country has for centuries stood at the crossroads of important trading routes between east and west. To the north, the Sredna Gora mountains (part of the Balkan range) drop to a wide, fertile plain of wheat fields and orchards. The region enjoys a temperate climate throughout the year with mild, short winters and an average temperature of 13°C (55°F).

The regional capital, Stara Zagora (population 180,000), was completely destroyed in 1877 and has been rebuilt on a grid plan, with leafy boulevards and outdoor cafes. The city is home to a range of galleries, museums and theatres and two opera houses, as well as ancient Thracian ruins, a massive park and thermal hot springs.

West of the city is Stara Zagora's main tourist attraction, Neolithic dwellings dating back to around 5500BC, while the nearby mountains have plenty of walking trails and fishing spots.

Stara Zagora has a regional development association and is positioning itself as a centre for investment in services (including tourism), agriculture and light industry. The area has long been a centre of textile production and the regional capital has a number of small, high-quality clothing manufacturers.

The region has numerous thermal mineral springs and a large number of spas and health centres. The town of Pavel Banya is a favourite health resort for people afflicted with arthritic and orthopaedic conditions, while the thermal waters and clean air around Starozagorski have made it an important healing centre for respiratory and other ailments. Pavel Banya is growing in popularity as a base for walking in the Balkan mountains. The eastern part of Stara Zagora is part of the 'Valley of the Roses' (see **Geography** on page 53).

As befits its strategic location, the region is easily accessed by road and rail and the completion of the E773 from Plovdiv should make journey times by road even shorter. The closest international airport is at Bourgas, around two hours by road and three to four hours by train.

Targovishte

The region of Targovishte (population 142,400) in the north-east of the country lies on the edge of the Danubian Plain and consists mostly of rolling hills and fertile agricultural land. It's another area that's relatively undiscovered by foreign property buyers, although its proximity to Varna and the Black Sea coast, as well as opportunities for eco-tourism in the mountains to the south, may see it increase in popularity. The climate is 'mild continental', with warm summers and cold winters. Targovishte can be subject to flooding and storms in early spring – in 2005 a combination of warm temperatures and fast melting snow led to floods across the region.

The regional capital, Targovishte (population 41,400), sits around 170m (550ft) above sea level. The town has a pleasant Old Quarter (*Varosh*) with over 30 original buildings in the Bulgarian Revival style. A few kilometres from Targovishte city are mineral springs renowned for their healing powers.

Close to the town are dozens of historic and cultural sites, including Zheravna and Kotel. The town of Kotel has a large number of older buildings protected against development in its Old Quarter and is a regional centre for carpet making, including handmade woollen rugs (*kilim*). Bulgaria's main folk music school is also located in Kotel and students travel from all over the country to learn to play traditional instruments. Zheravna, often referred to as a 'museum village', benefits from a beautiful location and has more than 200 wooden houses, some over 300 years old. While the village can be overrun with tourists in the summer, its winding cobbled streets and interesting museums make up for the crowds. There are also numerous old villages throughout the region with fine examples of traditional Bulgarian architecture and in picturesque mountain surroundings.

Targovishte town is around 110km (70mi) from Varna. There are no direct trains, as the nearest main station is at Shumen, around 30km (20mi) to the east. By road, Targovishte is around three hours from Varna and four hours from Bourgas.

Varna

With its favourable location on the central Black Sea coast, a Mediterranean climate, stunning coastal views and attractive villages (as well as huge tourist resorts) Varna (population 454,000) is one of the most popular regions in Bulgaria among foreign property buyers. The region also benefits from having an airport served by regular domestic and international flights for most of the year, ferry links with other Black Sea ports and excellent road and rail links with the rest of the country. And it has the country's highest concentration of English-speaking estate agents!

The regional capital, Varna (population 349,000), is Bulgaria's third-largest city (after Sofia and Plovdiv) and one of the most modern and westernised cities in the country. Varna has a fascinating history and was first inhabited around 4,000BC (the oldest gold treasure in the world was excavated near the city) and its long history is illustrated in its collection of ancient monuments, impressive old buildings and comprehensive Archaeological Museum. It has remained an important trading port to this day and is now the home of the Bulgarian Navy with a large shipbuilding industry, although this has gone into seemingly terminal decline along with most Bulgarian heavy industry. The city is pinning its hopes on tourism and already Varna and the nearby resorts of Golden Sands and Albena attract hundreds of thousands of tourists each year. Nevertheless, the city remains an important industrial centre, forming the Varna-Devnya Industrial Complex (with neighbouring inland town Devnya), home to some of the largest chemical, electrical and manufacturing plants in Bulgaria.

North of Varna, the tourist complexes at Golden Sands and Albena offer the potential for investment properties with summer lets, although much of the area is oversupplied. A growing number of people wanting to be close to Varna for its good transport links and range of facilities are purchasing properties inland – just a few kilometres from the beach. South of Varna, there are fewer large resorts and more small towns and villages, but all of them are easily accessible. Two popular locations are Byala and Obzor, relatively quiet seaside towns on the main road between Varna and Bourgas, and Kavarna (50km from Varna) is a small fishing port offering a more authentic seaside experience. Another attractive and as yet relatively undeveloped coastal resort is Kamchiya, between Varna and Byala.

Inland but within a few minutes of the coast are a number of attractive and popular villages, including Avren (at the region's highest point and enjoying spectacular views), Obrochishte (3km from Albena and with good amenities) and Rogachevo (the 'Beverly Hills' of Varna, with stunning views and just 3km from the sea). Other property 'hotspots' in Varna include Kitka, Kranovo, Priseltsi, Ravna Gora and Zdravets.

As befits Varna's size and popularity, transport links with Bulgaria and the rest of Europe are excellent. In summer, there are international trains to Istanbul, Kiev and Moscow, as well as buses to Istanbul and elsewhere in the Balkans. The train trip from Sofia to Varna city is best done overnight, as it takes from seven to nine hours, as does the journey by road (although this may improve as the main road is gradually upgraded with EU funding).

Veliko Tarnovo

The region of Veliko Tarnovo (population 290,000), located in central northern Bulgaria, is perhaps the best known area after the Black Sea resorts and certainly the most popular inland, rural region among foreign property buyers. It includes a variety of landscapes, from the fertile Danubian Plain in the north to the rugged Balkan mountains in the south.

The regional capital, Veliko Tarnovo (population 65,000), was the capital of the Bulgarian Second Kingdom (in medieval times) and its romantic mountainside location has made it a popular tourist destination. The town is spread across three hills and the Yantra river valley at the foot of the Balkan mountains and benefits from a mild climate, numerous natural and historical landmarks, nearby forests and a burgeoning local craft industry. Veliko Tarnovo dates back to around the fourth century BC and has been a centre of

Bulgarian culture for centuries. It's divided into a **New Town** and a picturesque Old Town, full of churches and museums and the remains of a palace and fortress. Veliko Tarnovo is home to the largest university in Bulgaria.

Just north of Veliko Tarnovo is the tiny, beautiful village of Arbanasi. Arbanasi was once a rich merchant town and its high-walled stone houses sit among churches and ancient monasteries with elaborately decorated interiors, carvings and murals. Property prices here are among the highest in Bulgaria and the village is a favourite among moneyed Bulgarians.

In the north of the region, the town of Svishtov has an attractive location on the banks of the Danube, quiet surroundings and a history dating back to Roman and Thracian times, with a good range of museums and important historic buildings. It's more affordable than Arbanasi if you're keen to live in the region but have a limited budget.

Veliko Tarnovo's central location means that it has good access to the rest of Bulgaria, with reasonable roads and public transport links. The train between Sofia and Varna stops at Gorna Oryahovitsa, 13km (8mi) north of Veliko Tarnovo town and linked by regular local trains. Travel time by train is around four to five hours to Sofia and three to four hours to Varna. By road, it should take three to four hours to reach Sofia and around the same time to get to Varna. There's an airport at Veliko Tarnovo town, but there are currently no scheduled domestic or international flights.

Vidin

Tucked away in the far north-west corner of the country on the border with Serbia and Romania, Vidin (population 131,000) is a predominantly agricultural region and an important transport hub for the rest of Bulgaria. The region includes part of the Danubian Plain, lowlands (in the centre) and uplands (in the south-west), marking the edge of the Balkan mountains. The banks of the Danube have beaches and forested areas on the Bulgarian side and low-lying, marshy land on the Romanian side.

The regional capital, Vidin (population 57,000), is an important river port, although trade with neighbouring Serbia suffered a major setback with the NATO bombing of the '90s. This is starting to improve, but some estimates put the proportion of Vidin's population that left in search of work elsewhere at over 30 per cent. Vidin is one of the oldest towns on the Bulgarian Danube, originally recorded as the Roman fortress Bononia, built on the foundations of a Thracian settlement. Several fortresses were built, destroyed and rebuilt by the Bulgarians and occupying Ottoman Turks over the centuries; the Baba Vida fortress, built on the ruins of a Roman fort, is a well preserved reminder of Vidin's strategic location.

In the south of the region, Belogradchik is a small town situated amongst stunning rock formations, stretching almost 100km (60mi) to the Macedonian border. Belogradchik sits at around 550m (1,800ft) above sea level at the edge of the Balkan mountains and functioned as a natural fortress for centuries. There are numerous caves and ravines to explore throughout the area, which could become a centre for adventure tourism.

Direct links with the Bulgarian capital are good: the E79 runs from Vidin town to Sofia – around three to four hours' drive. A new bridge across the Danube linking Vidin with Calafat on the Romanian side should be completed soon, making Vidin an important road link with western Europe. Trains between Vidin and Sofia take between five and six hours. Vidin's airport is currently closed.

Vratsa

In the north-west of the country and a few hours' drive from Sofia, the region of Vratsa (population 196,000) lies at the edge of the Balkan mountains. It's a rugged, mostly forest-covered area characterised by dramatic rock formations and so far mostly undiscovered by tourists and homebuyers.

The regional capital, Vratsa (population 58,000), has begun promoting itself as a tourist destination, based on the region's natural beauty and folk traditions. Vratsa is a pleasant town, situated on the banks of the river Leva and at the foot of the steep Vrachanska mountains (part of the Balkan range). Near the town is the huge Vrachanski Planina National Park, with excellent hiking and walking trails and spectacular scenery. There are over 500 caves and karst (limestone) precipices in the park, as well as the massive Ledenika cave, which gets its name from the icicles (*leden* means ice) that form there in the winter. The largest chamber at Ledenika, the 'Great Hall,' whose acoustics are unique, occasionally hosts classical music concerts. Several 'adventure tourism' companies have opened in Vratsa, promoting rock climbing, caving and canyoning, parasailing and downhill mountain biking.

Vratsa town is only 115km (72mi) from Sofia, and the journey takes around two hours by road. There are also direct trains, taking a similar time.

Yambol

Yambol in the south-east (population 144,000) is one of Bulgaria's most important agricultural regions. Bordering Turkey to the south, it's an increasingly popular area among property buyers as it's close to Varna and the Black Sea coast, yet relatively undeveloped. Property prices remain low and the region is diverse, taking in mountains, rolling hills and interesting towns. The climate is Mediterranean in the south of the province and more continental in the northern part, although the Balkan mountains in the north tend to shelter the region from cold winter winds. More than three-quarters of the land in Yambol is used for agriculture, although there are several forest reserves in the north.

The regional capital, Yambol (population 75,000), is situated on the banks of the Tundja river and dates back to Roman times (when it was known as Dianopolis). There are Roman baths in the city as well as numerous historic buildings and sites such as the mediaeval fortress, the churches of St George and St Nicholas, a covered market (dating back to the 16th century) and the Eski mosque.

The nearby town of Kabile is a well known archaeological site and one of the few surviving Thracian towns pre-dating the arrival of the Romans. The area around the town of Elhovo is popular with foreign (especially British) buyers, although some parts are rather isolated. In the south-east of the region, the village of Stefan Caradjovo is popular for its mineral springs, while the larger town of Straldja in the north-east is also renowned as a spa resort. Along the Tundja river valley there are guest houses and small tourist operators promoting hunting and 'ecological tourism'.

The town of Yambol is on the main railway between Sofia and Bourgas, with journey times around two to three hours to Bourgas and six to nine hours to Sofia. By road it's less than two hours from Yambol to Bourgas.

LOCATION

The most important thing to consider when buying a home anywhere is its location – or, as the old saying goes, the three most important considerations in buying property are location, location and location! Especially if you're buying as an investment, an average property in a great location is always preferable to a great property in an average location. Even if you aren't interested in making money from your property, there's no point in spending your money on a 'dream home' that's next to an industrial area or a busy road, or is so far from anywhere it takes you a whole day just to buy a loaf of bread. In the popular property-buying areas of Bulgaria amenities and facilities are all you could wish for, but you still need to make sure you choose the right property in the right spot.

 The wrong decision about location is one of the major causes of disenchantment among foreigners buying property in Bulgaria.

Many people come to Bulgaria on holiday and look to buy property in the same area, or base their decision on recommendations from friends, an area's reputation or on how easy it is to access. But if you're planning on retiring to a home in Bulgaria or even just spending a few weeks a year there on holiday, it's important to take your time and consider every aspect of its location. When it comes to choosing a place to live, don't be unduly influenced by the fact you've spent an enjoyable holiday or two there. A great holiday resort or place that was comfortable for a few weeks' holiday may be less than suitable for year-round living.

The 'best' place to buy a home in Bulgaria of course depends on your preferences and what you want from a property. It's important to sit down and evaluate the positive and negative aspects of every location you think may be suitable, to help you choose the place that suits you and your family best.

If you have a job in Bulgaria or plan to work there, the location of a home will probably be determined by how close it is to your place of work. Buy a map of the area and calculate the maximum distance you're prepared to travel to work each day, taking into account the quality of the roads and potential traffic. Draw a circle of appropriate radius with your workplace in the middle. If you're going to look for employment or start a business, choose an area that gives you the maximum scope. Unless you have reason to believe otherwise, don't rely on the romantic notion that everything will work out once you arrive in an area!

However, if you're looking for a retirement home, you must choose somewhere that's easily accessible, low maintenance and close to essential services and amenities. A holiday home may be in a popular resort, but think what you may want to do with it in five, ten or 20 years' time; will it be suitable as a retirement home, will you be able to sell it, will the resort be overcrowded?

If you don't know where you want to live, read as much as you can about the different areas of Bulgaria (see **Regions** above and the books listed in **Appendix B**) and spend as much time as possible looking at those that interest you. The climate, cost of living and way of life can vary dramatically from one area to another. If you choose to live in the mountains or in a rural area, the type of life you lead will be as dramatically different as the scenery from a coastal resort location.

If you want to live in or near a village, be sure to investigate it, as Bulgarian villages vary enormously in attractiveness and amenities. As a result of the government's 'Beautiful Bulgaria' initiative, many are clean, pretty and inviting, while others are run-down and unwelcoming.

Before looking at properties, it's best to have an idea of the type of home you're looking for (see **Types of Property** on page 115) and how much you want to spend (see **Property Prices** on page 107). With this information you should be able to draw up a shortlist of the areas and towns that interest you. If you don't do this, you're likely to be overwhelmed by the sheer number of properties to be looked at. To cut down the time you spend viewing properties, it can help to have an idea of where you want to buy within a 30 to 40km (20 to 25mi) radius, or even narrow your choices down to specific towns and villages.

Verify all travel times yourself – and don't rely on what estate agents tell you! There's no point in buying a delightful house in a picturesque village if you want to visit for weekends and it takes you three hours to drive there from the nearest airport. Especially if you think you will be relying on public transport, try to visit an area a number of times over a period of a few weeks, during the week and at weekends, to get a feel for the neighbourhood or village (and make sure you walk around!). A property viewed at the end of a pleasant holiday after a tasty lunch and a few beers or glasses of wine may look entirely different another time.

Try also to visit an area at different times of the year to get an idea of whether the climate is suitable, whether services and amenities are available outside the holiday season, and what restrictions there are on transport – public and private – in winter. While the climate is generally mild along the coast, in the mountains and further inland a place that's wonderful in summer can be forbidding and inhospitable in winter. Similarly, in summer the crowds, noise, heat and traffic pollution can be oppressive. If you're planning to buy a winter holiday home, you should also try to view it in the summer, as snow can conceal all manner of faults – structural as well as cosmetic (see **Doing Your Own Checks** on page 127).

If you're unfamiliar with an area, many experts recommend that you rent for a while before deciding to buy (see **Renting Before Buying** on page 98). This is particularly important if you're planning to buy a permanent or retirement home in an unfamiliar area. Many people change their minds about location after renting for a while and it isn't unusual for families to rent in two or three different places before settling down permanently.

When house hunting, it's advisable to buy large-scale maps of the area where you're looking and to mark off the places you've seen, perhaps using a grading system to record your impressions. If you use an estate agent, he will usually drive you around and you can use your annotated map to return later to those you like the most. One of the best series of maps of Bulgaria is published by a local company, Domino; the maps cover all the regions and most major towns and surrounding areas. Although printed in Bulgarian and English, they're currently only available in bookshops and travel agencies in Bulgaria. Another good map is the Bulgarian road atlas published by Global (🖳 http://www.mapsbg.com), which covers the whole country to a scale of

1:250,000. In Sofia, a good source of maps and information is Odysseia-In, 20-V Al. Stamboliiski Boulevard (🖳 www.odysseia-in.com).

In resorts – whether in the mountains or on the coast – you should always try to find out the medium-term infrastructure plans for the area, especially for road construction and development of vacant land (see **Doing Your Own Checks** on page 127). Your home with splendid sea views and open fields for neighbours might be crowded out and the view blocked by other buildings in a few years' time.

Foreign buyers are generally welcome everywhere in Bulgaria, particularly in rural areas, where they're seen as bringing life and valuable business to villages whose population is being depleted, while the Black Sea coast has long been a tourist destination, where people are used to large numbers of foreigners. Given Bulgaria's population decline and high unemployment, anyone who brings opportunity and 'hard currency' is usually welcomed with open arms. In any case, most Bulgarians are naturally friendly towards outsiders. In some of the poorer regions in the south, however, people can be inhospitable, particularly in regions with a history of ethnic tension, but these areas tend to be the poorest and least attractive parts of a region and so are of less interest to foreign buyers.

When assessing the advantages and disadvantages of a location, take into account the following factors.

Accessibility

Is the proximity to public transport, e.g. to an international airport, bus terminal or railway station, or to a main road important?

Road building continues apace in Bulgaria, but years of underinvestment have left many roads in a poor and crumbling state. There's only one motorway-quality road, running from Sofia to the border with Turkey, and even that isn't yet complete (see **Bulgarian Roads** on page 93). The rail network is extensive but doesn't reach all parts of the country (see **Regions** above and **Domestic Rail Services** on page 92). Budget airlines don't yet fly to Bulgaria, but many people believe that when Bulgaria joins the EU this will change. Certainly the growing number of people buying property in Bulgaria may encourage budget airlines to start flying to the country, although most tourists come to Bulgaria as part of a package using charter flights. You will need to check that there are flights from your home country throughout the year if you plan to visit outside the peak tourist season.

Don't always believe everything you're told about the distance or travelling times to the nearest main road, airport, train station beach or town; check them for yourself.

SURVIVAL TIP
One of the major considerations when buying a holiday home is communications (road, rail and air links) with your home country.

If you buy a property in a small or remote village, the distance to local amenities and services could become a problem, particularly if you're planning to retire to Bulgaria. If you're buying a home with a view to retiring there later, check the local public transport services, as you may not always be able (or want) to drive. See also **Getting Around** on page 91 and **Retirement** on page 41. Some remote areas can be snowed in during winter, cutting them off for several days.

Remember that a lot of the public transport in Bulgaria is seasonal and you will need to think carefully about whether you will need a car or not. If you don't plan to live permanently in Bulgaria you will usually be better off hiring a car, as prices are much lower than elsewhere in Europe. If you can live without a car you will spend much less money.

Amenities

What local health and social services are provided? How far is the nearest hospital with an emergency department? What shopping facilities are available in the town or village where a property is situated? How far is it to the nearest major town with a range of shopping facilities such as a supermarket or department store? How would you get there without a car? If you live in a village or rural area you will need to be much more self-sufficient than if you live in a town.

Climate

For most people the climate (see page 28) is one of the most important factors when buying a home in Bulgaria, especially a holiday or retirement home. Owing to the country's varied topography, the climate varies considerably across the country. Make sure you're familiar with the local summer and winter climate, as well as the position of the sun and direction of the prevailing wind. The orientation or aspect of a building is vital and you should make sure that balconies, terraces and gardens will be sunny or shady depending on your requirements. Depending on where you choose to live, air-conditioning may be a necessity, particularly if you're elderly and aren't used to intense heat.

Community

Do you want to live among people from your own country and other foreigners in a largely expatriate community such as those around Sunny Beach, Varna and Nesebar, or would you prefer (and be prepared) to fit into a more traditional Bulgarian environment?

You will find it difficult to integrate with the local community if you choose to live in a village and don't speak Bulgarian – and your enjoyment of the rural lifestyle will be diminished if you can't communicate with local people. On the other hand, if you settle in an expatriate enclave, you won't be deriving the full benefit from your Bulgarian home.

If you're buying permanently, it's important to check your prospective neighbours, particularly when buying a flat or apartment. Are they noisy, sociable, or absent for long periods? Do they have young children or babies that cry a lot? Do you think you will get along with them? **Good neighbours are invaluable, especially if you're buying a second home in Bulgaria.**

Crime

What's the local crime rate? In most areas the incidence of burglary is quite low, but you should check before narrowing your choice. Are rates increasing or decreasing? What sort of crimes are most common? Professional crooks like isolated houses, particularly those full of expensive furniture and other belongings, which they can remove at their leisure. You're much less likely to be a victim of theft if you live in a village, where everyone knows each other and strangers stand out instantly, although if your house appears to belong to a wealthy foreigner you may be a victim of opportunistic crime. Many people in rural areas who don't live there permanently employ a caretaker or gardener to make sure the property looks 'lived in'. See also **Crime** on page 236.

Employment

How secure is your job or business and are you likely to move to another area in the future? Can you find other work in the same area if necessary? If you might have to move in a few years' time, you should consider renting or at least buy a property that will be relatively easy to sell. Don't forget to take into account your partner's or children's actual or potential jobs.

Garden

If you're planning to buy a rural property with a large area of land attached, keep in the mind the cost and work involved in maintaining it. If it's to be a second home, who will look after the house and garden when you're away? Do you want to spend your holidays mowing the lawn and cutting back the undergrowth? Are you able to repair fences or build new ones? Maintenance contracts are reasonable on properties in or close to towns, but make sure you budget for them. In a village, you may have to pay a local person to look after your property if you aren't going to be there permanently.

Local Council

Is the local council well run? Despite the reorganisation of Bulgaria's regions in 1987 and 1999, many councils have a severe lack of funds. Bulgaria is working to improve municipal administration to meet EU standards, but the country remains highly centralised, and local councils are dependent on central government funding. What are the views of other residents? Are there good local social, sports and public transport facilities?

Natural Phenomena

Check whether an area is particularly susceptible to natural disasters, especially floods and landslides. Much of the coastal area along the southern Black Sea coast is susceptible to landslides and in some areas building restrictions have been ignored. Flooding has caused extensive damage in Bulgaria in the past few years. If a property is located near a waterway it may be expensive to insure against floods, which are a regular threat in some areas (see **Doing Your Own Checks** on page 127).

Noise

Noise can be a problem in some towns, resorts and developments. Although you might not be able to choose your neighbours, you can at least ensure that your property isn't next to a busy road, industrial plant, commercial area, nightclub, bar or restaurant. Look out for neighbouring properties that are too close to the one you're considering or are poorly cared for, and check whether nearby vacant land has been set aside for further building or commercial use.

In community developments, such as apartment blocks or villa complexes, many properties are second homes and are let short term, which means you may need to tolerate boisterous holidaymakers as neighbours throughout the year (or at least during the summer months).

Don't assume either that rural life is all peace and quiet. Other kinds of noise can disturb your peace and quiet, including ringing church bells, crowing roosters, braying donkeys, wedding celebrations and poorly maintained cars and tractors wheezing along the road. Most rural Bulgarian families have a dog (or several dogs) to guard the home, and they often bark at anything that moves throughout the day and night. You might be able to adjust to this background noise, or it may drive you mad!

Parking

If you're planning to buy in a town or city, is there adequate private or free on-street parking for your family and visitors? Is it safe to park in the street? Parking can be a problem in cities and busy resort areas, where private garages or parking spaces can be very expensive (e.g. over €3,000 for a space in some villa developments). Keep in mind that an apartment or townhouse in a new or community development may be some distance from the nearest road or car park. How do you feel about carrying heavy shopping hundreds of meters to your home and possibly up several flights of stairs?

Property Market

Do houses sell quickly in the area, e.g. in less than six months? You should try to avoid neighbourhoods where desirable houses stay on the market for six months or longer (unless of course, the property market is in a slump and nothing is selling).

Schools

What about your children's current and future schooling? Is there an international school nearby? How much will school fees be and how easy is it for your children to get to school? Even if your family has no need or plans to use nearby schools, the value of a home may be influenced by its proximity to an international or private school.

Sports & Leisure Facilities

What is the range and quality of local leisure, sports, community and cultural facilities? How close are sports facilities such as a beach, golf course or ski resort? Properties close to beach or mountain resorts are always more expensive but they will have the best letting potential.

Tourists

If you choose to live in a popular tourist area, you will have to put up with multitudes of holidaymakers in the summer (or winter) months. They won't only clog the roads and pack the public transport, they may even take your favourite table at the local cafe or restaurant!

Although a property right on the beach may sound attractive and be ideal for short-term holidays, it isn't usually the best choice for permanent residents. Many beaches are hopelessly crowded during the summer, the streets overrun with people eating and drinking outside, parking impossible and services stretched to breaking point, and the constant noise and hassle can drive you crazy. The same applies to many of Bulgaria's ski resorts.

Town or Country?

Do you want to live in a town or do you prefer the country? If you buy a property in the country, you will probably have to deal with irregular or non-existent public transport, long travelling times to a town where you can shop for anything other than necessities, and isolation from people who speak your native language. There won't be a choice of bars or restaurants on your doorstep and if you need a doctor or a post office you may have to travel some distance. In a town, there will usually be a good weekly market, a variety of places to eat, drink and be entertained, and a doctor and chemist nearby.

In the country you will get more of an 'authentic' Bulgarian experience, you will be closer to nature, as well as having more freedom (for example, to make as much noise as you like). Living in a village or a rural area will suit nature lovers looking to 'get away from it all' but even they might find that the attractions pall after a while. Remember that many people who move to a rural area to escape the city find they miss distractions and entertainment.

> **SURVIVAL TIP**
> **If you've never lived in the country before, it's a good idea to rent before you buy where possible.**

Remember also that while it's often much cheaper to buy in a remote location, it's usually much more difficult to find a buyer when you want to sell.

GETTING THERE

One of the major considerations when buying a holiday home is the cost of getting to and from Bulgaria and the time it will take. You should find the answers to the following questions:

- How long will it take to get to my home in Bulgaria, taking into account journeys to and from airports, train and bus stations?

- How frequent are flights, ferries, buses or trains at the time(s) of year when I plan to travel?

- Are direct flights available?

- Is it feasible to get there by car?

- What's the cost of travel from door to door?

- Are off-season discounts or inexpensive charter flights available?

If a long journey is involved, you should keep in mind that it may take a day or two to recover, especially if you're crossing time zones (Bulgaria is two hours ahead of GMT). Obviously, your travelling time and costs will be greater if you plan to spend frequent weekends there, rather than a few long visits a year. When comparing costs between public transport and driving, take into account depreciation and wear and tear on your car, the cost of additional insurance and the price of motorway tolls (see **Driving** on page 89) and fuel.

> **SURVIVAL TIP**
> **Allow plenty of time to get to and from airports, ports and bus stations, especially when travelling during peak times, when traffic congestion can be horrendous, and also take into account the time that security checks can take.**

Airline Services

Currently only British Airways and the national carrier Bulgaria Air (formerly Balkan Air) fly directly from the UK. Flight time direct from most UK airports is just over three hours. Most European carriers offer connecting flights to Sofia, usually via the airline's hub (e.g. Lufthansa flights usually stop in Frankfurt); while these are often good value, they can involve long flight times, as stopovers can add four or five hours to your flight. If you are unlucky enough to have an overnight stopover, the cost of the flight rarely includes hotel accommodation or breakfast. If you're flexible as to the times and dates you can travel, a good travel agent should be able to find routes that don't sacrifice convenience for cost.

Bulgaria Air flies to major European destinations and has a fleet of nine aircraft, mostly Boeing 737s. Service is reasonable (although not at premium level) and fares are generally lower than their British Airways equivalents. Services from the UK include daily flights between London Gatwick and Sofia, flights from London Heathrow to Bourgas on Tuesdays and Fridays and flights between Gatwick and Varna on Mondays, Wednesdays and Fridays. British Airways (BA) currently flies daily between London Heathrow and Sofia and four times a week from London Gatwick to Varna during the summer. Bulgarian airline Hemus Air offers direct flights between London Heathrow and Sofia four times a week, and Hungarian-based budget operator Wizz Air flies from London Luton to Sofia and Bourgas. While fares are substantially cheaper than those of other airlines, some Wizz Air flights stop in Budapest, which increases flying times.

Charter flights are operated by a number of companies, but these usually require you to book accommodation as part of a package. Some charter operators may have flight-only tickets but these are rarely advertised, so you will have to contact the operator directly. See **Appendix F** for a list of airlines (including charter operators) flying to Bulgaria.

Internet Booking

There's a range of internet flight and holiday booking sites, some of which offer flight deals not available elsewhere. It's advisable to check fares online and then ask if your travel agent has a better offer. The main booking websites are listed below.

- **Deckchair** (⌨ http://www.deckchair.com);
- **Expedia** (⌨ http://www.expedia.co.uk);

- **Last Minute** (💻 http://www.lastminute.com) – not as many cheap fares as it used to have;

- **Opodo** (💻 http://www.opodo.co.uk);

- **Orbitz** (💻 http://www.orbitz.com) – only for holders of a credit card with an address in the US;

- **Priceline** (💻 http://www.priceline.co.uk) – allows you to name a price and see if the airline will accept it;

- **Qixo** (💻 http://www.qixo.com) – currently US only;

- **Travelocity** (💻 http://www.travelocity.co.uk).

Airports

There are four international airports in Bulgaria: at Bourgas, Sofia, Plovdiv and Varna (see map in **Appendix E**). Those at Bourgas and Varna are currently undergoing construction of new terminals, the former due to be completed in August 2006, the latter ... some time later. Plovdiv is mainly used for charter flights to the ski resort at Pamporovo. To reach a property in the far north-east of Bulgaria, it may be quicker to fly to Bucharest in neighbouring Romania.

Car hire is available at all major airports, although booking is recommended. You should also check with a car hire company what time the rental desk closes if you will be arriving on a late evening flight. Information about car hire can be found on 💻 http://www.rentacarbulgaria.com.

International Rail Services

There's little point in travelling to Bulgaria by train unless you want to visit other countries en route. However, with the re-opening of the train line through Belgrade a few years ago there are now a number of options for getting to Sofia from the UK. The most direct routes are via France, Italy, Croatia and Serbia and via Belgium, Germany and Croatia. The most comfortable (and most expensive!) method is to travel from Paris to Vienna on the Orient Express, take an 'InterCity' train to Budapest, and then the Balkan Express to Sofia. This takes around three days and, if you're travelling from the UK, involves a trip on the Eurostar (see below).

Eurostar

The Channel Tunnel joins France with the UK by rail and links London Waterloo (until 2007, when trains will start operating from St Pancras) with Paris in just 2h35m. Depending on when and how you plan to travel it can be an expensive journey. A standard return fare costs over €400, although a return trip booked well in advance for a weekend costs around €150 and promotional fares are available for less than €100. For train information in English or to make a booking, call ☎ 08705-186186 in the UK or visit the Eurostar website (⌨ http://www.eurostar.com). A £5 booking fee applies to telephone bookings. For car-train services through the Channel Tunnel, see **Eurotunnel** on page 90.

International Bus Services

Eurolines (⌨ http://www.eurolines.com) operates regular services from London Victoria to destinations in Bulgaria, including Sofia. The bus fare isn't particularly cheap compared to discount flights and the journey time may be off-putting – it currently takes 48 hours from London to Sofia, including a 90-minute stopover in Frankfurt, Germany.

Driving

If you plan to drive to Bulgaria you will need an International Driving Permit (as well as your national licence) and an international Green Card from your insurance company. If you will be driving through the countries of the former Yugoslavia you will have to pay for a local insurance policy at the border.

Be aware of high motorway tolls in France and Switzerland; travelling via Germany is toll-free. If you don't travel through Switzerland, there are no border checks or formalities until you reach Bulgaria. The recommended route from Vienna is via Budapest and Belgrade to Sofia. It will take around three days to drive the approximately 2,300km (1,400mi) from London to Sofia. A longer, but more enjoyable, journey is through Italy to catch a ferry to Greece, then drive on to Sofia. There are ferries throughout the year to Greek destinations departing from Venice, Ancona and Brindisi.

The RAC has a useful journey planner (⌨ http://rp.rac.co.uk/routeplanner), which covers routes across Europe to Bulgaria.

Eurotunnel

If you plan to drive from the UK, Eurotunnel operates a shuttle car train service between the UK and France, through the Channel Tunnel. Trains carry all types of vehicle, including bicycles, motorcycles, cars, trucks, buses, caravans and motor-homes, although you pay more for larger vehicles.

There are five trains per hour during peak periods and the crossing takes just 35 minutes. Prices have come down recently and journeys start from €69 one way. It's usually advisable to book and you shouldn't expect to get a place in summer if you haven't, particularly on Fridays, Saturdays and Sundays. The cheapest way of travelling through the Tunnel is to buy a day return ticket, which can be had for as little as €44, using the outbound portion and simply discarding the return ticket. Eurotunnel prohibits this and may log numberplates on the outbound journey, then charge the maximum fare for the return (although whether this is legal is debatable), but if you're moving permanently to Bulgaria or plan to return a different way, this won't concern you.

Eurotunnel also has a Frequent Traveller scheme, which allows you to purchase ten single 'off-peak' journeys in advance for €57 each, to be used within a 12-month period. Further information is available by telephone (☎ 08705-353535) or from the Eurotunnel website (💻 http://www.euro tunnel.com).

International Ferry Services

Ferry services across the English Channel operate year-round between France and the UK/Ireland. There's a wide choice of routes for travellers between France and the UK but only one for Irish travellers (Cork/Roscoff). Some services operate during the summer months only and the frequency of services varies from dozens a day on the busiest Calais-Dover route during the summer peak period to one a week on longer routes. Services are less frequent during the winter months, when bad weather can also cause cancellations. On the longer routes (e.g. between Dover and Rotterdam/ Zeebrugge/Amsterdam and from Portsmouth to Le Havre), there are overnight services.

It's worthwhile shopping around for the best ferry deal, which is probably best done via a travel agent who has access to fares from all companies or by using a company specialising in discount Channel crossings. These include Channelcrossings.net (💻 http://www.channelcrossings.net), Cross-Channel Ferry Tickets (💻 http://www.cross-channel-ferry-tickets.co.uk),

Ferrybooker.com (🖳 http://www.ferrybooker.com), Ferrysavers.com (🖳 http://www.ferrysavers.com) and Into Ferries (🖳 http://www.intoferries.co.uk). It can be difficult to consult ferry company fares online, as you don't have access to the full range of fares and can often only find the price by filling in a time-consuming online booking form or quote facility.

GETTING AROUND

The lack of investment in public transport since the collapse of communism has left it in a dismal state. Bus and train stations are run down and dirty, trains are slow and often cancelled and buses are in poor condition. The frequent floods of recent years have seen east-west train services cancelled or re-routed for days at a time. Many private bus companies are now filling the gap left by the collapse of centralised transport services but improvement is slow.

Sofia is the exception, with an excellent network of trams, trolleybuses and buses (and an impressive new bus terminal) and swarms of inexpensive taxis (with typical fares between around €1 and €3). Taxis in smaller cities and towns can cost as little as 1 lev (€0.50). Sofia is also an easy city to negotiate by bicycle, with no large hills and wide boulevards (although stray dogs are often a problem after nightfall).

In rural areas, on the other hand, there's usually no public transport and locals often hitch a ride on the back of a neighbour's tractor. Where it exists, public transport is extremely cheap and, unless you're in a hurry, a good way to travel between the main cities.

Years of underinvestment have also left many roads in a poor state, and there's only one motorway-quality road, running from Sofia to the border with Turkey. Bulgaria's mountainous terrain and harsh winter conditions leave most roads potholed and dangerous and some impassable.

Domestic Flights

The only domestic flight operator in Bulgaria is the privately-owned Hemus Air (🖳 http://www.hemusair.bg), which operates a combination of BAe 146 and Russian-made Yakovlev and Tupolev aircraft between Sofia and Varna throughout the year and Sofia-Bourgas and Varna-Bourgas during the summer. Prices are reasonable compared to the train, especially considering the train takes six to eight hours to reach the coast from the capital. One-way fares in summer 2005 were Sofia-Varna €97, Sofia-Bourgas €97 and Varna-

Bourgas €25. At the time of writing Bulgaria Air was being privatised, which may affect some routes and fares.

Domestic Rail Services

The Bulgarian rail network is comprehensive and the state-owned railway company BDZ has services to most major towns and cities, the two main lines linking the capital with Bourgas and with Varna. However, trains are slow and delays or cancellations common, and rail travel is generally slower and less reliable than travelling by bus, although fares are comparable. To meet EU regulations, the government split the infrastructure and rail service of BDZ into to separate companies and investment in the railways has begun to increase, although BDZ still operates at a massive loss. Part of the problem is that passenger fares are below costs – the government subsidises the fares to make up the difference.

Despite being slow, Bulgarian trains are comfortable and a sleeper berth for longer journeys is excellent value (with an additional charge of just €3 or €4 for a first-class compartment for two!). There are three types of train: Express, Fast and Ordinary. Express trains operate only on the main routes, while Fast trains operate on almost all lines and are preferable to Ordinary trains, which stop at every station and take forever to get anywhere. There's usually a drinks and snacks trolley on intercity trains, although this rarely offers much more than peanuts and beer. Smoking is allowed only in designated carriages on all trains. BDZ has recently purchased new Siemens diesel trains to improve the quality of service on the Black Sea coast routes.

Booking is compulsory on all Express and Fast trains and if you want to travel in a sleeper compartment, you must book at least 24 hours in advance. Sleeper compartments are considered safe to travel in, although you should take the usual precautions and not leave valuables on display or unattended in your compartment.

BDZ has a surprisingly comprehensive website (🖳 http://www.bdz.bg/eng/index_eng.htm), with timetables for all destinations, information on ticket prices and discounts and a history of the company. In Sofia railway tickets must be purchased from the Central Railway Station (the booking office is beneath the main hall) or from the travel agency in the basement of the National Palace of Culture. Outside Sofia, tickets can be purchased only at railway stations. If you arrive at a station too late to buy a ticket (there's usually a queue) you can pay on the train, with a surcharge of around 30 per cent.

Main railway lines are shown on the map in **Appendix E**.

Domestic Bus Services

Competition from the private sector has seen a huge growth in the number of bus companies operating across Bulgaria. The bus is a comfortable and convenient option and it's often easier to travel by bus in mountainous regions as few towns in the mountains are reachable by train. Every town has a bus station, and sometimes two or three, as buses operated by private companies use different stations. The buses run by private companies are usually newer and more comfortable than those run by state-owned concerns. There's no national timetable for bus services; each company publishes its own timetable (although these aren't always easy to find) and services don't always link conveniently.

Bus transport is very cheap, a three-hour cross-country journey costing as little as 12 lev (€6), for example. It's usually easier to buy tickets either from the bus company office at the bus station or from a travel agent, as staff are more likely to speak English than bus drivers.

The private company ETAP runs one of the most modern and comfortable fleets of buses between the main cities and has timetables, fares and distance information on its website (🖳 http://etapgroup. com/etap/en). For services from Sofia's gleaming new bus station, the *Centralna Avtogara*, you can check timetables and destinations on its website (🖳 http://www.centralnaavtogara.bg – use the menu at the top right to change the language to English).

Bulgarian Roads

Bulgarian roads have a reputation for being potholed tracks frequented by farm animals and agricultural machinery. For the most part, that's correct. There are only four major sections of dual-carriageway in the country (see **Main Roads** below). Otherwise even main roads are often narrow, with long stretches of damaged tarmac. In rural areas and in the mountains there are numerous hairpin bends and wandering livestock to negotiate.

Bulgaria recently introduced a user-pays system for all roads. If you drive to Bulgaria, you will need to purchase a 'vignette', available at the border when you enter the country. Vignettes for a passenger car cost €59 for a year, €10 for a month or €4 for a week and cover you for travel on all roads. Police check vignettes and issue an on-the-spot fine of 1,000 lev (€500) for vehicles without one or with a vignette that has expired.

Speed limits are 60kph (35mph) in built-up areas and either 80kph (50mph) or 120kph (75mph) on main roads; speed limit signs are in Roman numerals. If you commit a traffic offence, the police are authorised only to issue you with a ticket (citation) and there are no on-the-spot fines, yet drivers of cars with foreign registration plates are sometimes stopped and 'fined' for minor (or non-existent) breaches of road rules. It is, however, compulsory for all vehicle occupants to wear seatbelts, and talking on a mobile phone while driving is illegal.

 Driving in Bulgaria is not for the faint-hearted and finding your way is often difficult or next-to-impossible, as most road signs are in Cyrillic script.

Main Roads

There are only four major sections of dual-carriageway in the country: from Sofia to Plovdiv, from Harmanli to the Turkish border, from Varna to Novi Pazar, and between Sofia and Jablanica (on the way to Pleven), only the first two of which are of motorway standard. The section of the A1/E80 between Plovdiv and Harmanli is under construction; when completed, there will be a dual-carriageway 'motorway' all the way from Sofia to the Turkish border, which should reduce some of the heavy, constant freight traffic on local roads between Plovdiv and Turkey. The Bulgarian government signed a contract early in 2005 for a private company to build a motorway running from the Serbian border in the west to Sofia and on to Varna; when complete, this road will have a user-pays toll. There are currently no other toll roads in Bulgaria, as the vignette system (see above) functions as a road toll for all drivers. Main roads are shown on the map in **Appendix E**.

Other Roads

The Bulgarian government is working to bring the main roads linking cities up to European standards. These are designated 'E' roads and are being slowly improved with EU funding. While some are in reasonable condition, be prepared to dodge potholes and to be stuck behind slow-moving HGVs en-route to western Europe for long periods.

Common hazards on Bulgarian roads include cars driving at night with damaged or no headlights, slow-moving or stationary livestock and farm machinery, people driving erratically (e.g. changing lanes with no indication and stopping suddenly for no apparent reason) and pedestrians. It's usually recommended not to drive after dark in rural areas.

3.

YOUR DREAM HOME

Once you've considered possible locations for your dream home in Bulgaria, you will need to decide on the type of property that will best suit your needs, compare the purchase options and calculate the costs, including the fees associated with buying.

There's an overwhelming choice of property for sale and it's a buyer's market in most areas, although less so along the Black Sea coast and in Sofia. Bulgarian property is very different from that in the UK and other western European countries, and there can be substantial differences between and even within regions. For these reasons it isn't necessary – and certainly isn't advisable – to be in too much of a hurry. As when making all major financial decisions, you should give yourself time to think (see **Renting Before Buying** below).

Have a good look around your chosen area(s) and get an accurate picture of the different types of property available, their relative values and what you can expect to get for your money. But before doing this you should make a comprehensive list of what you want (and don't want!) from a home, so you can narrow your search and avoid looking at unsuitable properties.

If you find something you fall head over heals in love with, wait and think about it for a week or two before rushing to the altar! One of the advantages of buying a home in Bulgaria is that there's usually another 'dream home' around the next corner or in the next village – and the second or third dream home is often even better than the first. On the other hand, **don't put off your decision too long, as good properties at the right price won't stay on the market for ever**.

RENTING BEFORE BUYING

To reduce the chance of making an expensive mistake when buying in an unfamiliar area, it's often sensible to rent a property for a while, taking in the worst part of the year (weather-wise). This allows you to become familiar with a region, with the weather and with the roads and transport, and gives you plenty of time to look around for a home at your leisure.

> **SURVIVAL TIP**
> **Unless you know exactly what you're looking for and where, it's best to rent a property for a while, especially if you're planning to buy in an unfamiliar area.**

This is even more important if you plan to set up a business or work in Bulgaria, when it isn't advisable to buy a home until you're sure that your business will be a success or you can survive financially without working. Renting long term before buying is sensible for anyone planning to live in Bulgaria permanently. Where possible, you should rent a similar property to the one you're planning to buy, during the time(s) of year when you plan to occupy it.

The advantages of renting include the following:

● It allows you to become familiar with the weather, the infrastructure and local people, to meet other foreigners who have made their homes in Bulgaria and share their experiences, and to discover the cost of living for yourself.

● It 'buys' you time to find your dream home at your leisure.

● It saves tying up your capital and can be surprisingly inexpensive in some regions. You may even want to think about renting a home in Bulgaria long-term (or 'permanently'). Some people let their family homes and rent one in Bulgaria for a period (you may even make a profit!).

On the other hand, the disadvantages of renting should also be taken into consideration, including the following:

● Annual property price increases in most areas are higher than interest rates, meaning you may be better off tying up your money in a property than investing it while you rent.

● Taking a long-term rental before buying means in effect moving house twice within a year or two; remember that moving is one life's most stressful experiences!

● You may not find the type of rental property you want, which will colour your experience of living in a particular area and possibly in Bulgaria generally. For example, most rental properties are apartments and rural homes are rarely available for rent.

If you're looking for a rental property for a few months, you may need to rent a holiday apartment or hotel room for a week or two to allow yourself time to find one that suits you. Remember that upon arrival in Bulgaria you must register your address with the local authorities and tell them how long you plan to stay (see **Permits & Visas** on page 36).

Short-term Rentals

The Bulgarian rental market is starting to grow rapidly, particularly in short-term holiday accommodation. You can choose from thousands of apartments, villas and homes. Short-term rental accommodation varies considerably, from smart one- and two-bedroom apartments to huge villas with swimming pools. However, the majority of property is available for holiday lets (i.e. one to two weeks) only, particularly during the peak summer season. The good news is that supply currently far exceeds demand so that competition for rental income is fierce and short-term rental prices have been dropping sharply. There's also an oversupply of hotel beds on much of the Black Sea coast and hotels regularly drop their rates or offer special deals. Note, however, that foreigners are normally charged higher rates than Bulgarians!

Alternatively, private rooms are usually available in most tourist resorts, including Bourgas, Plovdiv, Ruse, Sofia and Varna and along the coast. Rooms can be booked through the local tourist office or accommodation bureau or with a company specialising in room bookings, or you can book directly with owner. Size and quality range from large rooms in traditional old houses in historic towns to small apartments in larger cities. Rooms are often let by retired people and pensioners supplementing their income. Breakfast often isn't included in the rate but if you ask the owner nicely (or look hungry enough!), he will usually provide breakfast for a few lev more.

SURVIVAL TIP
If you will be renting in winter, remember to check that the property has central heating.

Long-term Rentals

A short-term rental may be suitable for house hunting but to get a feel for an area you will need to rent for more than a couple of weeks. Unfortunately, however, rural properties are rarely available for long-term rental and most long-term rental properties are unfurnished; long-term furnished properties are difficult to find outside Sofia. In the capital, the situation is different due to the huge demand for rental properties among expatriate workers.

In Bulgaria, 'unfurnished' can mean a number of things, although an unfurnished property should at least be equipped with major appliances such as an oven, washing machine and fridge. Always ask what's included before viewing, as you may save yourself a wasted trip.

Finding a Rental Property

Your success or failure in finding a suitable rental property will depend on many factors, not least the type of rental property you're looking for (a one-bedroom apartment is easier to find than a four-bedroom detached house, for example), how much you want to pay and the area you want to rent in. The Bulgarian rental market is concentrated on the coast and in the major towns and cities, although this may change as more people buy property for letting.

Ways of finding a property to rent include the following:

● Visit letting agents. Most estate agents also act as letting agents. Some agents are better than others; generally, those that advertise rentals on their website in English will be easier to deal with.

● Contact travel agents and local tourist information offices, who can book hotel rooms and private rooms and may also handle short-term rentals of apartments and houses.

● Look in newspapers and magazines, especially local papers and expatriate publications and foreign property publications (see **Appendix B** for a list).

● Look for advertisements in shop windows and on notice boards in shopping centres, supermarkets, universities and colleges, and company offices.

● Search on the internet – useful sites include 💻 http://www.bulgarianrentals.com, 💻 http://www.imotibg.com/en, 💻 http://www.mybulgaria.info, 💻 http://www.priderentals-bg.com and 💻 http://www.rentinbulgaria.com.

SURVIVAL TIP
It's often better to deal with an agent than directly with owners, especially when it comes to contracts and legal matters, in case there are any disputes over payment, damages or the cost of your stay.

Rental Costs

Rental costs vary considerably according to the size and quality of a property, its age and the facilities provided. Prices depend on the city the property is located in and the area. For example, a two-bedroom apartment in an area of Sofia popular with expatriates will cost much more than a similar property in a tower block on the outskirts of the city. In some areas at certain times of year, the rent on many properties is negotiable, but in cities with large numbers of expatriatess demand remains fairly constant and so do prices.

Rental prices are highest in Bourgas, Plovdiv, Sofia and Varna. Accommodation in Sofia is becoming increasingly expensive, particularly for larger and high-quality apartments and houses, and prices start at around €300 per week for a small (e.g. 90m^2) apartment and range from €350 to €450 for larger apartments. In Varna, small apartments can be had from €200 to €250 per week, while the average price for larger properties is around €300 to €350. Large houses and villas in and around Varna can be rented for €500 to €1,500 per week, depending on the quality of the property.

The lowest prices are found in small towns and rural areas, although there isn't as much choice. In rural areas, there are few if any properties for rent. Most of those that are available are large, renovated houses that can sleep between 6 and 15 people and are for short-term or holiday rental.

You may be able to negotiate a reduction in any quoted rate if you plan to stay for more than a week or two or will be staying outside the peak tourist season.

Lists of short-term rental accommodation in Sofia and Varna can be found on 🖳 http://www.sofiaapartments.com and 🖳 http://www.varna apartments.com.

Hotels

Bulgarian hotels range from excellent to atrocious and there's often little way of telling the good from the bad. Prices range from derisory to extortionate and often bear little resemblance to the quality of the hotel or the services and amenities provided. During the communist era hotels were run by the state, but almost all are now privately owned and in the main tourist towns and cities there's a reasonable selection of hotels, including at least one Western-owned hotel chain such as a Best Western, Novotel or Radisson. On the Black Sea coast and in popular resorts most former state-owned hotels have been renovated and refurbished to Western standards, but in small towns and rural areas, choice is often limited and there may be only an old, run-down state-owned hotel.

The international star system is used infrequently and it's recommended to base your choice of hotel on the age of the establishment – generally, the newer the better. You rarely need to book, as supply exceeds demand for hotels across Bulgaria. You may be able to negotiate a discount for room rates outside the summer season and for long stays.

Details of hotels in the main cities can be found on 💻 http://www.bourgashotels.com, 💻 http://www.plovdivhotels.com and 💻 http://www.varnahotels.com. To find a rural hotel, look on 💻 http://www.ruralbulgaria.com.

An alternative to a hotel is a private room (see **Short-term Rentals** on page 100), which can be booked through local accommodation bureaux and tourist offices.

HOME EXCHANGE

An alternative to renting is to exchange your home with one in Bulgaria. This way you can experience home living in Bulgaria for a relatively small cost and may save yourself the expense of a long-term rental. Although there's an element of risk associated with exchanging your home with another family, most agencies thoroughly vet clients.

There are home exchange agencies in most countries and, while there aren't a huge number of homes for exchange in Bulgaria yet, the number is bound to increase as more foreigners purchase homes and investment properties. Agencies in the US include Home Exchange.Com (💻 http://www.homeexchange.com) and Homelink International (💻 http://www.homelink.org or http://www.swapnow.com). Agencies based in the UK include Home Base Holidays (💻 http://www.homebase-hols.com) and Intervac Home Exchange (💻 http://www.intervac.com).

HOUSE HUNTING

There are many ways of finding homes for sale in Bulgaria, including the following:

- The internet, where Bulgarian estate agents selling property to foreigners usually have sites in English (and occasionally in German, Dutch or Russian). See **Appendix C** for a selection of addresses. Many people begin their search online to get an idea of prices in the areas they're interested in.

- Newspapers and magazines, including the English-language publications listed in **Appendix B**, national newspapers in your home country (if you're looking for an expensive property), local magazines, papers and newssheets.

- Property exhibitions (see **Appendix A**).

- Property viewing tours, which are organised by estate agents in Bulgaria and abroad, and often by property developers. These range from comprehensive viewing trips with a full itinerary and accommodation included to excursions where you're met by an agent at the airport or your hotel. Costs vary, but expect to pay around €350–400 for an all-inclusive weekend trip from the UK.

- Visiting an area yourself and contacting local estate agents. This is the only way to get a proper feel for an area.

- Developers, some of whom sell direct (usually off plan – see page 167), others via agents in Bulgaria and abroad.

- Estate agents (see below).

When you go house hunting in Bulgaria, remember to take a calculator (to convert prices quoted in lev or euros), a mobile phone that works in Bulgaria (and a charger and plug adapter), a notepad, maps and contact numbers. If you will be spending more than a few days looking at property, it's worth buying a Bulgarian 'pay as you go' SIM card for your mobile. It's usually a good idea to take a camera or video camera.

ESTATE AGENTS

While some foreigners have had success buying in Bulgaria directly from a seller, the majority of sales are handled by estate agents. The property boom in Bulgaria means that there's a huge choice of estate agents to choose from; it also means that some have little or no experience (estate agency is unregulated in Bulgaria) and a few are unreliable or even untrustworthy, and even those that aren't are often overwhelmed by enquiries and can therefore be less than efficient. You should therefore use only an agency that is registered as a 'property company' and accept that you may have to be persistent in your search for your dream home.

There are a growing number of estate agents based abroad who handle sales in Bulgaria, usually in partnership with a Bulgarian agency, while many Bulgarian estate agents are starting to advertise abroad, particularly in the publications listed in **Appendix B**, and many have English-speaking staff. Foreign agents may understand your needs better than a Bulgarian agent (and will often organise flights and accommodation for viewing trips and assist with the buying process, although services such as these will cost you more than arranging your own travel, accommodation and legal adviser) but they may have less knowledge of the market and of Bulgarian property law.

Many Bulgarian estate agents are starting to advertise abroad, particularly in the publications listed at **Appendix B**, and many have English-speaking staff. While it can be easier to work with an estate agent with English-speaking staff, you may fare just as well hiring a local translator. The going rate is around 30 lev (€15) per day.

As in most countries, agents vary widely in their professionalism, efficiency and enthusiasm, although the Bulgarian agents who advertise outside Bulgaria tend to provide accurate details and pictures of the properties they have for sale, especially for larger and more expensive properties. The best agents provide an abundance of information. On the other hand, some agents don't update their records frequently and their websites or property lists may be months out of date. If an agent isn't interested in helping you find what you want, go elsewhere.

Agents' Fees

There are no government controls or other limits on agents' fees, which are normally paid by the purchaser rather than the vendor owing to a traditional mistrust of property agents among Bulgarians!

 Unlike in most western European countries, it's standard practice in Bulgaria for the buyer to pay the agent's commission on top of the purchase price (i.e. it isn't included in the property price).

Most Bulgarian-based estate agents charge 3 per cent of the purchase price as commission but some charge as much as 10 per cent. In the case of low-value properties, a set 'minimum' fee is often charged, ranging between €500 and €1,000. The notary public's fees for administering the preliminary contract (see page 113) should be included in your estate agent's fee (but make sure you check this beforehand).

Some agents charge a fee to take you on property viewings, which is refunded if you buy a home through them. Other agents may charge you only the cost of the taxi fare. Make sure you establish what the fees are (for both commission and viewings) in advance.

Foreign agents' fees can vary dramatically (e.g. between 2 and 5 per cent) according to the level of service they provide. Some charge a fixed fee for lower-priced properties.

Viewing

Before visiting Bulgaria, obtain details of as many properties as possible of the appropriate type and price in your chosen area and make a shortlist of those you wish to view (marking their locations on a map). If you cannot decide where and what you you're looking for, at least tell the agent, so that he knows you're undecided. If you're 'window shopping', say so. Many agents will be happy to show you property anyway, as they're well aware that many people quickly change their minds and decide to buy on the spot.

If you're searching on the internet, keep in mind that many of the properties advertised might already be sold, that property descriptions – especially for rural properties – can be misleading and that photographs of picturesque properties in idyllic locations might be cleverly concealing something unpleasant, which may be just outside the shot!

If you've made an appointment to see specific properties, make a note of the reference numbers in case the Bulgarian agent doesn't have them (or has lost them), and confirm (and reconfirm) the price and that a particular property is still available before travelling to Bulgaria to view it.

 It isn't uncommon for agents to lure potential buyers with idyllic properties that are no longer for sale (or don't even exist!) and then try to sell them other properties that may not even match their requirements.

In Bulgaria, agents will show you properties themselves and won't give you the keys or expect you to deal with owners or tenants directly. In rural areas, property can be difficult to find (away from main roads, signs are all in Cyrillic) and agents themselves often get lost trying to find a particular address.

You should make an appointment to see properties, as agents usually won't have time to drive you around if you turn up at their office unannounced. If you make an appointment, you should keep it or cancel it. If you're on holiday, it's fine to walk in to see what's available, but don't expect to be able to view any properties. If you do view properties while you're on holiday, it's best to do so at the start of your holiday so that you can return later to review any you like. You should also dress appropriately, and not in a vest top and flip-flops. Bulgarian estate agents tend to work all hours so you can generally view property on any day of the week.

You should try to view as many properties as possible in the time available, but make sure you allow enough time to view each property thoroughly, to travel (and get lost) between houses and to take food and drink breaks. Although it's important to see enough properties to form an accurate opinion of price and quality, don't see too many in one day (between four and six is usually enough), as it's easy to become confused as to the pros and cons of each. If you're shown properties that don't meet your specifications, tell the agent straight away. You can also make the agent's job easier by telling them what you don't like about the properties you reject.

It's advisable to make notes of both the good and bad features and take lots of photographs of properties you like so that you can compare them later (but make sure you make a note of which photo is of which house!). It's also worth marking each property on a map so that if you want to return later on your own you can find them without getting lost.

SURVIVAL TIP
The more a property appeals to you, the more you should look for faults and negative points; if you still like it after stressing all the negative points, it must be worth considering seriously.

Note the following public holidays, which should be avoided on any viewing or house-hunting trip: 1st January, 3rd March, Easter (which is a week later than in western Europe), 1st, 6th and 24th May, 6th and 22nd September, and 25th and 26th December.

PROPERTY PRICES

Prices for most Bulgarian properties are quoted in euros, although in some areas popular with UK buyers prices are quoted in sterling. For a rough conversion of euros to sterling, multiply by 0.7; for US dollars, multiply by 1.25.

Apart from obvious points such as size, condition and land area, the most important factor influencing the price of a house is its location. A large two- or three-bedroom house with land can cost as little as €15,000 in a remote or undiscovered area but two or three times as much in a popular location. The closer you are to the Black Sea coast, a mountain resort or Sofia the more expensive a property will be, with properties in Sofia, Bourgas and Varna the most expensive in the country. The cheapest areas are in the north-east, around Vidin and Lovech, where property is on average around 65 per cent cheaper than on the coast and in Sofia.

In Bulgaria, a 'rural idyll' (i.e. a run-down property miles from anywhere) is still a bargain, and in many areas it's possible to buy a property for less than €5,000, although you will need to carry out major restoration work. In fact, when a property is described as 'inexpensive' or 'a bargain', it usually means that it needs restoring – and will therefore cost at least as much as the purchase price (and more likely two to three times more) to make habitable. Semi-restored small houses cost from around €10,000 and larger stone houses and villas from €15,000, while a rural two-bedroom renovated house costs from around €25,000.

Modern studio and one-bedroom apartments in towns cost from around €25,000 and two-bedroom apartments from €40,000, but an apartment in central Sofia can cost four times as much as a flat in a provincial town such as Pleven. A modern two-bedroom house in a small town will cost around €50,000. If you're looking for a home with several bedrooms, a big plot and a swimming pool, you can pay from €50,000 in rural areas away from the coast (but not too far from a town or city) and upwards of €150,000 along the coast. Luxury apartments in Sofia and villas on the coast can cost as much as €250,000.

Property in the four main ski resorts – Bansko, Borovets, Mount Vitosha (near Sofia) and Pamporovo – is expensive by Bulgarian standards. It also varies considerably in price according to the location and type of property. Bansko, the smallest (and newest) of the Bulgarian ski resorts, is by some distance the most expensive; for example, a two-bedroom apartment costs between €80,000 and €120,000, while a similar property in in Borovets, the largest ski resort, costs only around €60,000. Property in the villages surrounding the ski resorts is much less expensive, with building plots and stone houses starting from around €15,000 to €20,000.

The table below gives a rough idea of what you can expect to get for your money in Bulgaria. Unless otherwise stated, the prices listed below refer to property in all regions. Note, however, that properties under €20,000 are rare in the cities and in ski and beach resorts, but are common in rural areas and in the mountains. Inexpensive properties are also easier to find in the poorer regions of Bulgaria such as the far north-east and central south. Rural properties usually come with land attached and often have farm buildings included. Remember that if you buy a property with land attached, you must set up a limited company to get around the restriction on foreigners owning land in Bulgaria (see **Forming a Company** on page 162).

Price	Will Buy
Under €10,000	A house in the north-east; a house away from tourist areas requiring modernisation or renovation; a small house or bungalow in a ski resort.
€10,000 to €25,000	A large house or bungalow in a rural area; a small house or villa in the Sofia region (not in Sofia); a plot several kilometres from a ski resort or from the coast; an older house or stone cottage in a coastal area in need of renovation; or a house in a small village.
€25,000 to €50,000	A one or two-bedroom apartment in a ski resort or in one of the coastal resorts; a plot in a village near the coast or near a ski resort; a new house or villa in the mountains or inland from the coast; a renovated house in a village near the coast; an apartment on the outskirts of Sofia.
€50,000 to €75,000	An apartment in a suburb of Sofia; an apartment in the centre of a ski resort or in one of the popular coastal towns; a detached house or villa in a ski resort; a small new or renovated property in a coastal area; a large house near one of the bigger cities.
€75,000 to €100,000	A small off-plan villa or renovated house in a village in a coastal area or popular inland area; a large plot several kilometres from the sea; a two-bedroom apartment in Sofia.
€100,000 to €150,000	An apartment in the centre of a coastal town; a large house or villa in a village or near a tourist area; a plot near a tourist area; a large, quality apartment in Sofia.
€150,000 to €300,000	A large villa near the coast or in a mountain resort, usually with a swimming pool; a luxury apartment with sea views along the coast; land for development in a tourist area.
Over €300,000	A huge villa with swimming pool close to the beach or a large villa in one of the ski resorts; a working hotel or similar business in a popular area; a large plot in a tourist area or near Sofia for development; a luxury house in an upmarket neighbourhood of Sofia.

SURVIVAL TIP

Keep in mind that on many older properties the price is for the land and would be the same if the building weren't there!

In addition to the purchase price, you will need to allow for the various costs associated with buying a house in Bulgaria (see **Fees** on page 112). Property prices may be quoted inclusive or exclusive of agency fees (see page 114), so make sure you know in advance whether agency fees are included in the price quoted and, if not, who will pay them. You will also need to include the cost of setting up a limited company if you're buying anything other than an apartment (see **Forming a Company** on page 162).

Negotiating the Price

When buying a property it usually pays to haggle over the price, even if you think it's a bargain. While property prices in Bulgaria are usually much lower than in the UK and other western European countries, there's no point in paying more than you need to, although if a property has been realistically priced, you shouldn't expect to obtain a reduction of more than 5 or 10 per cent. Although negotiation isn't common in Bulgaria, some vendors take the view that all foreign buyers are fabulously wealthy and can afford whatever the asking price may be, and therefore aren't interested in negotiating. Be prepared to walk away from a deal if you think the price is inflated.

There has been some suspicion of dual pricing in the Bulgarian market, although local estate agents are quick to deny any such practice. It's more likely to occur in rural areas where demand from local buyers is low and many people have moved away in search of work. Often the only people interested in buying in these areas are foreigners and prices may be speculative rather than based on the local market value of a property.

It's wise to obtain an independent valuation (or appraisal) to determine a property's true value. If you're using an agent, it's worth asking him what to offer, although he may not tell you as he's acting on behalf of the seller and it may be worth paying another agent to value a property in order to obtain a less biased opinion.

Timing is important in the bargaining process. If a property has been on the market for a long time and the vendor is desperate to sell, a lower offer is more likely to be accepted. You may be able to find out from neighbours why someone is selling, and therefore whether an offer might be accepted.

SURVIVAL TIP

If there are many desirable properties for sale in a particular area or developments that have been on the market a long time, you should find out why, as there may be changes to planning restrictions about to occur or a new development planned.

Before making an offer, you should find out as much as possible about a property, such as the following:

● when it was built;

● whether it has been used as a permanent or holiday home and, if the former, whether it has been let;

● how long the owners have lived there;

● how keen they are to sell;

● how long it has been on the market;

● the condition of the property;

● what the neighbours and neighbourhood are like;

● whether the asking price is realistic.

For your part, you should ensure that you keep any 'sensitive' information from a seller and give the impression that you have all the time in the world (even if you have to buy immediately). All this 'cloak and dagger' stuff may seem unethical and it's up to you to decide how much skulduggery you wish to engage in to save a few thousand euros.

If you make an offer that's too low you can always raise it, but it's impossible to lower an offer once it has been accepted (and if your first offer is accepted without haggling, you will never know how low you could have gone!). If an offer is rejected, it may be worth waiting a week or two before making a higher offer, depending on the market and how keen you are to buy a particular property.

If you make a low offer, it's a good idea to indicate to the owner a few negative points (without being too critical) that merit a reduction in price. But keep in mind that if you make a very low offer, an owner may feel insulted and refuse to do business with you!

```
SURVIVAL TIP
Be prepared to walk away from a deal rather than pay
too high a price.
```

If you want a bargain property as an investment, shopping around and buying a 'distress sale' from an owner who simply must sell is likely to result in the best deal. But if you're looking for an investment property it's better to buy in an area that's in high demand, preferably with buyers and renters. Obviously you will be in a better position if you're a cash buyer and able to close quickly. Cash buyers in some areas may be able to negotiate a considerable price reduction for a quick sale, depending on the state of the local property market and how urgent the sale is.

An offer should always be made in writing, as it's likely to be taken more seriously than a verbal offer.

Buying at Auction

Property auctions are rare in Bulgaria, and most property sold at auction is owned by municipal or government authorities and consists of large blocks with (often run-down) local council or government buildings attached, which aren't of interest to home buyers. If you're interested in making a bid on a property at auction, you should talk to your solicitor about the process.

```
SURVIVAL TIP
Before making a bid, it's imperative to accurately
assess the market value of a property and (if applicable)
what it will cost to bring it habitable condition.
```

FEES

A variety of taxes and fees are payable when you buy a property in Bulgaria, most of which vary according to the price but which may also depend on whether the property has land attached, whether you're buying through an agent (as opposed to buying direct from the vendor), whether you've employed a lawyer and surveyor and whether you employ a translator.

Most property fees are based on the 'declared' purchase price, which may be less than the actual purchase price or its 'market' value.

You should never be tempted to under-declare the purchase price in order to pay lower fees, as it can have serious consequences if discovered (see Declared Price on page 166).

The fees associated with buying a property in Bulgaria are listed below, although not all will apply to all sales. Fees are usually payable on the completion of a sale if not before (see **Chapter 5**). Before signing a preliminary contract, check exactly what fees are payable and how much they are, and have these confirmed in writing.

Company Registration Fee

If the property you're interested in has land attached to it (i.e. is anything other than an apartment), you will need to form a limited company (see page 162). Under Bulgarian law, you must either be Bulgarian or buy through a Bulgarian limited company to own land. It's a relatively simple process but you must pay a deposit of between 3,500 lev (€1,800) and 5,000 lev (€2,500) into the company bank account. This isn't the cost of setting up the company, and once the company has been formed you will have access to this money, but you must pay fees and charges relating to the formation and registration of your company amounting to around €500 to €750.

Municipal Tax

Similar to stamp duty in the UK, a municipal tax of 2 per cent of the purchase price of the property is paid to the local council.

Property Tax

Property tax covers the cost of registering the title deeds with the municipality and is equal to 0.15 per cent of the purchase price.

Notary Public's Fees

A notary public charges for preparing the preliminary contract and notary deed and for any checks he makes on a property. The fees are set by the government and depend on the purchase price of a property, as follows:

Purchase Price (lev)	Notary Fee (lev)
Up to 100	15
100 to 1000	15 + 1.5% of the amount over 100
1000 to 10,000	28.5 + 1% of the amount over 1,000
10,000 to 50,000	118.5 + 0.5% of the amount over 10,000
50,000 to 100,000	318.5 + 0.2% of the amount over 50,000
Over 100,000	418 + 0.1% of the amount over 100,000

The maximum fee is 3,000 lev (€1,500). The notary's fees for preparing the preliminary contract should be included in your estate agent's fee (but make sure you check this beforehand).

Selling Agent's Fees

Selling agent's fees are usually around 3 per cent of the purchase price, but they can be as high as 10 per cent depending on the type and level of service provided (see **Agents' Fees** on page 105).

Other Fees

Other fees may include:

- lawyer's fees (see **Conveyancing** on page 164);
- translator's fees (normally around 30 lev/€15 per day);
- surveyor's fee (see **Professionals** on page 129);
- utility connection and registration fees (see page 265).

Value Added Tax

Sale of property for residential purposes and residential property rental are exempt from value added tax (VAT). Commercial property transactions are subject to VAT at 20 per cent, although VAT-registered entities are entitled to a refund.

Example

The following example of fees is based on a property costing €30,000 and assumes a 'cash' purchase (i.e. without a mortgage).

Fee	Amount
Limited company fees	€600
Municipal tax (2 per cent)	€600
Property tax (0.15 per cent)	€45
Notary public fees	€170
Selling agent's fees (3 per cent)	€900
Lawyer's fees (1 per cent)	€300
Surveyor's fee	€150
TOTAL	€2,765

Running Costs

As well as the fees associated with buying a property, you must take into account running costs. These include building and contents insurance (see page 210), standing charges for utilities (see page 265), maintenance (e.g. garden and pool, plus communal areas if you buy an apartment or a property in a development with shared facilities), plus a caretaker's or management fees if you leave a home empty or let it. Annual running costs usually average around 2 to 3 per cent of the cost of a property.

TYPES OF PROPERTY

For many foreign buyers, Bulgaria offers a chance to buy a size or style of home they might never be able to afford in their home countries. For others, it affords the opporunity to buy a rural property for next to nothing – albeit one in need of complete restoration and renovation. In most areas, properties range from rundown rural houses to modern apartments or townhouses and to luxury villas with ocean views and prices to match.

Standards of construction vary tremendously and the phrase 'you get what you pay for' is generally true. Most new properties tend to be of high quality, as the standard of construction in modern Bulgaria is good. On the other hand, while older properties can be sturdy affairs of stone and solid wood, they can often be tumbledown shacks. There are some beautiful older homes, although properties advertised as being 'good value' invariably need plenty of work to bring them up to an acceptable standard and are often quite remote.

Apartment or House?

Apartments are the most common type of new property in Bulgaria (see **New Property** below) and, of course, virtually the only type of property available in town and city centres. Whereas old apartments (particularly those built during the communist period) tend to be drab and poorly constructed, modern apartments are generally of a high standard, many of them aimed specifically at foreign buyers.

Apartments have a number of advantages: you don't have to form a company to buy one (with the attendant costs – see **Forming a Company** on page 162), they're generally cheaper than houses (for the same amount of accommodation), external and communal areas are often maintained for you, they're usually more secure than a house, and there may be shared facilities such as a swimming pool, jacuzzi, sauna, gym and tennis courts. Disadvantages include the lack of a garden and parking space (or this may cost extra) and possibly noisy neighbours.

A house has the opposite advantages and disadvantages, and can be expensive to maintain. The best of both worlds may be to buy a house in a development or complex where there are shared facilities, good security and a maintenance contract.

National Revival Style

So-called National Revival style properties, built between the late 16th and the late 19th centuries, are made of stone and wood, with intricately carved ceilings, wooden furniture and colourfully painted facades. Many of these properties were bought by the government in the '40s and '50s and turned into public buildings. Plovdiv's Old Town and parts of Shumen have some beautiful National Revival style houses and there are many such properties in and around Nessebar, Sozopol and Veliko Tarnovo, although they're in great demand and prices are correspondingly high. Many of them are protected or 'listed' (the title deeds will note this), which means that you must gain permission for any alterations or renovations (which won't usually be allowed to the exterior) and the building work will have to be supervised by the municipal council.

The Communist Period

Most of the property remaining from the communist period (1946–1989) is soulless apartment blocks, which are quite common in towns and cities, although it's unlikely that you will be tempted to buy one. Construction during the communist period tended to be fairly dire – as it was in most communist countries – so if you plan to purchase a property built during this era you will need to budget a substantial amount to bring it up to standard and cover any unforeseen problems.

Rural Properties

Rural properties are a popular choice if you're looking for a pleasant holiday home or somewhere to retire. They shouldn't be considered an investment, however, unless you plan to start a business (e.g. self-catering accommodation) and sell it with the property. Most rural properties need extensive renovation and modernisation to make them habitable.

Rural properties are usually timber-framed, one or two storey, and with two to three bedrooms. Toilets are normally outside and there's no internal bathroom or even an area for washing. If a property is connected to mains electricity, the wiring will need to be checked to ensure it's safe (wires are often not earthed properly). There may be running water but usually cold only. The kitchen will normally have a wood-fired stove, used for heating, cooking and boiling water. Wood floors are common but in older properties the floor may be stone. Fitted or 'wall-to-wall' carpet in rural homes is unknown; as in Turkey, floors are covered by woollen rugs and handmade carpets that families take with them when they move. There will be little or no insulation and poorly-fitted doors and windows. Where there are fences, these will usually be in poor condition and you will have to have them repaired, if not replaced, if you want to keep wandering animals out of your garden!

On the plus side, you will get a lot of space! Many rural properties have a large plot, including a small kitchen garden. Away from towns and villages, rural properties may also include farm buildings such as barns or hay sheds.

New Property

There's a huge variety of new property on the market, and an increasing number of developments aimed at foreign buyers are springing up, especially along the Black Sea coast. Choices range from apartments in coastal or mountain resorts and in the cities to architect-designed houses and villas. Most sales of new properties are in off-plan or purpose-built developments in the coastal and mountain resorts. However, these are often built as holiday homes and, while they can be comfortable for a few weeks at a time, they can be too small to live in permanently.

Apartments in the towns and the suburbs of Sofia can be good value but are often dark and small, although two- and three-bedroom apartments are springing up in many parts of the capital. The build quality and fittings are much better than in rural properties and even cheap apartments have windows that close properly and doors that keep out a draught. Recently-built apartments are increasingly being finished to 'Western' rather than Bulgarian standards (see page 119). In cheaper apartments, however, noise can be a problem due to thin, poorly insulated walls.

At the upper end of the scale, villas range from standard, medium-sized properties built by developers to beautiful, individual, architect-designed homes. Villas usually have their own pool or access to a shared pool, secure entry, air-conditioning and central heating, modern appliances and a well appointed kitchen, as well as open fireplaces in cooler locations. Many have landscaped gardens and car-parking away from the villa. Bedrooms range from three or four to as many as eight or ten.

Older villas will require renovating or modernising, but not to the extent of older rural houses, as they're still modern (by Bulgarian standards) with indoor toilets, bathrooms and hot water.

BUYING A NEW HOME

A 'new' home is usually defined as one built in the last five years. Although new properties can lack the charm and character of older buildings, they can offer attractive financial and other advantages, including the following:

- higher construction standards and lower maintenance costs;

- better insulation and therefore lower heating/air-conditioning bills;

- modern plumbing and electrics (including plenty of sockets);

- better security;

- no costs or problems associated with renovation or modernisation;

- greater resale value, particularly to foreign buyers.

The standard of new building in Bulgaria is usually quite high and new houses are built to higher specifications than old houses – particularly those built during the communist period (see above). Depending on the location, new houses usually include roof, cavity and under-floor insulation, central heating and air-conditioning; it can cost up to three times as much to heat an old home without proper insulation as to heat a new home.

It's often cheaper to buy a new home than to restore a derelict property, as the price is fixed, unlike the cost of renovation which can increase way beyond the original estimates (see **Renovation & Restoration** on page 133).

Security is a priority for most new developments (which often have security gates) and homes often have security blinds and other features.

There are also some disadvantages to buying a new home, including the following:

- New homes are usually smaller than old properties and rarely come with a large plot.

- The garden may lack mature trees and shrubs.

- There may be 'settling in' problems with a very new building, such as cracking plaster.

- Unless you've chosen the interior, you may wish to change it.

- It may have less letting potential than an older building.

Most new properties are sold by developers and builders and marketed by estate agents. You may see descriptions of new property as being to 'Bulgarian standard' (or 'Bulgarian national standard' or 'BDS'), which means the exterior is complete but the interior is unfinished. There will generally be plastered but unpainted walls and bare concrete floors, and no toilet, shower or wash basin in the bathroom, let alone tiling. Plumbing and wiring throughout the house is usually connected but capped (i.e. no electricity sockets, taps or fittings) and internal doors will be hung, but unpainted and without handles or locks. This is because most Bulgarian buyers prefer to decorate and furnish a new property themselves. It means, however, that you must budget for finishing the property on top of the purchase price, the cost of which is normally (i.e. unless you want gold taps) between €50 and €100 per square metre – often less for houses in rural areas.

It can cost €10,000 or more to finish a brand new home in Bulgaria, *excluding* furniture and furnishing.

Off-plan Homes

When buying a new property in a development, you're usually obliged to commit to a purchase before it's completed (or even before it's begun!) – a process known as buying 'off plan'. In fact, if a development is built and largely unsold, particularly a quality development in a popular area, it usually means there's something wrong with it!

Buying a home that hasn't been built may seem a risky business, but the procedure is usually safe and there can be several advantages. Off-plan properties are generally cheaper than built homes. You can often choose your bathroom suite, kitchen, wallpaper, paint, wall and floor tiles and carpet in the bedrooms, all of which may be included in the price. You may sometimes be able to alter the interior room layout, although this will increase the price, but you won't be able to make major structural alterations or changes of material or design. Most developers will negotiate over the price or include 'free' extras (such as a fitted kitchen that isn't included in the price) if a development isn't selling well.

All fixtures and fittings will, of course, be brand new and you will benefit from modern insulation, ventilation, heating and other materials and systems, plus a ten-year guarantee on these and the building itself.

Disadvantages of buying off plan include the fact that you must pay VAT at 20 per cent on building costs, although this is usually included in the price quoted to you, and you must start paying for your home long before you can actually live in it.

If you have the time, it's a good idea to visit other developments that the developer has completed to see what the finished product is like and check the build quality. There's a lot of building going on in Bulgaria and, while most new developments are of good quality, some developers will inevitably cut corners.

You should, of course, make regular checks (in person where possible) that everything is going to plan, although it's unlikely that you will be allowed onto the construction site itself. When the property is finished, you will normally have a site meeting to check its condition, although this isn't necessary, as an independent inspector should have approved each stage of the construction.

If you aren't happy with anything, you should make your complaints in writing and send it to the developer. In extreme circumstances, you can refuse to go through with the purchase, in which case a new completion date must be agreed by the developer; failing this, you can take him to court, although this is obviously a last resort. (See also **Buying Off Plan** on page 167.)

Resale Homes

Buying 'new' doesn't necessarily mean buying a brand new home no one has lived in before. There can be many advantages in buying a resale home less than five years old rather than a brand new one, including better value, an established development with a range of local services and facilities in one place, more individual design and style, no problems when settling in, furniture and other extras included in the price, and a mature garden and trees. With a resale property you can see exactly what you get for your money and the previous owners may have made improvements or added extras such as a swimming pool that may not be fully reflected in the asking price. The disadvantages of buying a resale home can include decor that isn't to your taste or a poor state of repair.

BUYING AN OLD HOME

The term 'old home' usually refers to a building that's pre-Second World War (or pre-Soviet era) and possibly over 100 years old, which is either in need of restoration and modernisation or has already been restored. If you want a very cheap property, a property with charm and character, a building for renovation or conversion, outbuildings, or a large area of land, you must usually buy an old property. The advantages and disadvantages of buying a new home (see above) apply in reverse to an old home.

Many old properties purchased by foreigners in Bulgaria are in need of restoration, renovation or modernisation. The most common examples are the many old stone houses and cottages in rural areas that have either been left empty for years or previously owned by families that have moved to the cities in search of better opportunity. Depending on the area and the condition of the building, you can buy a stone cottage for as little as €5,000 or €10,000, or a larger building either in better quality or near a popular tourist area for €15,000 to €25,000.

 Most properties listed as 'in need of renovation' will probably lack a proper bathroom and inside toilet and may not even be connected to basic services such as electricity and a reliable water supply.

Before buying a property requiring restoration or modernisation, you should consider the alternatives. An extra €10,000 or €20,000 spent on a purchase can be better value than spending a similar amount on building work. It often works out cheaper to buy a renovated property than a ruin in need of total restoration, unless you're going to do most of the work yourself. On the other hand, if you like a challenge and want something you've designed and built yourself that's therefore unique, buying an old home and 'doing it up' may be for you.

If you're planning to buy a property that needs restoration or renovation, obtain an accurate assessment of the costs before signing a contract. Many foreign buyers are tempted by the low cost of old homes and believe they're getting a wonderful bargain, without fully realising the costs of restoration or bringing it up to a 'liveable' standard. **Don't buy a derelict property unless you have the courage, determination and money to overcome the many problems you will certainly face.**

 Keep in mind that renovation or restoration costs will invariably be higher than you imagined or planned – often much higher!

Unless you're prepared to wait until you can occupy it or are willing to live in a caravan or rent for a long time while you work on it, it's better to spend a bit more and buy something habitable but untidy than buy a property that needs gutting before you can move in.

SURVIVAL TIP
As with all things, you get what you pay for, so you shouldn't expect a charming, quaint and fully modernised property for €15,000.

PART-OWNERSHIP SCHEME

If you're looking for a holiday home abroad, you may wish to investigate a scheme that provides sole occupancy of a property for a number of weeks each year. These include co-ownership, leaseback and timeshare (or timesharing).

⚠️ **Don't rush into any of these schemes without fully researching the market and before you're absolutely clear what you want and what you will get for your money.**

Co-ownership

Co-ownership – also known as part-ownership and fractional ownership – is an agreement between several buyers to share ownership of a property and includes schemes such as a consortium of people buying shares in a property-owning company. Co-owners may be members of a family, friends or strangers. Co-ownership allows you to save on holiday costs while retaining equity in a property. A common deal is a four-owner scheme, where you buy a quarter of a property and can occupy it for up to three months a year. But there's no reason why there cannot be as many as 12 co-owners, each with a month's occupancy each year (usually shared between high, mid and low seasons).

Co-ownership provides access to a size and quality of property that would otherwise be unimaginable. It can be a good choice for a family or group of friends seeking a holiday home for a few weeks or months a year and has the added advantage that (because of the lower cost) a mortgage may be unnecessary. Co-ownership is much better value than a timeshare (see below) and needn't cost more.

A purchase should be treated like a business venture, even (or especially!) if you're buying with friends or relatives. In particular, you should do the following:

- agree on occupancy periods for each co-owner (e.g. a share of high-, mid- and low-season weeks);

- agree on any restrictions that will apply to users (e.g. regarding smoking, children and pets);

- decide on the decor and furnishing of the property, who is to do it, and how it's to be paid for;

- decide whether or not the property is to be let when not being used by any of the co-owners and, if so, how the letting is to be managed and the income apportioned and paid;

- decide on notice periods and procedures if one party wishes to withdraw from the arrangement;

- set annual maintenance fees for each co-owner (which should be on the high side to allow for unforeseen expenses);

- establish a procedure for dealing with problems;

- have a detailed contract drawn up by an experienced lawyer to protect the co-owners' interests.

One of the best ways to set up a co-ownership, if you can afford it, is to buy a house yourself and offer 'shares' to others. This overcomes the problem of finding a group of would-be owners and trying to agree on a purchase in advance, which is difficult unless it's just a few friends or family members. Each co-owner is given a number of shares according to how much he has paid, entitling them to so many weeks' occupancy a year. Owners don't need to have equal shares and all can be made title holders. If a co-owner wishes to sell his shares, he must give first refusal to other co-owners. If they don't wish to buy them and a new co-owner cannot be found (which is unlikely), the property must be sold.

Timesharing

Timesharing (also called 'holiday ownership', 'vacation ownership' and 'holidays for life') is an arrangement whereby you purchase the right to occupy a property at designated times but don't in fact own any part of the property itself. Timesharing is uncommon in Bulgaria and isn't as popular as in countries such as Spain and the US.

Timesharing has earned a poor reputation in the past few decades. Since 1998 the Organisation for Timesharing in Europe (OTE, 🖳 http://www.ote-info.com) has been trying to restore respectability to timesharing and its members are bound by a code of conduct. This includes a requirement that buyers have secure occupancy rights and that their money is properly protected before completion of a new property. A recent EU directive requires timeshare companies to disclose information about the vendor and the property and to allow prospective buyers a ten-day 'cooling off period', during which they may cancel any sales agreement they've signed without penalty. But although the directive technically binds timeshare companies, if they flout it you will need to seek redress through the courts, which may not be something you want (or can afford) to do. In any case, Bulgaria doesn't yet have a national association affiliated to the OTE, although Bulgarian laws on consumer protection were recently harmonised with those of the EU.

The best timeshare developments are on a par with luxury hotels and offer a wide range of facilities. If you don't wish to take a holiday in the same place each year, you can choose a timeshare development that's a member of an international organisation such as Resort Condominium International (RCI, 🖳 http://www.rci.com) or Interval International (II, 🖳 http://www.intervalworld.com), which allow you (usually for a fee) to exchange your timeshare with one in another area or country.

Bulgaria doesn't as yet have the timeshare touts common in some other countries (such as Spain) but it may be only a matter of time before they start to appear. You may be invited to a presentation in a popular resort, so it's best to know what to expect. If you're tempted to attend a sales pitch (usually lasting for one or two hours but which can be up to four hours) you need to be aware you will be subjected to some of the most high-pressure sales methods employed anywhere on earth. If you do attend, don't take any cash, credit cards or cheque books with you so you won't be pressured into paying a deposit without thinking it over. Although it's illegal for a timeshare company to accept a deposit during the cooling-off period, many companies will try to persuade you to pay one. Don't rely on being able to get your money back if you pay by credit card. If you do pay a deposit, your chance of getting it back is slim; if it is repaid, it's likely to take a long time. If you're an EU citizen and get into a dispute over a timeshare purchase in Bulgaria, you can take legal action in your home country ... when Bulgaria joins the EU.

SURVIVAL TIP

Of those who agree to buy a timeshare, around half cancel within the cooling off period, and many people bitterly regret the day they signed up for a timeshare. If you're considering a timeshare, always keep in mind the old adage that if it sounds too good to be true, it usually is!

Most experts believe there's little or no advantage in a timeshare over a normal holiday rental and that you're better off putting your money into a long-term investment, where you retain your capital and may even earn sufficient interest to pay for a few weeks' holiday each year.

Further information about timesharing can be obtained from the Timeshare Council (🖳 http://www.timesharecouncil.co.uk) in the UK. The Timeshare Consumers Association (Hodsock, Worksop, Notts S81 0TF, UK, ☎ 01909-591100, 🖳 http://www.timeshare.org.uk) has a wealth of advice and information for anyone considering buying into a timeshare (or interested in how to avoid scams).

BUYING A BUSINESS PROPERTY

With the growing number of tourists visiting Bulgaria, you may be looking to purchase a residential property with a business attached, such as a farm, vineyard, hotel, restaurant or bar. (For the purposes of this section a business property doesn't include a secondary or 'part-time' business such as bed and breakfast accommodation.)

There are usually separate prices for business premises and for the business itself (i.e. its value as a 'going concern'). In some cases the premises are rented. Where possible, however, you should buy a business with the premises, especially if you need to raise a loan. You can obtain a mortgage on premises, but you will need to fund the business yourself.

> **SURVIVAL TIP**
> **If you rent business premises, it's essential to take legal advice about the lease, which must contain a right-to-rent clause to ensure the future value of the business.**

Before buying any property-based business, you must do your homework thoroughly, especially regarding the history and viability of the business. You must also be certain that you already have or can quickly pick up the skills necessary to run the business successfully. Many people wear (thick!) rose-tinted glasses when looking for a business property in Bulgaria and only go into the pros and cons **after** they've committed themselves.

 Buying a business in Bulgaria is a complicated undertaking that should be concluded only after taking expert legal and professional advice.

INSPECTIONS & SURVEYS

When you've found a property you like, you should not only make a close inspection of its condition, even if it's a fairly new building, but also ensure that 'what you see is what you get'. In many rural areas, boundaries aren't always clearly drawn and nearby land may or may not be part of your property, despite what an estate agent may tell you!

There are various ways you can carry out an inspection; which one you choose will depend largely on whether a property is a ruin in need of complete restoration, partly or totally renovated, or a modern home.

Doing Your Own Checks

There are a number of checks you can carry out yourself, including the following (although you will probably need to take a translator with you if you don't speak Bulgarian):

- Visit the local town hall and check the development plan of the land on which the property stands.

- While you're at the town hall, ask for details of any areas that are liable to flooding (see **Earthquakes & Flooding** on page 29). In an area that's liable to flooding, storms and subsidence, it's wise to check an old property after heavy rainfall, when any leaks should come to light.

- If you buy a property near a river, you should ensure that it has been designed with floods in mind, e.g. with electrical installations above flood level and solid tiled floors.

- Ask the vendor or agent for a copy of the title deeds, which should contain a copy of the relevant section of the local land registry plan. This is a check that will be made by the notary handling the sale (see **Conveyancing** on page 164), but it's worth anticipating any doubts or disputes by checking at this stage.

- Check the condition of any boundary walls, fences or hedges and find out who they belong to and therefore who is responsible for their upkeep.

- If you're planning to make extensions or alterations (e.g. putting in a swimming pool) that may require planning permission, find out whether such permission is likely to be granted (see page 139).

- When it comes to examining the building itself, check the outside first, where there may be signs of damage and decay, such as bulging or cracked walls, damp, missing roof tiles and rusty or insecure gutters and drainpipes, dry or wet rot in beams and other woodwork, and doors and windows that no longer hinge, lock or fit properly. Plants growing up or against walls can cause damp and damage, and the roots of trees and shrubs close to a building can undermine foundations (look for telltale cracks). Use binoculars to inspect the roof and a torch to investigate the loft, noting any cracks or damp patches using a camera and notepad. If you see a damp patch on the outside, check whether it runs right through the wall when you go inside.

● In the case of a property that has been restored, if work has been carried out by registered builders (see page 140), ask to see the bills. If the current (or a previous) owner did the work themselves, it's essential to consult an expert to ascertain whether it has been done properly (see **Professionals** on page 129); otherwise, you may end up having to redo everything.

● If the property has a swimming pool, check that planning permission was granted for its construction. Check also the type of pool structure and its condition and that the filtration and cleaning systems work as they should. If you know little or nothing about swimming pools, it's worthwhile getting an expert to make the checks for you. The small cost of an inspection should be set against the potentially astronomical cost of repairing an unsound pool and, if repairs are required, these may be paid for by the vendor or covered by a reduction in the price of the property.

More generally, consider the location of the pool, the local climate and your inclinations, and ask yourself (honestly) how often you're likely to use it and whether its maintenance will be more trouble and expense than it's worth.

● Test the electrical system, plumbing, mains water, hot water boiler and central heating systems as applicable. **Don't take someone's word that these work, but check for yourself and, at the same time, find out how these systems work**.

● If the property doesn't have electricity or mains water, check the nearest connection point and cost of extending the service to the property, as it can be very expensive in remote rural areas (see **Utilities** on page 265). If a property has a well or a septic tank, you should have them tested (see **Septic Tanks** on page 131).

● Check also whether the property can be connected to main drainage (if it isn't already) – see **Sewerage** on page 272.

● Check the quality of the water in the area of the property; for example, is it soft or hard?

- Locate the stop cock for the mains water supply, if there is one, and test the water pressure (turn on the highest tap). Ask where the meter is and check it.

- If a building has a ventilation space beneath the ground floor, check that this hasn't become blocked by plants or been filled with debris; if it has, this could have caused ground-level wooden floors to rot and damp to rise up walls.

- Check the local crime rate by asking neighbours and local police to find out whether any existing security measures, such as shutters and locks, are likely to be adequate or whether you will need to install additional systems, such as an alarm or window bars, which will affect not only your budget but also the appearance of your property. Take into account that neighbours may be reluctant to tell you if burglary is prevalent, and the local police may have different standards of comparison from your own!

It's strongly recommended that, if possible, you visit your prospective home at least once in winter to get an idea of what the climate is like at that time of year and whether you will want to spend any length of time there. Such a visit may also reveal problems that weren't apparent at another time, such pipes freezing or local shops being closed until spring. Winter visits also help you to find accommodation for when a property is being built or renovated, if a house is uninhabitable.

Although you can make such obvious checks yourself, the cost of a professional inspection (see below) is a small price to pay for the peace of mind it affords.

```
SURVIVAL TIP
If you would have a survey carried out if you were
buying the same property in your home country, you
should have one done in Bulgaria.
```

Professionals

An estate agent can carry out a 'survey' but it's usually little more than a valuation (see **Negotiating the Price** on page 110).

Licensed Property Surveyors

A licensed property surveyor (often referred to as a building and structural engineer) performs a range of services from a basic assessment of the value of a property to a full inspection of its quality and condition. Your lawyer can arrange this inspection. You will need to specify whether you just want a basic valuation or a full inspection, and the fee charged will reflect the amount of work carried out. A full inspection should cost between €1 and €2 per square metre.

 A survey isn't legally required as part of the purchase process in Bulgaria. (Because there were no mortgages until recently, banks didn't insist on buyers having a survey carried out.) There are therefore few private property surveyors.

Foreign Surveyors

It may be possible to employ a surveyor practising in Bulgaria who speaks (and will write a report in) your language. If you employ a foreign surveyor, however, you must ensure he's experienced with Bulgarian property and has professional indemnity insurance covering Bulgaria (which means you can sue him if he does a bad job!).

Architects

An architect is usually best qualified to check a modern home (unless he designed it himself!). You may be able to hire an architect through the Bulgarian Union of Architects, 11 Krakra Street, Sofia 1504 (☎ 02-943 8321, ✉ sab@bgnet.bg).

Builders

You can employ a builder or building company to check an older property for soundness. A builder will also be able to give you an idea of the extent and likely cost of work needing to be done. You could ask for a detailed quote, although a builder may be reluctant to provide one if you haven't yet bought the property. If you decide to buy the property and have work done by the builder in question, you may pay nothing for the inspection, although you should get at least one other quote for comparison before engaging him.

Survey Report

If you decide to use a qualified surveyor or similar professional, discuss in advance what exactly will be included in his report and, more importantly, what will be excluded (you may need to pay extra to include certain checks and tests). Whatever else it includes, a report should establish that the land being offered for sale with the property matches the land registry plan (it isn't unknown for the area of land stated in an agent's details to differ from the land registry record) and that there are no rights of way over the property. You should also ask a surveyor to check that there aren't any buried electricity cables or water pipes that may affect renovation and building work.

In the case of an old property, perhaps the most important part of a survey is to make sure that, in order to make any necessary repairs, you won't be spending any more than the amount by which the value of the property will increase if you need or want to sell it. This involves determining what essential work needs to be done, the likely cost of such work and the estimated value of the property once it has been done; the difference between the two figures is the correct purchase price for the un-renovated property.

SEPTIC TANKS

If a property is connected to a mains sewerage system, you're very lucky! Most rural properties and many in small towns aren't on mains drainage and so have individual sewerage systems, which consist of a septic tank (if you're lucky) or more likely a cesspit. Bulgarians often refer to 'septic tanks' and 'cesspits' interchangeably, but they're quite different things.

A cesspit is a hole in the ground, usually lined with stone or gravel, that collects all the wastewater from your house. Some of the water evaporates or soaks away, but most of it remains and cesspits need to be emptied once a year (sometimes more).

A septic tank is an enclosed system that breaks down solids with bacteria and discharges the filtered water. Septic tanks must still be emptied (usually around every five to ten years) and household chemicals such as bleach and non-biodegradable detergents must be kept out of the system, or it loses its effectiveness.

Older rural properties usually have only a cesspit. Such properties often didn't have running water, so showers were non-existent, baths rare and washing-up water was used to water the garden. If you install hot running water and a shower, you might find your cesspit filling up rapidly! If you plan to spend more than a few weeks a year in your home or let it, you will therefore have to install a septic tank.

A new fibreglass septic tank will cost around €500–750. Installing a tank and connecting the pipes to your house will cost another €500–750, depending on the length of the pipes and the complexity of the system. If the property is in a mountainous or rocky area, the cost of installation will be higher.

Unless you think you can live with a cesspit, it's a good idea to check that a septic tank can be installed before you commit to buying a property. If you plan to install a septic tank, you should check the following:

- that there's enough available land, keeping in mind that the drains for a septic tank must be installed a certain minimum distance from the boundaries of a property;

- whether there are rivers, canals or other watercourses (including underground springs and waterways) that might affect the siting of the tank and the soak-away;

- whether the ground is marshy or rocky, in which case installation could be difficult and/or expensive;

- whether the land slopes upwards away from the house, which may mean that waste water must be pumped up to the soak-away – another additional expense;

- whether there's access to the site for a lorry (delivering the tank and subsequently emptying it) and a digger to install the tank and soak-away.

Make sure that a tank is large enough for your property, e.g. 2,500 litres for two bedrooms and up to 4,000 litres for five bedrooms. **It's essential to check these things before buying a property**.

SWIMMING POOLS

It's quite common for foreign buyers to install a swimming pool at a home in Bulgaria, which will greatly increase your rental prospects and the rent you can charge if you plan to let it. There are only a few swimming pool installation companies in Bulgaria, mostly in Sofia, although there are also companies in Albena, Bourgas, Plovdiv and Varna.

There are various types of pool, each with advantages and disadvantages. Above-ground pools are the cheapest but can be unsightly. Small plastic above-ground 'splasher' pools can be purchased for as little as €75–100 from DIY stores, while more elaborate fibreglass or wooden pools usually require professional installation and will be more expensive.

In-ground pools come in three general types: moulded fibreglass (or 'one-piece' pools), which can simply be 'dropped' into a hole in the ground and cost around €4,000–5,000 for a reasonable-size moulding; panelled pools, which can be bought in kit form and put together without professional help and cost from around €10,000; and concrete block pools, which normally require professional installation and are therefore the most expensive option, costing from around €28,000 for an 8m x 5m pool. If you get a quote from a pool company to install a pool for you, make sure it includes the cost of digging the hole, which can be between €1,000 and €1,500 or more.

You will need planning permission to install an in-ground pool and you should apply a few months in advance; the pool company may apply on your behalf.

Pools require regular maintenance and cleaning, which is also expensive – and heating a pool can cost a fortune, especially in cooler regions. If you have a holiday home in Bulgaria or let a property, you will need to employ someone to maintain your pool (you may be able to get a local family to look after it in return for using it).

SURVIVAL TIP
If you won't swim in water below 25ºC, you shouldn't even think about installing a pool in Bulgaria unless you're prepared to spend a fortune heating it.

RENOVATION & RESTORATION

Once you've decided to buy a property requiring renovation or restoration – a decision not to be taken lightly (see **Buying an Old Home** on page 121) – there are a number of important checks to be made before committing yourself to a purchase (see below). These should be made in addition to those listed on page 127.

Land

If a property will need extensive restoration or renovation, you should check that there's access to the site for the necessary machinery and materials. Ask yourself whether vehicles can pass safely under overhead cables and power lines and whether they will be able to turn around or reverse out, for example. Check also that there's room for the storage of demolished and new materials.

The condition of a garden should be taken into consideration. A badly overgrown garden can take years to restore to an acceptable state, let along turn into an orderly and attractive garden, especially if most of your time is taken up with renovating the house.

Planning Permission

You must obtain planning permission if a planned renovation will affect the height, size, position or structural integrity of the building (see **Obtaining Planning Permission** on page 139).

DIY or Builders?

One of the first decisions you need to make about restoration or modernisation is whether to do all or most of the work yourself or have it done by professional builders and specialist tradesmen. A working knowledge of Bulgarian is essential for DIY, especially the words associated with building materials and measurements.

When restoring a period (e.g. National Revival) property, it's important to have an informed and sensitive approach. You shouldn't tackle jobs yourself or with friends unless you're sure that you're capable – when renovations and 'improvements' have been botched, there's often little that can be done except to start again from scratch.

Even if you do much of the work yourself, you will still need to hire specialists for certain jobs.

Cost

How much you spend on restoring a property depends on your purpose and the depth of your pockets. If you're restoring a property as a holiday or permanent home, money can be no object. On the other hand, if you're restoring a property as an investment, it's easy to spend more than you can ever hope to recoup when you let or sell it. Keep an eye on your budget (which will usually be less than half the actual cost!) and don't be in too much of a hurry. Some people take many years to restore a holiday home, particularly when they're doing most of the work themselves.

 You should expect the cost of the renovating an old building to be at least equal to its purchase price – and possibly much more. It isn't unusual for buyers to start out on a grandiose renovation scheme and run out of money before it's completed, then be forced to sell at a huge loss.

Renovation costs vary considerably. How much you're quoted by a builder will depend on where your property is (in popular areas, materials and labour are more expensive), the complexity of the job and the quality of materials and fittings you specify. As a very rough guide, €250–350 per square metre should be enough to renovate your property to a modern standard, with fittings, windows and doors included (but not appliances such as water or heaters or central heating systems). It's possible to pay up to €600 per square metre in popular areas along the Black Sea coast. If you're buying a property in a rural area, keep these figures in mind when planning your budget. Old properties can be incredibly cheap – as low as €5,000 for a house and land – but at this price you will virtually (if not actually!) have to build a new house.

Quotations

Before you buy a property that needs renovation or restoration, it's vital to obtain accurate estimates of the work involved from one or more reliable local builders. Note, however, builders' quotations aren't legally binding. To minimise the risk of being 'stung', as well as using a registered builder, you must detail exactly the work that's required; e.g. for electrical work this would include the number of lights, points and switches, their exact location and the quality of materials to be used. If you have only a vague idea of what you want, you will receive a vague and unreliable quotation, and extras added or alterations made to your building plan after work starts can escalate costs wildly, even up to 100 per cent. Make sure that a quotation includes everything you want done and that you fully understand it (if you don't, get it translated). Look out for any terms in the quotation allowing the price to be increased for inflation or a general rise in prices, and check whether it's definitive or provisional, i.e. dependent on further exploratory work.

You should obtain written quotations from at least two (preferably three) builders before employing anyone. Before signing a contract for the building work, agree on a schedule of payments against work completed and make sure this is written into the contract. If you have the budget you will save considerable peace of mind (especially if you will not be in Bulgaria for the construction) by employing a professional project manager. When it comes to builder's quotations it can often help if you offer to pay a fee, which should be reimbursed by the builder who gets the job.

Supervision

If you aren't on the spot and able to supervise work, you should hire a building supervisor or architect to oversee a job; otherwise it may drag on for months or be left half-finished. Be extremely careful who you employ, particularly if you intend to authorise materials to be purchased and documents signed in your absence, and ensure that your instructions are accurate in every detail. Make absolutely certain that you understand what has been agreed and if necessary get it in writing (with drawings). It pays to keep everything connected with a job, from the first letters, including old drawings and even bits of paper with scribbles on them. Project supervision should cost around €5 per hour, or you may be able to negotiate a set fee.

SURVIVAL TIP
If you don't speak Bulgarian, it's even more important to employ someone to oversee building work. Progressing on sign language is a recipe for disaster!

Make sure that a job is completely finished (including repairing any damage done by workmen) before paying bills. Never pay a builder in advance, especially a large sum, as he may disappear with your money. It's best to pay one month in arrears, which most builders will agree to. On the other hand, if you want a job done while you're away, you will need to pay a builder a sum in advance or get someone local to supervise the work and pay him regularly, or the builder is unlikely to finish the job.

BUILDING YOUR OWN HOME

If you want a bespoke modern home, you can buy a plot and have a house built to your own design or to a standard design provided by a local builder. You can even buy a 'kit' house, offered by several companies for installation in Bulgaria. Although most Bulgarian builders have a smallish range of standard designs, they will be able to include almost any interior of exterior variations (for a price), as long as they meet local building regulations. Building work takes around six months from start to finish for an average-size property.

SURVIVAL TIP
In the Black Sea resorts, there's a ban on construction work during the summer months.

Finding a Plot

Building plots are available in most areas of Bulgaria and range in size from small town plots to large areas of farmland. The average urban building plot size is around 850m^2 (around a quarter of an acre), while in rural and village areas plots are likely to be between 3,000m^2 and 5,000m^2 (around an acre). For a villa by the sea, where land is most expensive, you may be able to make do with 300m^2, depending on the proportion of the land that can be built on (see **Obtaining Planning Permission** below), but it's generally recommended to buy at least 500m^2.

Restrictions on land ownership by foreigners apply to building plots as well, so you will need to form a limited company and complete the associated legal procedures before you can purchase land (see **Forming a Company** on page 162).

Land can be bought through estate agents or directly from the owner (e.g. a farmer). Most Bulgarian estate agents have land listed for sale and some specialise in finding large plots for investment and development. The UK website Plot World (🖳 http://www.plotworld.co.uk) lists land for sale and has a specific page for Bulgaria.

Checks

You should take the same care when buying land as you would when buying a home, particularly when it comes to ownership, local development plans and planning permission.

Land in Bulgaria – especially farmland – is often owned by more than one person, which can make conveyancing a nightmare, if not impossible. Furthermore, land may not even belong to the person purporting to be the owner, who may have only a right to buy it from the government ... In such cases, it's usually wise to find another plot!

Land is classified as regulated, unregulated or agricultural. Regulated land can be built on, while unregulated and agricultural land needs to be changed to regulated land before building can commence. Unregulated and agricultural land is much cheaper than regulated land for obvious reasons: it can take up to 12 months for a decision to be made on changing the status of land and even then the application may not be successful. That said, the process can be simple.

You must have the land surveyed by the municipal surveyor. This should cost around €1–2 per square metre. The surveyor will handle all the paperwork and tell you the likelihood of regulation being granted and whether there are regulated plots nearby. It's usually easier to get your lawyer or the estate agent selling the land to organise the survey. If there are no impediments, the process should take around six months. Keep in mind that you need to change the status only of the land you intend to build on, not the entire plot.

Before commencing any building you must obtain planning permission (see below).

 Never believe an owner or estate agent keen to sell you a plot who says there will 'no problem' getting land regulated or obtaining planning permission; always check with the local town hall and make permission a condition of the purchase of a building plot.

Keep in mind that the cost of having services connected to a property in a remote rural area may be prohibitive (see **Utilities** on page 265) and it must have a reliable water supply. Many villages don't have mains water and houses often draw their water supply from a well, which in some cases is of poor quality. If you don't have mains water and need to rely on other sources such as wells, you should ensure that the supply is adequate for your needs.

> **SURVIVAL TIP**
> Before buying land, especially agricultural or rural land, seek advice from a lawyer or similar professional who can thoroughly investigate the conditions and regulations affecting the land.

Cost

The cost of land varies considerably, according to location and to whether it's regulated or unregulated (see above). The most expensive land is along the Black Sea coast, where plots are keenly sought by developers, especially 'front line' plots (i.e. those with sea views), which are becoming scarce and can command prices of €100 per square metre or more.

In other areas, an average building plot (the most common size for building a two- or three-bedroom house is between 500 and 1,000 square metres) costs around €20–30 per square metre. Unregulated or agricultural land costs around €3–5 per square metre.

You will need to set up a company before you can buy land (see **Forming a Company** on page 162), which will cost around €500–750. If you buy through an agent, expect to pay him a 3 per cent commission on the cost of the land, a lawyer's fee for conveyancing will be around 1 per cent, and other fees (e.g. municipal tax and a notary public's fee) will add a further 3.5 per cent (see **Fees** on page 112).

Costs for building a new property are similar to the cost of renovation and, like those, vary across Bulgaria. Between €250 and €350 per square metre is normal for a fully finished home, although €450 per metre isn't uncommon and you can pay up to €600 in some of the Black Sea resorts.

Obtaining Planning Permission

Before commencing any building you must obtain planning permission or a building permit (sometimes referred to as a 'PUP'). To do so, you must employ a Bulgarian architect (see below) to draw up plans, which will cost at least €15 per square metre. The architect will then submit the plans to the local municipality for approval.

When applying for planning permission, keep in mind that regulations, such as the proportion of a plot that may be built on, vary from region to region (you may be limited to 20 per cent of a plot or allowed to build on twice that amount); don't even assume that you will be able to build the same size or type of house as your neighbours, as regulations can vary according to location and type of plot, and rules may have changed since other houses were built. Don't rely on a builder or developer to obtain planning permission for you; do it yourself or have your lawyer make the application. **If a mistake is made, a building may have to be demolished!**

The process for obtaining planning permission for regulated land usually takes around 30 days but can take up to six months; unregulated or agricultural land must first be regulated, which can take up to a year (see above). Once you've obtained permission, you must start building within three years and complete the basic structure within five years; otherwise, you must reapply for permission.

Finding an Architect & Builder

When looking for an architect or builder, it's wise to obtain recommendations from local people you can trust, e.g. a notary, local mayor or neighbours. Professionals aren't always the best people to ask as they may receive a commission. Always obtain references (e.g. from previous customers) before employing a builder or architect.

All bona fide architects are required to have a licence, which you should ask to see. A good architect should be able to recommend a number of reliable builders, but you should do your own research, as the most important consideration when choosing a new home is the reputation (and financial standing) of the builder. You should be wary of an architect with his 'own' builder (or a builder with his own architect); as it's the architect's job to ensure that the builder does his work according to the plans and specifications, you don't want their relationship to be too cosy! Inspect other homes the builder has completed and check whether the owners are satisfied.

It's wise to use a Bulgarian building company, which should have an English-speaking project manager. The project manager will keep you updated with photographs of work in progress (if you aren't in Bulgaria) and will liaise with the builders to ensure that your requirements are met. In any case, you should only use a builder who is registered with the Bulgarian Builders' Association.

SURVIVAL TIP
Your best insurance when building a property is the reputation of the builder and his liquidity.

Contracts

If you're buying land for building, you should make it a condition of the purchase that a building permit is granted; otherwise, you could be forced to buy land on which you cannot build. If you're having a home built to your specifications, you should ensure that the building contract includes the following:

- a detailed description and a list of the materials to be used (with reference to the architect's plans);
- the exact location of the building on the plot;
- the building and payment schedule, which must be made in stages according to building progress;
- the retention of a percentage (e.g. 5 to 10 per cent) of the building costs as a guarantee against defects;
- an explanation of how disputes will be settled.

It's worth trying to get a penalty clause for late completion included in the contract, though few builders will agree to this. Note, however, that it isn't common in Bulgaria for builders to provide bank guarantees in case they go bust.

Ensure that the contract includes all costs, including the architect's fees (unless contracted separately), planning application fees, landscaping (if applicable), and the connection of utilities (e.g. electricity and water) to the house, not just to the building site.

> **SURVIVAL TIP**
> It isn't uncommon to have problems during construction, particularly relating to material defects, so it's vital to have a contract checked by a lawyer, as building contracts are often heavily biased in the builder's favour and give clients very few rights.

If you're buying a property off plan, the developer should provide a standard contract (see **Buying Off Plan** on page 167).

Avoiding & Resolving Problems

Builders should be registered with the Bulgarian Builders' Association, and you should never use an unregistered builder. Similarly, an architect must be licensed. An architect may suggest a preliminary study to bring to light any potential problems with your proposed construction, such as the lack of a nearby water or electricity supply or rocky or unstable ground. This should cost in the region of 400 lev (€200) but may be money well spent. A full geological survey will cost a further 200 lev (€100).

If you want a house built in Bulgaria exactly to your specifications, you will need to supervise it every step of the way or employ an architect or engineer to do this for you (see **Supervision** on page 136). Without close supervision it's highly likely that your instructions won't be followed or that inevitable problems won't be resolved to your satisfaction. You must usually be extremely patient when trying to resolve problems and should keep a record of every conversation and take relevant photographs as evidence. Always budget a contingency fund in case of unforeseen problems.

4.

MONEY MATTERS

One of the most important aspects of buying a property in Bulgaria is finance, including transferring and changing money, opening a bank account and obtaining a mortgage, all of which are covered in this chapter. The fees involved in purchasing a property are discussed on page 112. Depending on whether or not you plan to live permanently in Bulgaria, you may also have to pay Bulgarian taxes, which are covered in **Chapter 7**.

If you're planning to buy a property (or a business) in Bulgaria with foreign currency (e.g. GB£ or US$; the euro is tied to the lev and may become Bulgaria's currency in 2009 – see below), it's important to consider both the present and possible future exchange rates. If you need to borrow money to buy property or for a business venture in Bulgaria, you should carefully consider where – and in what currency – to raise finance.

 If your income will be paid in a currency other than lev or euros it can be exposed to risks beyond your control when you live in Bulgaria, particularly inflation and exchange rate fluctuations.

Conversely, if you live and work in Bulgaria, this may affect your financial obligations abroad. If you own a home in Bulgaria, you can employ a local accountant or tax adviser to look after your financial affairs there and declare and pay your local taxes. You can also have your financial representative receive your bank statements, ensure that your bank is paying your standing orders (e.g. for utilities and property taxes) and that you have sufficient funds to pay for them. If you let a home in Bulgaria through a Bulgarian company, it may provide these services.

SURVIVAL TIP
You should ensure that your income is (and will remain) sufficient to live on, keeping in mind devaluations, rises in the cost of living, unforeseen expenses such as medical bills and anything else that may reduce your income (such as stock market crashes and recessions).

While the cost of living in Bulgaria is very low compared to most Western countries (see **Cost of Living** on page 32), it's easy to underestimate the cost of living abroad, especially if you plan to return to your home country regularly.

Bulgaria is still a mainly cash economy and credit cards are generally accepted only at large hotels and in payment for items such as airline tickets. Nevertheless, it's wise to carry at least one credit card in Bulgaria; as well as for emergencies they can be used for deposits on hire cars and to pay for hotel rooms. Most banks won't issue cash advances on credit cards outside Sofia, but nearly all cash machines (ATMs) are linked to the global Maestro or Cirrus networks and can therefore be used to obtain cash up to your specified limit.

 You shouldn't make any major financial decisions based on the information in this chapter, which is provided as advice only and is not intended to replace the guidance of a financial advisor or accountant.

BULGARIAN CURRENCY

Bulgaria's official currency is the lev. The lev is fixed to the euro, one euro equalling 1.95583 lev. One lev is therefore worth around €0.50 or £0.35 or $0.60. (For the sake of convenience, euro equivalents in this book are given at the rate of €1 = 2 lev.) Inflation in the 1990s was so great that in 1999 the Central Bank took devalued the currency, making 1,000 old leva worth one new lev. The official abbreviation for the new lev is BGN (the old leva was referred to as BGL). To make matters somewhat confusing, the plural of lev is leva and the abbreviation 'lv' is generally used on price tags; to avoid confusion in this book, only the word lev is used, for both the singular and the plural.

> **SURVIVAL TIP**
> **The leva is no longer legal tender, so you should get used to the new currency as quickly as possible in order to be able to recognise worthless leva notes, which are sometimes given as change to unwary visitors.**

The lev is divided into 100 stotinka and coins come in denominations of 1 lev and 50, 20, 10, 5, 2 and 1 stotinkas. The 1, 2 and 5 stotinka coins are bronze-yellow in colour, while the 10, 20 and 50 stotinka coins are silver-white. The 1 lev coin is silver-coloured in the centre with a bronze-coloured rim (similar to the 1 euro coin) with a serrated edge. Note that when buying something in a shop you should try to give the exact amount, as you may not receive the proper change; it's common practice to round prices up to the nearest lev!

Bulgarian banknotes come in denominations of 1, 2, 5, 10, 20, 50 and 100 lev. Notes feature images and motifs from the lives of famous Bulgarians. Notes increase in size as their value increases and have similar security features to the current euro notes. The 100 lev note isn't common and you should be wary of them – if only because of the risk of losing them!

The Bulgarian National Bank website (🖥 http://www.bnb.bg) has pictures and descriptions of the notes and coins in circulation.

Although less common than a few years ago, some businesses insist on payment in 'hard currency' (e.g. euros, sterling or dollars) for items such as airline tickets. Many hotels quote their prices in dollars or euros, and property prices are commonly given in euros and sometimes in sterling, although payment in lev is generally accepted.

IMPORTING & EXPORTING MONEY

Shop around for the best exchange rate and the lowest costs when transferring money to Bulgaria. Banks are often willing to negotiate on fees and exchange rates when you're transferring a large amount of cash.

 The Bulgarian lev is pegged to the euro and its value therefore varies with that of the euro and can fluctuate accordingly in relation to other world currencies.

Don't be too optimistic about the exchange rate and bear in mind that a sudden fluctuation can cost you thousands of lev (or euros, pounds or dollars). For example, if you're buying a home in Bulgaria costing €50,000 and paying in sterling, this would be equal to £33,333, at an exchange rate of £1 = €1.50. But if the £/€ exchange rate falls to €1.40 between the time your purchase offer is accepted and the time you come to pay, it will cost you £35,714 – an increase of £2,381!

It's possible to 'fix' the exchange rate to guard against unexpected devaluations by purchasing a 'forward time option' or 'limit order' from your bank or from a specialised currency exchange firm; the further in advance you buy, the more you pay. The only downside is that you may regret doing so if there's a big swing in your favour!

It's recommended that you open an account with a Bulgarian bank if you decide to purchase a property there. This will make it easier for you to set up a limited company, which is necessary to buy land in Bulgaria (see **Forming a Company** on page 162), and make it **much easier** to transfer money to Bulgaria (see **Opening an Account** on page 154).

Declaration

The Bulgarian lev is a 'controlled' currency, which means that there are certain restrictions on the import and export of funds. These are constantly changing so you should check the latest regulations before importing or exporting currency. You cannot currently buy lev outside Bulgaria, but you can take lev out of Bulgaria and bring them back with you, subject to the following restrictions:

● You can import lev or foreign currency up to the value of 8,000 lev (€4,000) without having to make a declaration. If you're carrying between 8,000 and 25,000 lev or the equivalent in foreign currency, you must fill out a Customs Currency Declaration and go though the red channel at Customs when you arrive in Bulgaria.

● If you're carrying over 25,000 lev or its equivalent, you must show how you acquired the money and produce a certificate from the tax authorities in Bulgaria or your home country proving that you don't have any unpaid taxes.

● Restrictions on exporting currency apply only to commercial transactions (i.e. foreign currency trading) and not to individuals (unless you're a currency speculator!).

 If you fail to make a declaration, you risk being fined or having your money confiscated.

Transfers

There are the following methods of transferring money to or from Bulgaria.

● **Bank transfer** – A 'normal' transfer should take three to seven days, but can often take longer, depending on the bank in your home country and the receiving bank in Bulgaria.

- **SWIFT transfer** – One of the safest and fastest methods of transferring money is via the Society of Worldwide Interbank Financial Telecommunications (SWIFT) system. A SWIFT transfer should be completed in a few hours, although even SWIFT transfers can take five working days, especially from small branches that are unused to dealing with foreign transfers. The cost of transfers varies between banks – not only commission and exchange rates, but also transfer charges – but is usually between €30 and €50.

- **Currency dealer** – It can be quicker to use a specialist currency dealer to carry out the transfer for you, and you may get a better exchange rate than from a bank. In effect, you transfer money to the dealer's account and the dealer pays it into the third party account. Dealer transfers can work out cheaper than using banks; some charge no fee and make their money solely on commission so you should shop around for the best rate. An increasing number of dealers offer an online service, whereby you can arrange a transfer via the internet. Companies specialising in foreign transfers include the following:

  - **Currency Solutions** (🖥 http://www.currencysolutions.co.uk);

  - **Foreign Currency Direct** (🖥 http://www.currencies.co.uk);

  - **Global Currency Exchange Network** (🖥 http://www.gcen.co.uk);

  - **HIFX plc** (🖥 http://www.hifx.co.uk) – currency exchange and brokerage;

  - **Moneybookers.com** (🖥 http://www.moneybookers.com);

  - **Sterling Exchange** (🖥 http://www.sterlingexchange.co.uk) – based in the City of London;

  - **Worldwide Currencies** (🖥 http://www.worldwidecurrencies.com) – offers a range of financial products and services;

  - **XE.com** (🖥 http://www.xe.com) – apparently the world's most popular currency site.

When you have money transferred to Bulgaria, make sure you give the name, branch number and bank code of the receiving bank and your account number. Otherwise, it's possible for you money to be 'lost' in the system and it can take weeks to locate.

Always check charges and exchange rates in advance and agree them with your bank and/or dealer – you may be able to negotiate a lower charge or a better exchange rate. You should also check what fees are charged by the Bulgarian bank for receiving the money, as this can be a percentage of the amount transferred, which can amount to a large sum on a major transfer.

SURVIVAL TIP

If you plan to send a large amount of money to Bulgaria or abroad for a business transaction such as buying property, you should ensure that you receive the commercial exchange rate, rather than the tourist rate.

It isn't advisable to close your bank accounts abroad, unless you're certain you won't need them in the future. Even if you're resident in Bulgaria, it's cheaper to keep money in the currency of your home country if you visit regularly than it is to pay overseas withdrawal fees to your Bulgarian bank.

Obtaining Cash

There are various methods of obtaining small amounts of money for everyday use. These include the following:

- **Banks & post offices** – Most banks in Bourgas, Plovdiv, Sofia and Varna, and a growing number in the larger regional capitals, have foreign exchange windows, where you can buy and sell foreign currencies, buy and cash travellers' cheques and obtain a cash advance on a credit card.

- **Exchange bureaux** – Exchange bureaux have longer business hours than banks and are usually open at the weekend. Exchange bureaux are usually open from 09.00 until 17.00 or 18.00 and stay open later in the summer. Some exchange bureaux in Sofia and the major tourist destinations are open 24 hours throughout the summer. Most offer competitive exchange rates and low or no commission (but check the small print before you sign for the transaction). They're easier to deal with than banks, but often have much lower rates as they make their profit on the exchange rate, rather than on commission. There are private exchange bureaux at airports, in Sofia and in the major tourist destinations. Airport exchange bureaux usually offer the worst exchange rates and charge the highest fees (e.g. 'handling charges').

There's still a black market for hard currency in Bulgaria, but never be tempted to change money unofficially, as you will probably be short-changed or given a wad of useless old leva.

- **Cards** – If you need instant cash, you can draw on debit, credit or charge cards, although there's usually a daily limit. Many foreigners living in Bulgaria keep the bulk of their money in a foreign or 'offshore' account and draw on it with a cash or credit card. This is an ideal solution for holidaymakers and holiday homeowners, although the latter will still need a Bulgarian bank account to pay bills. Exchange rates are better when obtaining cash with a credit or debit card as you're given the wholesale rate, although there's a charge of between 1.5 and 2.5 per cent on cash advances and ATM transactions in foreign currencies. A popular bank account in the UK is the Nationwide FlexAccount, which has no charges on withdrawals from overseas ATMs and a high rate of interest (💻 http://www.nationwide.co.uk/banking). Some ATMs may reject foreign cards – if it happens, try again and if necessary try another ATM.

- **Telegraphic transfer** – One of the quickest (it takes around ten minutes) and safest methods of transferring cash is via a telegraphic (or wire) transfer, such as Moneygram (💻 http://www.moneygram.com) or Western Union (UK ☎ 0800-833 833, 💻 http://www.westernunion.co.uk), but it's also one of the most expensive, with commissions of between 5 and 10 per cent of the amount sent! Money can be sent via American Express offices by Amex cardholders.

- **Travellers' cheques** – If you're visiting Bulgaria, it's much safer to carry travellers' cheques than cash. The three major denominations are accepted (GB£, US$ and euros), although if you plan to use your travellers' cheques in another country it's better to buy in US$ or GB£. Travellers' cheques aren't accepted as cash by businesses in Bulgaria, and you must cash them at a bank or large hotel. To cash them at a bank you will need your passport.

  You can buy travellers' cheques from most large banks, although commission charges vary between banks. You may also be charged a commission to cash your cheques and the exchange rate can be much worse than the market rate, so it pays to shop around.

  Always keep a record of cheque numbers and note where and when they were cashed. All companies provide a local number for reporting lost or stolen travellers' cheques. American Express provides a free, 24-hour replacement service for lost or stolen travellers' cheques at any of their offices worldwide, provided you know the serial numbers of the lost cheques; without the serial numbers, replacement can take three days or longer.

SURVIVAL TIP
One thing to remember when travelling in Bulgaria (or any other country) is not to rely on one source of funds only.

BANKS

After the national banking crisis of the mid-'90s, a Banking Consolidation Company was set up in 1996 to restructure and consolidate Bulgaria's banking sector. All state-owned banks were privatised in 2000, when smaller commercial banks were either taken over by larger Bulgarian banks or bought out by foreign banks. Commercial banks provide a full range of banking services. There are currently 28 commercial banks, over 90 per cent of which are foreign-owned, and six branches of foreign banks (see below).

The largest Bulgarian bank is Bulbank, which was taken over in 2000 by Italy's Unicredito; second-largest is DSK Bank, owned by the Hungarian OTP Bank; and the National Bank of Greece holds a majority stake in United Bulgarian Bank, the country's third-largest bank.

The Bulgarian National Bank (BNB) is the authority which sets interest rates and regulates other banks; you cannot open an account with the BNB.

Post Office Banking

As in many countries, the most popular banking facility (and the bank with the most branches) is the Post Bank (🖳 http://www.postbank.bg, click on the link at the top left for the English version), which is jointly owned by the American insurance group AIG and an international private bank, EFG. The Post Bank has 30 branches and a presence in over 2,300 post offices. In rural areas, where the nearest bank is often many kilometres away, many people use the post office for banking. Another advantage of the post office is that many branches are open for longer hours than banks (although many aren't!). Post office accounts provide the same services as bank accounts, including international money transfers (by post and Western Union telegraph) and payment of bills. The Post Bank also offers internet banking (see **Internet Banking** below).

Foreign Banks

Foreign banks with a substantial presence in Bulgaria include the French banks Société Générale (through its subsidiary SG Express Bank) and BNP Paribas, the Austrian Raiffeisen Bank, Dutch bank ING and American bank Citibank. There are also a number of Greek banks with branches in Bulgaria, including the National Bank of Greece and Piraeus Bank.

If you do a lot of travelling abroad or carry out international business transactions, you may find that the services provided by a foreign bank are more suited to your needs. They're also more likely to have staff who speak English and other foreign languages.

Internet Banking

Internet banking is growing in popularity in Bulgaria but is still limited by the poor quality of the telecommunications network (see **Internet** on page 260). A number of banks offer online banking services, but the range of services available and the cost varies from bank to bank. Some banks allow you only to view your account balance. If you register for internet banking, your access details will normally be posted to you around a week later, so you will either need to be in Bulgaria for at least a week or have someone collecting your post.

Opening Hours

Normal bank opening hours are from 09.00 to 16.00, Mondays to Fridays, although banks may open any time between 08.00 and 10.00 and close between 15.00 and 17.00.

Opening an Account

You can open a bank account in Bulgaria whether you're a resident or a non-resident. It's advisable to check which banks have branches nearby and whether they have staff who speak your language. This is unlikely in the smaller towns, so you may want to open an account at a bank's Bourgas, Plovdiv, Sofia or Varna branch.

© Penka Uzunova (shutterstock.com)

© Victor I Maknanov (shutterstock.com)

© Matt Paschke (shutterstock.com)

© Ljupco Smokovski (shutterstock.com)

© Anton Gavrailov (shutterstock.com)

© Penka Uzunova (shutterstock.com)

© Bogdan Postelnicu (istockphoto.com)

© monokul (istockphoto.com)

© Alexander Tasevski (shutterstock.com)

© Paparazzio (shutterstock.com)

© Anton Gavrailov (shutterstock.com)

© Andy Didyk (istockphoto.com)

© Alexander Tasevski (shutterstock.com)

© Boris Vasilev Neshev (shutterstock.com)

© Elisa Locci (shutterstock.com)

To open an account in Bulgaria, all you need is your passport and evidence of your address in Bulgaria (if you have one); a utility bill usually suffices. There's no charge, but you must make an opening deposit of at least a few lev or euros.

Most banks offer the choice between a lev account and a euro account – or you can open one of each. If you plan to transfer money using a foreign exchange dealer (see **Transfers** above), you will need a lev account, as many dealers can deposit money only in the local currency. Euro accounts are often used for paying larger sums such as management fees or building work invoices and for handling rent payments if you're letting a property. A euro account is a form of guarantee against currency fluctuation in the unlikely event that the lev is 'unpegged' from the euro by the Central Bank. You can transfer money from your lev account into your euro account as necessary.

Bulgarian banks commonly charge for **everything** – even withdrawing money, so shop around for the best deal, i.e. the lowest fees and an interest-bearing account.

MORTGAGES

To finance your purchase of a home in Bulgaria, you have three main options: you can pay outright using resources such as savings, you can release equity in your current home by remortgaging, or you can take out a foreign or Bulgarian mortgage on your Bulgarian property.

Only a few years ago, mortgages were a novel idea in Bulgaria and interest rates were prohibitively high. But since 2005, the big Bulgarian banks have started to realise the potential for providing loans to foreigners buying property in Bulgaria and not only to reduce lending rates but also to introduce new types of loan. Nevertheless, the process of obtaining a local mortgage can be slow (delays are common) and Bulgarian lenders usually require you to have a 'clean' credit record and a substantial (by Bulgarian standards) minimum income. Moreover, not all Bulgarian lenders offer mortgages to Bulgarian limited companies (see **Forming a Company** on page 162).

The main Bulgarian banks offering home loans to foreigners are Bulbank, DSK Bank, First Investment Bank, Invest Bank (I-Bank) and United Bulgarian Bank (UBB). The Greek bank Piraeus, which has 13 branches in Bulgaria, also offers 'Bulgarian' mortgages. Interest rates are usually around 6.5 to 7.5 per cent and can be fixed or variable. If you apply directly to a bank for a loan, keep an eye on the various costs such as application fees, completion fees and legal fees. These can be expensive (up to €1,200 for legal fees and around €200 to €300 for application fees) and won't be refunded if your loan application is unsuccessful.

The maximum mortgage term in Bulgaria is 20 years, and Bulgarian banks won't lend you the full amount of a property's value. The average 'loan to value' ratio is 70 per cent for properties under €100,000, 75 per cent for properties over €100,000 and usually around 60 to 65 per cent for brand new properties (including off-plan purchases). This means that you must be able to pay a cash deposit of 30 to 40 per cent of the purchase price. In the case of a brand new property, finance isn't available until the property is complete and registered in your name (i.e. you're the legal owner). You must therefore finance any deposit and stage payments using other resources.

Some of the established Bulgarian estate agents (such as Barrasford & Bird, 🖳 www.barrasfordandbird.co.uk) are now offering 'buy-to-let' mortgages arranged through Bulgarian banks to those who wish to invest in Bulgarian property. Keep in mind, however, that these mortgages carry a high element of risk: the mortgage must still be paid even if there's no rental income!

As well as buying an existing or new property, Bulgarian mortgages can be used to finance improvements to a property.

SURVIVAL TIP
If you need to obtain a mortgage to buy a home in Bulgaria, you should shop around and compare interest rates, terms and fees (which can be very high) from a number of banks and financial institutions.

Bulgarian mortgages are paid in euros and there's an element of risk in taking out a euro loan if you aren't paid in euros. You will need to weight up these risks with an independent financial advisor before committing to a loan. One way of decreasing risk is by fixing the exchange rate in advance with a specialist foreign currency broker such as HiFX (🖳 http://www.hifx.co.uk) or Travelex (🖳 http://www.travelex.com). Using these services you can agree to make a payment at a future date at a rate agreed in advance.

Remortgaging

If you have spare equity in an existing property, it can be more cost-effective to remortgage (or take out a second mortgage) on that property than to take out a new mortgage for a second home. Depending on the equity in your existing property and the cost of the Bulgarian property, this may allow you to pay cash for a second home. There may be several advantages to remortgaging, including the following:

● Remortgaging involves less paperwork and therefore lower legal fees.

● You may not require additional life insurance.

● All documentation will be in English.

● You can take advantage of any types of mortgage not available in Bulgaria (e.g. endowment or pension mortgage) if appropriate.

The disadvantages of remortgaging or taking out a second mortgage on an existing property include the following:

● You may have to pay higher interest rates (e.g. in the UK) than in Bulgaria (this is unlikely in the short to medium term).

● If you plan to let the property, you may not be eligible for tax relief on mortgage interest payments in Bulgaria.

● You reduce the amount of equity available in the property.

● If your mortgage payments are in a different currency to your income, you put yourself at risk of currency fluctuation and devaluations.

In the present Bulgarian property market, it's generally thought to be preferable to release equity in your current home than to take out a separate mortgage on a Bulgarian property. The main reason is simplicity: you're dealing with a bank which knows you and therefore most of the paperwork has already been done. It doesn't always make the best financial sense, however, as you're vulnerable to currency fluctuations between the euro and your home currency.

Foreign Mortgages

While some high street banks in the UK offer foreign mortgages, these tend to be only in well established property markets such as France, Spain and Portugal. Bulgaria is considered an emerging market and so only a few financial institutions will lend for property purchased in Bulgaria. Banks that offer loans for foreigners to purchase property in Bulgaria include the Greek-based Piraeus Bank (🖳 http://www.piraeusbank.gr), although these can be difficult and time-consuming to arrange. Specialist companies such as Bulgarian Home Loans (UK ☎ 0114-252 5062, 💻 http://www.bulgarian homeloans.com) and Conti Financial Services (UK ☎ 01273-772811, 💻 http://www.mortgagesoverseas.com) offer mortgages for UK and Irish nationals secured on Bulgarian properties (and other nationals on a 'case by case' basis). If you're in the UK, make sure that any mortgage broker or financial adviser you use is accredited by the Financial Services Authority.

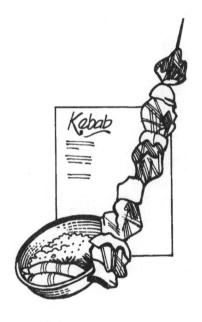

5.

THE PURCHASE PROCEDURE

This chapter details the purchase procedure for buying a home in Bulgaria, which is slightly different from that in most Western countries. Although relatively straightforward, the procedure isn't without potential problems and it's therefore highly advisable to engage a lawyer who's familiar with it before paying any money or signing a contract (see **Avoiding Problems** on page 22).

Once you've found a home you plan to buy and agreed the selling price, you will need to take the following steps:

1. If the property has land (i.e. is anything other than an apartment), form a limited company (see **Forming a Company** below).

2. Sign a preliminary contract and pay a deposit (see **Preliminary Contract** on page 166).

3. Sign the notary act and make the final payment (see **Completion** on page 170).

The buying process is generally straightforward and is often completed within a month.

FORMING A COMPANY

If you're purchasing a property that has no land attached (i.e. an apartment or flat) you don't have to form a limited company; otherwise, you must do so. Bulgarian law currently forbids foreigners from owning land in Bulgaria and the only way around this is to form a company, registered in Bulgaria. This is not illegal or a 'tax dodge' but an accepted and recognised practice. The requirement will change once Bulgaria joins the EU, which is scheduled for 2007. According to the latest government information, citizens of EU countries and citizens of non-EU countries that have reciprocal agreements with Bulgaria on land ownership will be allowed to buy land without restriction. Other foreigners will have to wait at least another five years (i.e. until at least 2012) before the requirement to form a company will be lifted.

Normally, you must go to a notary public's office to sign the requisite documents, but most estate agents can organise company registration for you or you can use the services of a local lawyer, although this requires you to set up a power of attorney (see page 163).

The process of registering a limited company can take a single day or several weeks but normally takes between three and four weeks, so you should allow at least this amount of time between signing the preliminary contract and completion. Note, however, that a streamlined registration procedure is due to be introduced in October 2006, when a new Registry Agency will be formed; this may also reduce and standardise the cost of registration. Existing companies will have to re-register with the new agency.

The cost of registration currently varies between regions, ranging from around €500 to around €750. (Some agents offer an accelerated registration service, but this can double the price!) Although it may cost a little extra, using a lawyer who speaks your language will make the process much simpler.

The minimum amount of capital required to set up a company is 5,000 lev (€2,500), although you usually need to deposit only 70 per cent of this amount, i.e. 3,500 lev (€1,750). This isn't the cost of setting up a company but the amount that must be deposited into a bank account in order to set up a company. Once the company has been formed, you can access the money.

You must give your company a name (which will have the suffix 'OOD', equivalent to Ltd in the UK or Inc. in the US), determine a registered office address and appoint directors/shareholders. These are normally the buyers themselves, e.g. a husband and wife, although you should check the tax, inheritance and other implications of your choice of shareholders. If you're a non-EU citizen, your company must employ at least ten Bulgarians, although this can be on a part-time or occasional basis. Following protests by the EU, this requirement was dropped for EU citizens.

Your company must be registered with the National Insurance Institute (NOI) within seven days of its formation and with the local tax authority within 14 days. You will receive confirmation of the company's registration, a tax registration card (with the company's tax numbers on it) and a stamp to be used on all official documents.

At the end of the financial year (March) you will need to file an annual tax return for your company. In almost every case your account will be 'zero' (i.e. no trading for the entire year). Nevertheless, unless you can read and write in Bulgarian and are familiar with the Bulgarian tax system, you will need a lawyer to ensure that your tax return is filled out correctly; he shouldn't charge more than 100 lev (€50).

POWER OF ATTORNEY

Many people are unable to be in Bulgaria for the whole of the purchase process, particularly those buying a holiday home or investment property. If this is your case, you can give power of attorney to your lawyer or estate agent to handle the formation of a limited company and/or the purchase of a property. If you need to provide power of attorney to anyone, it's essential that you know exactly what it authorises.

Power of attorney can allow unscrupulous people to withdraw money from your bank account without your permission, buy and sell property without your knowledge and commit you to unfavourable contracts.

You can prevent such eventualities by stating exactly what your power of attorney permits and forbids and by setting a time limit for its applicability.

Usually power of attorney allows your lawyer to establish a limited company for you and deposit the initial capital in the account, then pay any fees and withdraw money for the final payment. You can also provide power of attorney to your estate agent to withdraw money from your account to pay a deposit on the property.

You may be sent documents for the provision of power of attorney by your lawyer or an estate agent in your home country. For these to be binding legal documents, you must normally sign them in front of a witness (usually a notary public or lawyer) and pay a fee.

SURVIVAL TIP
If you plan to retire to Bulgaria, it's often wise to provide power of attorney to a member of your family or trusted friend to look after your financial affairs if you're no longer able to do so.

CONVEYANCING

Conveyancing (the legal term is conveyance, but conveyancing is more commonly used) is the processing of paperwork involved in buying and selling property and transferring the deeds of ownership. In Bulgaria, all legal procedures must be completed before a notary public.

 Don't expect the notary to speak any language other than Bulgarian or to explain the intricacies of Bulgarian property law, for which you will need to engage a lawyer (see Legal Advice on page 168).

Conveyancing includes the following:

- checking the title deed and ensuring the land is correctly registered at the land registry;

- verifying the identity of the vendor(s) and buyer(s);

- checking that there aren't any restrictions on the transfer of ownership, e.g. any outstanding debts or a mortgage greater than the selling price;

- establishing the terms of the contract.

A notary checks only planned developments directly affecting a property, such as a road running through the garden, and not those that may affect its value, such as the building of a power plant or waste handling facility nearby.

 A notary public won't necessarily protect or act in your interests, and you should engage a lawyer to ensure that everything is carried out to your satisfaction.

Obviously a new motorway that disturbs the peace of your home would be something of a disaster; on the other hand, upgraded roads or a motorway junction within a few kilometres may improve the value of your home. It's therefore essential to check local development plans.

Unfortunately, there's no single office or government department that provides this information, although you (or your lawyer) may be able to contact the relevant public works department and check building projects planned for the area. You could also ask local residents if they know of anything planned that may adversely affect a property.

The main problem is usually unsympathetic or poorly planned development in resort areas along the coast, where your sea view may suddenly become a view of an apartment block. If you do buy an apartment with a 'sea view', make sure it's zoned as a 'front line' property (usually along the beach or cliff front). Front line property cannot be built in front of.

 Even if you make all necessary checks, zoning regulations may change or the municipal council may decide to build a new road or waste processing facility that will be 'of benefit' to the community!

PRELIMINARY CONTRACT

The first stage in buying a home in Bulgaria is the signing of a preliminary contract. Your lawyer is responsible for ensuring that this is drawn up correctly and you shouldn't rely on an estate agent to do so. While some agents or developers will provide a properly-drawn up contract, some won't – and unless you're a Bulgarian-speaking lawyer you won't be able to tell which is which! For peace of mind it's recommended that you have the contract drawn up or at least checked by a Bulgarian lawyer.

There are a number of types of preliminary contract, depending on whether you're buying an existing (built) property or a new property off plan (i.e. yet to be built or under construction).

Buying an Existing Property

The preliminary contract will describe exactly what you're buying, including the amount of land associated with the property. The contract will also state the amount of the deposit you've agreed with the vendor (see page 169) and any conditional clauses (see page 169). Contracts must be in Bulgarian to meet legal requirements, so you should have a translator with you if necessary. As more foreigners purchase property in Bulgaria, some developers and estate agents are beginning to provide contracts in English, which makes the process easier, but remember that to be legally binding a contract must also be in Bulgarian. **Anything written in English isn't a legal document.**

Once the preliminary contract has been signed and the deposit paid (see **Deposit** below), the property should be removed from the market by the seller and the preliminary contract verified by the notary public, who will also check the identity of the seller and buyer. This stage can usually be handled by your estate agent or lawyer if you've given them power of attorney (see page 163), in which case the notary public will also authenticate your power of attorney documents. The notary's fees for administering the preliminary contract should be included in your estate agent's fee (but make sure you check this beforehand).

Declared Price

Don't be tempted by the Bulgarian practice of tax evasion, where the sale price declared to the tax authorities (sometimes euphemistically referred to as the 'tax estimation price' or TEP) is lower than the actual price paid for a property. If you're buying directly from a vendor, he may suggest this, and some estate agents may state that the practice is 'normal'. New (including off-plan) property is subject to 20 per cent VAT on the sale price. Some unscrupulous developers either don't include VAT in their quoted price or ask you to declare a lower value on the notary deed. The advantage for the seller is that he pays less tax on the profit from the sale.

You will also save money on taxes and fees (see page 112), but you will have a higher capital gains tax bill if you sell the property and it's a second home. For example, if you buy a property for €80,000 but declare a value of €50,000, then (if you're lucky) sell the property a few years later for €100,000, the tax man will see this as a profit of €50,000 and you will be taxed on this amount, not the actual profit of €20,000. What's more, if you're resident in the UK for tax purposes you will be subject to capital gains tax of 40 per cent on the same amount! If you keep the property for more than five years, your CGT liability will be zero – but don't rely on this law remaining unchanged! To avoid this increased tax payment, you will have to sell the property to someone who is also willing to underdeclare the value of the property ...

In any case, the practice underdeclaring the value of your property is illegal. The authorities can revalue the property and demand that you pay the shortfall in tax, as well as other taxes and fines. If a seller will accept an offer only on condition you underdeclare, you should talk to your solicitor.

 Declaring a lower price than the actual sale price of a property is illegal in Bulgaria and you may be prosecuted for tax evasion.

Buying Off Plan

If you're buying an off-plan property, the preliminary contract should include full details of the property to be built (including a copy of the plans and drawings showing its exact location within a plot or development, the number of rooms and the estimated total living area, and the type of materials to be used in its construction), what extras are included (e.g. swimming pool or parking space), any services to be provided, the timetable for construction, the price (including any possible variations or additions), a schedule of payments, details of penalties for non-completion and circumstances under which the deposit is to be refunded and details of any guarantees applicable (see **Off-plan Homes** on page 167).

In an off-plan purchase, payments are spread over 12 to 18 months, depending on when you put down a deposit and when the development is due for completion. Payment schedules vary; a typical schedule is shown below:

Stage	Payment
Initial deposit	10%
30 days after signing preliminary contract	40%
Completion of 'shell stage' (external walls)	40%
Signing of final contract	10%

Depending on the agent and developer you're purchasing from, you may also have to pay a commission on top of the purchase price as well as notary fees and local taxes (see **Fees** on page 112). In almost every case VAT is included in the quoted price for off-plan property, but you should check. The final contract isn't signed until building is complete (see **Signing the Notary Act** on page 172).

Legal Advice

The preliminary contract is binding on both parties, so it's important to obtain legal advice before signing it. It isn't necessary to have a preliminary contract signed in front on a notary public and a notary public won't necessarily protect your rights, although he will ensure that a contract has been drawn up correctly.

In any case, if a preliminary contract has been drawn up by a developer or estate agent, it's worth paying for an independent lawyer to check it before you sign it to make sure that your rights and interests are fully protected.

SURVIVAL TIP
Unless you're confident in Bulgarian property law and speak fluent Bulgarian, it's highly recommended to have all documents checked by a lawyer. A lawyer should, of course, also speak your language.

Before hiring a lawyer, compare the fees charged by a number of practices and get quotations in writing. Check what's included in the fee and whether it's 'full and binding' or just an estimate (a low basic rate can be supplemented by much more expensive 'extras'). A lawyer's fees may be calculated at an hourly rate or as a percentage of the purchase price of the property, e.g. 1 to 2 per cent, with a minimum fee (e.g. €400). In the case of an off-plan purchase, there may be a basic fee based on the value of the property plus an hourly charge for unforeseen extra work.

Deposit

You will usually be expected to pay a 10 per cent deposit to the seller once you've signed the preliminary contract. While this is usually paid in cash, you should be able to negotiate for a bank transfer for larger amounts, which may incur lower charges (check with your bank). In some situations you can pay a small amount of the deposit as a 'goodwill' gesture and pay the remainder of the deposit seven to ten days later. The preliminary contract will state the amount and the period in which you have to pay.

You should try to have a clause inserted into the preliminary contract requiring that the deposit be held by a third party until completion. This way, if the seller changes his mind or the sale falls through for any reason beyond your control, you will receive your deposit back.

 It isn't uncommon for sellers to register their property with several estate agents and pull out of a sale if they think they can get a better price from someone else.

Conditional Clauses

One of the main reasons for engaging a lawyer is to protect your interests by inserting any necessary conditional clauses in the preliminary contract, which are of little concern to a notary public. Conditional clauses stipulate requirements that must be met to ensure the validity of a contract. Conditions usually apply to events out of control of the vendor or buyer, although almost anything the buyer agrees with the vendor can be included in a preliminary contract. If any of the conditions aren't met, the contract can be suspended or declared null and void, and the deposit returned. But if you fail to go through with a purchase and aren't covered by a clause in the contract, you will forfeit your deposit or could even be compelled to go through with a purchase.

If you're buying anything from the vendor such as carpets, curtains or furniture that are included in the purchase price, there should be a clause to this effect and they should be listed and attached as an addendum to the contract. Any fixtures and fittings present in a property when you view it (and agree to buy it) should still be there when you take possession, unless otherwise stated in the contract (see also **Completion** below).

There are many possible conditional clauses concerning a range of subjects, including the following:

- obtaining a mortgage (see below);

- obtaining planning permission, e.g. for renovation or improvements;

- confirming that the land area being purchased with a property matches the land register;

- selling another property;

- obtaining a satisfactory building survey or inspection.

Mortgage Clause

A mortgage clause states that a buyer is released from the contract if he cannot obtain a mortgage. It's a good idea to include this clause, even if you don't plan to obtain a mortgage, just in case your circumstances change.

A mortgage clause should state the amount, term and interest rate expected or agreed with a lender, plus the lender's name (if known). If you can't obtain a mortgage for the agreed amount and terms, you won't lose your deposit. You must make an application for the loan within a certain time after signing the contract and have a specified period in which to secure it.

 If you're unable to obtain a loan for reasons that could reasonably have been foreseen, you can still lose your deposit.

COMPLETION

Once the preliminary contract has been signed and the deposit paid (see **Deposit** on page 169), the property is 'sold subject to contract', as in the UK.

It should be removed from the market by the seller and the preliminary contract verified by a notary public (if this hasn't already been done), who will also check the identity of the seller and buyer and authenticate your power of attorney documents. This stage can usually be handled by your estate agent or lawyer if you've given him power of attorney. If you've use an estate agent to draw up the preliminary contract (which is common practice for off-plan purchases), this service should be included in his fee.

Your lawyer should now carry out the necessary checks on the property, including verifying the authenticity of title documents, making sure licences and permissions are in order, ascertaining whether there are any debts on the property and observing the terms of the contract. This process can take three to four weeks.

Final Checks

Property is sold on the condition that the buyer accepts it in the state it's in at the time of completion, so you should be aware of anything that occurs between the signing of the preliminary contract and completion. It isn't unknown for vendors to remove all the fittings – or even the boiler!

 Before signing the final contract, it's imperative to check that the property hasn't fallen down or been damaged in any way, e.g. by a storm or the owners.

If you've employed a lawyer or are buying through an agent, he should accompany you on this visit (the previous owner should have already vacated the property). You should check off an inventory of the fixtures and fittings and anything that was included in the contract or purchased separately, e.g. carpets, light fittings, curtains or kitchen appliances, and make sure that they're present and in working order. This is especially important if furniture and furnishings (and major appliances) were included in the price. You should also ensure that expensive items (e.g. baths, basins and kitchen fittings) haven't been replaced by inferior ones. Any fixtures and fittings (and garden plants and shrubs) present in a property when you viewed it should still be there when you take possession, unless otherwise stated in the contract.

If you find that anything is missing, damaged or isn't in working order, you should make a note and insist on immediate restitution, such as a reduction in the amount to be paid. In cases such as these the notary can withhold an appropriate amount in escrow from the vendor's proceeds to pay for repairs or replacements.

SURVIVAL TIP

You should refuse to go through with a purchase if you aren't completely satisfied, as it will be difficult or impossible to obtain redress later.

If it isn't possible to complete a purchase, you should consult your lawyer about your rights and the return of your deposit and any other funds already paid.

Signing the Notary Act

Signing the notary act (sometimes referred to as the notary deed, purchase contract or final contract, which is equivalent to a title deed) is the final step in taking ownership of your property. If you're unable to be present at the signing, you can have your agent or lawyer sign it on your behalf if you've given him power of attorney.

SURVIVAL TIP

You should always sign the notary act in person if you're buying a brand new or off-plan property, to make sure that all the requirements of the preliminary contract have been met.

The signing of the notary act takes place in front of a notary public, who first checks that all the conditions contained in the preliminary contract have been fulfilled. It's normal for all parties concerned to be present when the final contract is read, signed and witnessed by the notary, including the estate agent, developer (for new or off-plan property), your lawyer and your translator. Either party (buyer or seller) can give a representative power of attorney (see page 163). In the case of an off-plan purchase, the final contract isn't signed until building is complete.

Payment

To make payment of the final amount to the seller it's preferable to have a bank account in Bulgaria. That way you can transfer the money from your home country to your Bulgarian currency (or local euro) account and withdraw it when you're in Bulgaria. It isn't advisable to carry large amounts of cash into Bulgaria (or anywhere for that matter!) and you must declare any amount over 8,000 lev (€4,000) in cash or its equivalent.

Most sellers will be unwilling to accept a payment from your home bank account, as they will usually have to pay a fee for receiving a foreign currency and may be at the mercy of foreign exchange rates. Some sellers will ask for the final payment in cash (usually for smaller amounts), but most will accept payment in the form of a bank transfer, telegraphic transfer or bank draft from a Bulgarian account. If you cannot be present at the signing of the final contract, you can authorise your lawyer or another agent to transfer the money on your behalf (see **Power of Attorney** on page 163). In the case of an off-plan purchase, payment is made in stages (see **Buying Off Plan** on page 167).

Registration

When the notary act has been signed, your property must be registered with various authorities. The registration process depends on whether the property has land or doesn't (e.g. is an apartment).

Properties With Land

Your property must be registered with the National Insurance Institute (NOI) within seven days of your signing the notary act and with the local tax authority within 14 days. Property registration is normally done by the notary between one and three days after the signing.

Properties Without Land

Since early 2006, buyers of property without land (e.g. an apartment) have been required to complete a BULSTAT registration and send it to the Registry Agency within seven days. Previously, property without land didn't have to be registered and owners were slipping through the tax net. Unless you speak fluent Bulgaria, registration should be done by your lawyer, as all the forms are in Bulgarian, although some agents and developers will do it for you. Registration should cost only around 20–40 lev (€10–20).

Occupancy Permit

All new property (including off-plan purchases) must be issued with an 'Act 16' (or 'Akt 16') certificate – sometimes referred to as an occupancy permit

– by the municipal authority. Under Bulgarian law a property isn't complete until is has been granted an Act 16 certificate, which confirms that the building has been 'finished', i.e. that all electricity, plumbing, insulation, walls, doors and windows have been installed (but see page 119 for details of the Bulgarian standard of finishing). Your builder or the developer organises the Act 16 certificate.

An Act 16 certificate isn't to be confused with an Act 15 certificate, which is issued when the basic construction is finished (and usually coincides with one of the stage payments in an off-plan purchase). **This does not constitute an occupancy permit.**

It's highly recommended that you write a clause into the preliminary contract that you won't pay the final instalment on a property until the Act 16 certificate is granted (most reputable developers will include this anyway). That way there is a financial imperative for the developer to complete the project – and you aren't paying for work that hasn't been completed.

If you're buying off plan, the Act 16 certificate must be issued before you sign the notary act, as ownership of an unfinished property cannot be legally transferred.

SURVIVAL TIP
Despite what you may hear, it's illegal to live in a property that hasn't been issued with an Act 16 certificate.

6.

<u>MOVING HOUSE</u>

Moving into your new Bulgarian home is the culmination of your dreams – but it can also be a highly stressful experience. It's possible to limit the strain on your mental and physical health by careful planning and preparation. This chapter contains checklists that should help to ensure that you don't forget anything important and your move runs as smoothly as you can reasonably hope.

SHIPPING YOUR BELONGINGS

It usually takes two to three days to ship your belongings to Bulgaria from western Europe or the UK. From anywhere else the time varies considerably, e.g. over four weeks from the east coast of America, over six weeks from the US west coast or the Far East and around eight weeks from Australasia.

It's essential to find out about customs requirements and formalities in advance (see **Customs** on page 182). If you're using a removal or shipping company, they should be able to advise you of these. Otherwise, check with the local Bulgarian embassy or consulate, and don't forget to check the customs requirements in the countries you need to pass through. **If you fail to meet all requirements or follow the correct procedure, you can encounter numerous problems and delays and may be charged duty or fined.**

It isn't usually a good idea to do your own move unless it's a simple job, e.g. a few items of furniture and personal effects only. It's no fun heaving beds and wardrobes up stairs and squeezing them into improbably tight spaces. If you're taking pets with you, you may need to ask your vet to tranquillise them, as many pets are frightened (even more than people) by the chaos and stress of moving house. (See also **Pets** on page 47.)

If you're moving permanently to Bulgaria, take the opportunity to sell, give away or throw out at least half your possessions. It will cut down on your removal bill, clear your mind and make life simpler – and you will have the fun of buying new furniture that really suits your new home. In any case, after considering the shipping costs, you may decide to ship only selected items of furniture and personal effects and buy new furniture and appliances in Bulgaria!

Keep in mind when moving house that everything that can go wrong often does, so allow plenty of time and try not to arrange your move from your old home on the same day as the new owner is moving in – that's just asking for fate to intervene! See also the **Checklists** on page 186.

Removal Companies

It's recommended to use a major shipping company with a good reputation. For international moves it's best to use a company that's a member of the

International Federation of Furniture Removers (FIDI) or the Overseas Moving Network International (OMNI), with experience in Bulgaria. Members of FIDI and OMNI usually subscribe to an advance payment scheme providing a guarantee: if a member company fails to fulfil its commitments to a client, the removal is completed at the agreed cost by another member company or your money is refunded. Major international moving companies usually provide a wealth of information about relocation abroad and can advise you on a wide range of related matters, including travel and health insurance. Some removal companies have subsidiaries or affiliates in Bulgaria, which can be convenient if you encounter problems or need to make an insurance claim.

You should obtain at least three written quotations – as well as references – before choosing a company, as costs and standard of service vary considerably. If you will be moving more than just boxes (that you can pack yourself), the moving company should send a representative to provide a detailed quotation. Most companies will pack your belongings and provide packing cases and special containers, although this will be more expensive than if you pack everything yourself. Ask a company how fragile and valuable items are packed and whether the cost of packing cases, materials and insurance (see below) is included in a quotation. If you want to do your own packing, most shipping companies will provide packing crates and boxes. Shipments are charged by volume, e.g. by the square metre in Europe and the square foot in the US.

If you're flexible about the delivery date, shipping companies will quote a lower price based on a 'part load', where the cost is shared with other deliveries. This can result in savings of 50 per cent or more compared with an individual delivery. Whether you have an individual or shared delivery, make sure you get the maximum transit period in writing; otherwise you might have to wait months for delivery!

Be sure to fully insure your belongings during removal with a well established insurance company. Don't insure through your shipping company, as rates are often high and a claim may be contested. Insurance premiums are usually 1 to 2 per cent of the declared value of your goods, depending on the type of cover chosen.

SURVIVAL TIP
Most companies recommend that you make a
photographic or video record of your valuables for
insurance purposes.

Most insurance policies provide cover for 'all risks' on a replacement value basis. Note, however, that china, glass and other breakables can usually be included in an all-risks policy only when they're packed by the removal company. Insurance usually covers total loss or loss of a particular crate only, rather than individual items (unless they were packed by the shipping company). If there are any breakages or damaged items, they must in theory be noted and listed before you sign the delivery bill, although it's obviously impractical to check everything on delivery; check the procedure before taking out insurance.

If you need to make a claim, be sure to read the small print, as some companies require clients to make a claim within a few days, although seven is usual. Send a claim by registered post. Some insurance companies apply an 'excess' of around 1 per cent of the total shipment value when assessing claims. This means that if your shipment is valued at €30,000 and you make a claim for less than €300, you won't receive anything.

If you're unable to ship your belongings directly to Bulgaria, most shipping companies will put them in storage and some allow a limited free storage period before shipment, e.g. 14 days, after which you may be charged from €50 to €100 per month for an average-size container.

 If you need to put your household effects into storage, it's imperative to have them fully insured, as warehouses have been known to burn down!

Make a complete list of everything to be moved and give a copy to the removal company. Don't include anything illegal (i.e. guns, explosives, drugs or pornographic material), as customs checks are rigorous and the penalties severe.

Provide the shipping company with **detailed** instructions as to how to find your Bulgarian address from the nearest main road and a telephone number where you can be contacted. If your property has difficult or impossible access for a large truck, you must inform the shipping company (the ground must also be firm enough to support a heavy vehicle). Note also that, if furniture needs to be taken in through an upstairs window, you may need to pay extra. You should also make a simple floor plan of your new home with rooms numbered and mark corresponding numbers on furniture and boxes as they're packed, so that the removal company will know where everything is to go and you can leave them to it.

PRE-DEPARTURE HEALTH CHECK

If you're planning to take up residence in Bulgaria, even if only for a part of the year, it's a good idea to have a full health check (including general health, eyes, ears, teeth, etc.) before you depart, especially if you have a record of poor health or are elderly. If you're taking medicine regularly, you should keep in mind that the brand names of drugs and medicines vary from country to country; ask your doctor for the generic name.

IMMIGRATION

Citizens of most European countries don't require a visa to visit Bulgaria (see **Permits & Visas** on page 36) and border and immigration restrictions will be eased considerably when Bulgaria joins the EU – scheduled for 2007. If you have a single-entry visa, it will be cancelled by the immigration official. **If you require a visa to enter Bulgaria and attempt to enter without one, you will be refused entry.**

Immigration officials may ask visitors to produce a return ticket and proof of accommodation, health insurance and adequate financial resources (e.g. cash, travellers' cheques and credit cards). The onus is on visitors to show that they won't violate Bulgarian law; immigration officials aren't required to prove that you will breach the law and can refuse you entry on the grounds of suspicion only. Young people may be more susceptible to interrogation, especially ones with 'strange' attire, and therefore should carry international credit or charge cards, a student identity card or a letter from an employer or college stating that they're on holiday, as appropriate.

All foreigners must register with the local police within five days of arrival (see **Registration** on page 183). If you intend to stay for more than 90 days (in the case of most EU citizens) or 30 days (for US, UK, Australian and other citizens) – see **Visitors** on page 36 – you will need to apply for a Type D visa from the Bulgarian embassy or consulate in your home country (see **Visas** on page 36). A Type D visa is valid for 12 months from the date of issue for a stay of up to 90 days in succession, which is long enough to obtain a residence permit (see page 39).

SURVIVAL TIP
Bulgarian immigration officials' 'customer service' is improving, but as in all countries it pays to be calm and polite and speak clearly when passing through immigration.

CUSTOMS

Prohibited & Restricted Goods

Certain goods may not be imported (or exported) or are subject to restrictions or special regulations. This applies to historical artefacts, precious metals and gems, plants (see below), guns and ammunition, tobacco, drugs (including medicines and medicinal products but excluding prescribed medicines), alcohol and pornographic material. If you're unsure whether any goods you're importing fall into the above categories, check with your removal company or a Bulgarian consulate or embassy.

Customs duty is payable if you're carrying more than one litre of spirits and two litres of wine; and more than 200 cigarettes, 100 cigarillos, 50 cigars or 250g of tobacco. However, there's little point in bringing alcohol into Bulgaria, as it can be purchased cheaply in the country.

To import certain types of plant into Bulgaria, you require a phytosanitary health certificate issued by your country's customs department and a certificate (issued upon entry) by the Bulgarian National Service for Plant Protection, Quarantine and Agrochemistry. Information can be obtained from this service at 17 Hristo Botev blv, Sofia (⊠ prong@mbox.infotel.bg, 🖳 http://www.mzgar.government.bg/MZ_eng).

If you bring more than 8,000 lev (or the equivalent in another currency) in cash into Bulgaria, you must declare it. There are no restrictions on the import or export of currency by individuals (see **Declaration** on page 149).

Visitors

Visitors' belongings aren't subject to duty or tax and can be imported without formality, provided they aren't prohibited or restricted (see above) and their nature and quality doesn't imply any commercial aim. This applies to private cars, camping vehicles, motorcycles, boats (see below) and personal effects. All means of transport and personal effects imported duty-free mustn't be sold, loaned or given away in Bulgaria, and must be re-exported at the end of the permitted 90- or 30-day period (see **Visitors** on page 36). Information about duty-free allowances can be found on page 253.

Bulgaria has been relaxing its regulations on entry to seaports and cruising is now allowed along the Black Sea coast. The ports of entry are Bourgas and Varna, where you will undergo immigration checks (see page 181), subject to which you will be issued with a Temporary Navigation Certificate, valid for 30 days.

Residents

If you plan to take up permanent or temporary residence in Bulgaria, you're permitted to import your furniture and personal effects free of duty, but import is subject to customs regulations. When shipping belongings, you must provide a copy of your passport and residence permit (if applicable), evidence that you've formed a limited company in Bulgaria (if you've bought a property with land) or a letter from your employer in Bulgaria, plus an inventory (in English) of the goods being shipped and their value. The inventory must include all electrical or electronic devices, with the brand names and serial numbers. Information about the import of pets on page 47.

If you use a removal company to transport your belongings to Bulgaria, they will usually provide the necessary forms and take care of the paperwork. If the removal company packs your belongings, ask them to mark the containers 'Mover Packed', as this will speed up the customs clearance process. If you want an agent (e.g. of the removal company) to deal with customs, you must usually give him power of attorney (see page 163).

Until regulations come into line with those of the EU, you may be charged VAT at 20 per cent, dependent on the discretion of the customs officer. Generally, if articles have been owned and used for at least six months you won't have to pay VAT on them.

All personal effects must be imported within three months of your arrival in Bulgaria, either in one or in a number of consignments, although it's better to have one consignment only.

There's a high rate of vehicle theft in Bulgaria and many cars are fitted with new registration plates. If you're importing a privately owned vehicle, you will therefore need to produce proof of ownership, the vehicle's registration document, your Bulgarian visa (if applicable), your driving licence and insurance Green Card. Check with your removal company what the current regulations are for importing a motor vehicle and the documentation required. To qualify for duty-free entry, a vehicle must have been used for at least six months before your departure from your home country.

Always keep a copy of forms and communications with customs officials, both Bulgarian officials and those in your previous or permanent country of residence. You should also obtain an official record of the export of valuables from any country in case you wish to re-import them later.

REGISTRATION

All foreigners staying for more than five days in Bulgaria must register with the local police within five days of arrival. If you're staying in a hotel, this is normally done by staff, but if you're in private accommodation you will need to register yourself. This involves simply providing the address of where you're staying, your name and your passport details (number and expiry date).

You're also recommended to register with your local embassy or consulate – registration isn't usually compulsory, but most embassies likes to keep a record of their country's citizens in Bulgaria in case of a major accident or natural disaster.

FINDING HELP

One of the biggest difficulties facing new arrivals in Bulgaria is finding help with everyday problems, particularly as many administrative matters are handled at the provincial or local level, rather than nationally. How successful you are at finding local information depends on the town or area where you live (e.g. residents of Sofia are better served than those living in rural areas), your nationality and your command of Bulgarian (there's plenty of information in Bulgarian, but much less available in English and other foreign languages). A further problem is that much of the available information isn't intended for foreigners and their particular needs. Nevertheless, you should make use of the following sources of information.

Colleagues & Friends

As in almost any country with a strong bureaucratic culture, it isn't so much what you know as who you know that counts. String-pulling or the use of contacts is widespread in Bulgaria, particularly as many former public servants and bureaucrats lost their jobs after the fall of communism but kept in touch with their former colleagues. Often a telephone call on your behalf by a Bulgarian neighbour or friend can work wonders. But take care: although friends, neighbours or work colleagues (either existing or new) can often offer advice based on their own experiences and mistakes and invariably mean well, you're likely to receive misleading and conflicting information (it may not necessarily be wrong but irrelevant to your particular situation).

Local Community

Your local community is usually an excellent source of reliable information, but most often you will need to speak Bulgarian to benefit from it. Your town hall serves as the local registry of births, deaths and marriages, council offices and land registry. The local post office often doubles as the tourist office and citizens' advice bureau.

Embassy or Consulate

Most embassies and consulates provide their nationals with local information including details of lawyers, interpreters, doctors, dentists, schools, and social and expatriate organisations. The British Embassy (🖳 http://www.britishembassy.gov.uk) has an excellent website, which includes plenty of information (in English) about living in Bulgaria, including a list of English-speaking lawyers, and general guidelines for buying property and relocating to Bulgaria.

Internet

The main online resource for information about national rules and regulations is the government website (🖳 http://www.government.bg – click the link on the left for the English version). Other regions have websites and information portals, but the amount of useful information depends on how developed the tourist infrastructure is in the area; for example, the Varna District Administration has an informative website in English, with details of local government services and other information about the area (🖳 http://www.vn.government.bg/en).

The Disabled

The standard of access for disabled people in Bulgaria is poor, with few ramped kerbs on roads, disabled parking spaces or even disabled toilets. While the standard is improving in major tourist destinations such as Varna and Bourgas, Bulgaria has a long way to go before it reaches the standards of access in western European countries.

MOVING IN

One of the most important tasks to perform after moving into a new home is to check that the previous owner hasn't absconded with any fixtures and fittings that were included in the price, or anything that you specifically paid for, such as carpets, light fittings, curtains, furniture, kitchen appliances, garden ornaments, plants or doors (see **Final Checks** on page 171).

When moving into a long-term rental property it's necessary to complete an inventory of its contents and a report on its condition. This includes the condition of fixtures and fittings, the state of furniture and furnishings, the cleanliness and state of the decoration, anything that's damaged, missing or in need of repair. An inventory should be provided by your landlord or agent and may include every single item in a furnished property (even the number of teaspoons!). The inventory should be completed in your presence. If an inventory isn't provided, you should insist on one being prepared and annexed to the lease. If you find a serious fault after signing an inventory, ask (in writing) for it to be attached to the inventory. An inventory should also be drawn up when vacating a rented property. If the two inventories don't correspond, you must make good any damages or deficiencies or the landlord can do so and deduct the cost from your deposit.

Whether buying or renting, note the reading on your utility meters (e.g. electricity, gas, water) and check you aren't overcharged on your first bill. The meters should be read by the utility company before you move in, although you might need to organise this yourself.

It's worth obtaining written instructions from the previous owner regarding access to shared facilities and for operating entry systems and any appliances such as heating and air-conditioning systems, the maintenance of the garden and swimming pool, and the care of surfaces such wooden or marble floors, as well as the names of reliable local maintenance men who might know the property. Check with your local town hall about local regulations on such things as rubbish collection, recycling and on-road parking.

Finally, you should introduce yourselves to neighbours as soon as you can, even if your Bulgarian is basic.

CHECKLISTS

When moving permanently to Bulgaria there are many things to be considered and people to be informed. Even if you only plan to spend a few months per year in Bulgaria, it may be necessary to inform a number of individuals and companies in your home country. The checklists below are designed to make the task easier and help prevent an ulcer or nervous breakdown (provided, of course, you don't leave everything until the last minute). Not all the points below are applicable to non-residents or those spending only a few weeks per year in Bulgaria.

Before Arrival

The following are tasks that should be completed (if possible) before your arrival in France:

- Check that your and your family's passports are valid.

- Obtain a visa if necessary, for you and your family members.

- Arrange inoculations and shipment for any pets you're taking with you.

- Visit Bulgaria before your move to compare schools and arrange schooling for your children.

- If you're living in rented accommodation, give your landlord adequate notice that you're moving out (check your contract).

- Arrange to sell and dispose of anything you aren't taking with you, e.g. house, car and furniture. If you're selling a home or business, you should obtain expert legal advice, as you may be able to save tax by establishing a trust or other legal vehicle. Note that if you own more than one property, you may have to pay capital gains tax on any profits from the sale of second and subsequent homes.

- Arrange shipment of your furniture and belongings by booking a shipping company well in advance.

- Check whether you need an international driving licence or a translation of your national driving licence(s).

- Before exporting a car to Bulgaria, complete the relevant paperwork required by your current vehicle licensing authority (e.g. the DVLA in the UK).

- Check whether you're entitled to a rebate on your road tax, car and other insurance. Obtain a letter from your vehicle insurance company stating your no-claims discount.

- You may qualify for a rebate on your tax and social security contributions. If you're leaving a country permanently and have been a member of a company or state pension scheme, you may be entitled to a refund or be able to continue payments to qualify for a full (or larger) pension when you retire. Contact your company personnel office, local tax office or pension company for more information.

- Arrange health insurance for yourself and your family. This is essential if you aren't covered by a private insurance policy.

- Open a bank account in Bulgaria (see page 154) and transfer funds (see page 148). Give the details to any companies that you plan to pay by standing order (e.g. utility companies).

- Arrange health, dental and eye check-ups for your family before you leave your home country. Also, obtain a copy of any health records and a statement from your private health insurance company stating your present level of cover.

- Terminate any outstanding loan, lease or hire purchase contracts and pay all bills (allow plenty of time, as some companies are slow to respond).

- Return any library books!

- If you don't already have one, it's wise to obtain an international credit or charge card, which may be useful during your first few months in Bulgaria, particularly until you've opened a bank account.

- Don't forget to take all your family's official documents, including birth certificates, driving licences, marriage certificate, divorce papers or death certificate (if a widow or widower), educational diplomas, professional certificates and job references, school records and student identity cards, copies of medical and dental records, bank account and credit card details, insurance policies and receipts for any valuables. You will also need the documents necessary to obtain a residence permit (see page 39) plus certified copies, official translations and numerous passport-size photographs (students should take at least a dozen).

- Inform the following people:

    - your employer (e.g. give notice) or clients and customers if self-employed;

    - your town hall or municipality (you may be entitled to a refund of your local property or income taxes);

    - the police if it was necessary to register with them in your home country or present country of residence;

    - your electricity, gas, water, telephone, internet and cable TV companies (contact companies well in advance, particularly if you need to have a deposit refunded);

- your insurance companies (e.g. health, car, home contents and private pension), banks, post office (if you have a post office account), stockbroker and other financial institutions, credit card, charge card and hire purchase companies, lawyer and accountant, and local businesses where you have accounts;

- your family doctor, dentist and other health practitioners (health records should be transferred to your new doctor and dentist in Bulgaria, if applicable);

- your children's schools (try to give a term's notice and obtain a copy of any relevant school reports or records from your children's current schools;

- all regular correspondents, social and sports clubs, professional and trade journals, friends and relatives (give them your new address and telephone number and arrange to have your post redirected by the post office or by a friend;

- your local or national vehicle registration office if you have a driving licence or car (return your registration plates if applicable).

● If you will be living in Bulgaria for an extended period (but not permanently) you may wish to give someone power of attorney over your financial affairs in your home country so he can act for you in your absence. This can be for a fixed or unlimited period and can be for a specific purpose only. **You should always take expert legal advice before giving someone power of attorney over any of your financial affairs!**

● Finally, allow plenty of time to get to the airport or ferry, register your luggage, and clear security and immigration.

After Arrival

The following tasks should be completed after arrival in Bulgaria (if not done before):

● If you've exported a vehicle, re-register it in Bulgaria.

● If you aren't taking a car with you, you may wish to rent one for a week or two before buying one locally. Keep in mind that it's practically impossible to get around in rural areas without a car. If you purchase a car in Bulgaria, register it and arrange insurance.

- Apply for a Type D visa (see page 37) at the Ministry of Interior within 90 or 30 days of your arrival.

- Arrange schooling for your children.

- Find a local doctor and dentist.

- Arrange whatever insurance is necessary, including health, car, household and third-party liability insurance.

- Make courtesy calls on your neighbours and the local mayor within a few weeks of your arrival. This is particularly important in villages if you want to be accepted and become part of the community.

7.

TAXATION

An important consideration when you're buying a home in Bulgaria, even if you don't plan to live there permanently, is taxation, which includes property tax, wealth tax, capital gains tax (CGT) and inheritance tax. You will also have to pay income tax if you live permanently in Bulgaria or earn an income from a property there.

While Bulgaria has much lower tax rates than western Europe (particularly France and the UK), you should obtain expert advice on Bulgarian taxes before deciding to settle there permanently. This will (hopefully) ensure that you take maximum advantage of your current tax status and that you don't make any mistakes you will regret later.

Most foreigners buying property in Bulgaria must form a limited company to purchase land, so they will be subject to corporation tax (see **Corporation Tax** on page 197). If you earn an income in Bulgaria, either from employment or from property letting, you must also pay personal income tax (see below).

INCOME TAX

Bulgarian residents are taxed in Bulgaria on their worldwide income, subject to relevant treaty obligations; non-residents are only taxed on their income in Bulgaria. Personal income tax in Bulgaria is much lower than in western European countries and is roughly comparable to other eastern European countries, including those that joined the European Union (EU) in 2004.

Liability

Your liability for Bulgarian taxes depends on where you're 'domiciled'. Your domicile is normally the country you regard as your permanent home and where you live for most of the year. A foreigner working in Bulgaria for a Bulgarian company who has taken up residence in Bulgaria and has no income tax liability abroad is considered to have his tax domicile in Bulgaria. A person can be resident in more than one country at any given time, but can be domiciled in only one country. The domicile of a married woman isn't necessarily the same as her husband's but is determined using the same criteria as for anyone capable of having an independent domicile. Your country of domicile is particularly important when it comes to inheritance tax (see page 199).

Under the Bulgarian tax code, your domicile is decided under the 183-day rule. You're considered to be a Bulgarian resident for taxation purposes if any of the following applies:

● your permanent home, i.e. family or principal residence, is in Bulgaria;

- you spend over 183 days in Bulgaria (i.e. more than half the year) in Bulgaria during any calendar year;

- you carry out paid professional activities or employment in Bulgaria, except when secondary to business activities conducted in another country;

- your centre of economic interest, e.g. investments or business, is in Bulgaria.

If you intend to live in Bulgaria permanently, you should notify the tax authorities in your present country (you will be asked to complete a form, e.g. a P85 in the UK) and you may be entitled to a tax refund if you depart during the tax year. The tax authorities may require evidence that you're leaving the country, e.g. evidence of forming a limited company in Bulgaria or of having bought or rented a property there.

Double Taxation

Citizens of most countries are exempt from paying taxes in their home country when they spend a minimum period abroad, e.g. a year. Bulgaria has double-taxation treaties with over 50 countries, including the members of the 15-state EU (i.e. excluding the states that joined in 2004), China, India, Japan, Russia and Singapore.

Treaties are designed to ensure that income taxed in one treaty country isn't taxed again in another treaty country. The treaty establishes a tax credit or exemption on certain kinds of income, either in the country of residence or the country where the income is earned. Where applicable, a double-taxation treaty prevails over domestic law. Many people living abroad switch their investments to offshore holdings to avoid the often complicated double-taxation agreements, although offshore accounts aren't always suitable for income. The US is the only country that requires its citizens to file a tax return, even if they aren't living in the US or, indeed, have never set foot in the country (e.g. a child born to US parents in another country).

Leaving Bulgaria

Before leaving Bulgaria, foreigners must pay any tax due for the previous year and the year of departure. Leaving (as well as moving to) Bulgaria may offer you an opportunity for 'favourable tax planning' (i.e. tax avoidance rather than tax evasion). To get the most out of your situation, you should obtain professional advice from a tax adviser familiar with both the Bulgarian tax system and that of your present or future country of residence.

Exemptions

Income from the sale of 'immovable' property (i.e. houses and apartments) is tax exempt (but may be subject to capital gains tax – see page 198). There's no tax on income earned from bank deposits.

Taxation of Property Income

Income tax is payable in Bulgaria on rental income from a Bulgarian property, even if you live abroad and the money is paid there. All rental income must be declared, irrespective of how long you let a property. Twenty per cent of rental income isn't taxed; the remainder is taxed at your personal income (or corporation) tax rate. If you receive rent and aren't resident in Bulgaria for tax purposes, a 15 per cent withholding tax is levied, minus deductions for allowable expenses such as mortgage interest.

If you've purchased a property through a limited company, you may be subject to corporation rather than personal income tax (see page 194).

Calculation

The tax year in Bulgaria runs for the calendar year (i.e. from 1st January to 31st December). The income tax rates for a single person for 2005 income (2006 tax return) are shown below.

Taxable Income	Tax Rate
Up to 2,160 lev	0%
2,161 to 3,000 lev	20%
3,001 to 7,200 lev	22%
Over 7,200 lev	24%

If you're working and receiving a salary in Bulgaria you must also pay social security contributions of 1 per cent of income and unemployment fund contributions of 0.5 per cent of gross (pre-tax) salary.

Tax Returns

Tax returns must be filed by 15th April for individuals and by 31st March for companies. It's recommended that you engage an accountant in Bulgaria to complete your tax return. To file a tax return yourself, either as an individual or as a company, you will need a solid grasp of Bulgarian and an understanding of the taxation system. Most estate agents offer a tax return filing service but the cost varies dramatically (the average charge is around €100, although the fee can be as low as €25 and as high as €300), so it's worth shopping around and not relying on the agent who sold you your property.

CORPORATION TAX

If you buy a property with land in Bulgaria, you must form a limited company (see **Forming a Company** on page 162) and pay corporation tax.

Corporation tax has been cut several times in the past few years by the Bulgarian government to encourage inward investment and now stands at 15 per cent. This means that if you sell your property, any gain you've made on it will count as a profit for your limited company and will be taxed at 15 per cent. Any profit you make from rental income will also be taxed at 15 per cent, although you may make certain deductions, including depreciation (calculated at 4 per cent per year) and expenses such as repairs, maintenance, renovation and interest on loans used for the acquisition of the property.

If you don't have any business activity during the year (i.e. you don't sell your property and you have no rental income), you will still need to file a 'zero' tax return. Your accountant will be able to file your return in your absence if you provide him with power of attorney and many estate agents offer a tax return service (see **Tax Returns** above).

VALUE ADDED TAX

There's a single rate of value added tax (VAT) in Bulgaria, which is 20 per cent. VAT is payable on all products and services in Bulgaria and on imports to the country. Every business that has an annual turnover of more than 50,000 lev (€25,000) must register for VAT. If you've purchased your property as an individual (i.e. not through a limited company) you don't have to worry about VAT, but if you purchased it through a limited company (i.e. if it has land) you may have to add VAT to the selling price. If it's your first property, you will most likely **not** be registered for VAT (because your company will almost certainly have a turnover of less than 50,000 lev even if you've been letting it), so you will only need to register for VAT after the sale (and if the selling price is over 50,000 lev). If and when you come to sell a second property, you will then need to add 20 per cent VAT to the selling price, as well as adding VAT to any rental charges. You must also open a separate bank account for VAT payments.

PROPERTY TAXES

There are usually two property taxes to be paid: one is a tax at 0.15 per cent on the declared purchase price of the property (see **Declared Price** on page 166), e.g. €7.50 for a property worth €50,000, and the other a small levy for waste collection, although in some villages there's no collection service and therefore no tax. You must pay both taxes (if applicable) at the municipal council offices. Some agents and accountants offer a property tax payment service, but the fee can often be out of proportion to the amount of tax due.

CAPITAL GAINS TAX

Technically, there's no capital gains tax (CGT) in Bulgaria, but under certain circumstances capital gains are taxed at 15 per cent (and if that isn't a capital gains tax, what is!?).

 Beware of the practice of understating a property sale price on the contract (see Declared Price on page 166): while this may reduce the vendor's tax bill and some of your fees, when you come to sell the property it will appear as if you've made a larger capital gain than you actually have and you will be taxed accordingly.

Your liability for tax depends on various factors and differs according to whether you're a resident or non-resident of Bulgaria (see below).

> **SURVIVAL TIP**
> Capital gains gax is a complex subject, particularly if you aren't a Bulgarian resident for tax purposes, and you should consult an independent financial adviser before making any major financial decisions.

Non-residents

If you aren't resident in Bulgaria for tax purposes (see **Liability** on page 194), i.e. your Bulgarian property isn't your principal residence but a second home or investment property, any gain you make on its sale is taxed at 15 per cent. If you've bought a Bulgarian property as an individual non-resident (i.e. a property without land), you must pay tax on the difference between the purchase and sale price; **there are no allowances or adjustments for inflation**.

 Because this tax isn't classed as CGT, you will still be liable for capital gains in your the country where you're resident and won't be able to offset the Bulgarian tax payment against it but will effectively pay CGT twice – 15 per cent in Bulgaria and whatever rate applies in your home country.

If you purchased through a limited company (i.e. a property with land), you will be subject to corporation tax on the profit (also at 15 per cent) and may also be liable for CGT in your country of residence (see **Capital Gains Tax** on page 248).

Residents

If you're a resident of Bulgaria for tax purposes and not taxed as a limited company (i.e. you've bought a property without land), you don't have to pay tax on the sale of a property if it's your primary residence **and** you've owned it for more than five years. If your property isn't exempt, you must pay tax at 15 per cent on any gain as if you were a non-resident (see above).

INHERITANCE & GIFT TAX

Inheritance tax was partially abolished in 2005. Currently, your immediate relatives and surviving spouse won't have to pay inheritance tax, while brothers, sisters and their children will have to pay 0.7 per cent on amounts above 250,000 lev (€125,000).

Gift tax is payable at fixed rates depending on the relationship between the donor and the recipient. Spouses and direct line inheritors are exempt.

Gifts between brothers and sisters are taxable at 0.7 per cent, and all other beneficiaries are taxed at 5 per cent.

WILLS

It's an unfortunate fact of life that you're unable to take your hard-earned assets with you when you take your final bow (or come back and reclaim them in a later life!). All adults should make a will, irrespective of how large of small their assets. The disposal of your estate depends on your country of domicile (see **Liability** on page 194). It's possible to make two wills, one relating to Bulgarian property and the other to foreign property. Opinion differs on whether you should have separate wills for Bulgarian and foreign property, or a foreign will with a codicil (appendix) dealing with your Bulgarian property, or vice versa. Most experts believe that it's better to have a Bulgarian will from the perspective of winding up your Bulgarian estate and a separate will for any other country where you own assets. Note, however, that getting a Bulgarian will drawn up may be next to impossible!

SURVIVAL TIP
If you do have Bulgarian and foreign wills, make sure they don't contradict one another – or worse, cancel each other out (e.g. when a will contains a clause revoking all other wills)!

8.

<u>I</u>NSURANCE

An important aspect of owning a holiday home in Bulgaria is insurance, not only for your home and its contents, but also for you and your family when visiting.

SURVIVAL TIP
It's vital to ensure that you have sufficient insurance when visiting your home abroad, which includes travel insurance, car insurance (including breakdown insurance), building and contents insurance, public liability insurance and health insurance.

If you live in Bulgaria permanently, the only compulsory insurance is third-party liability car insurance. However, it's recommended that you take out, at a minimum, property/building insurance and public liability insurance if you will be letting out your property. You may be required to take out life insurance if you have a mortgage, depending on the amount borrowed. Other voluntary insurances you should have are health, household (contents) and travel insurance.

 It's your responsibility to ensure that you and your family are legally insured, and Bulgarian law is likely to differ from that in your home country or your previous country of residence, so never assume that it's the same.

It's unnecessary to spend half your income insuring yourself against every eventuality from the common cold to being sued for your last *stotinka*, but it's important to insure against any event that could precipitate a major financial disaster, such as a serious illness or your house falling down.

When buying insurance, shop until you drop! Obtain recommendations from friends, colleagues and neighbours (but don't believe everything they tell you!). Compare the costs, terms and benefits provided by a number of companies before making a decision. **Simply collecting a few brochures from insurance agents or making a few telephone calls could save you a lot of money**. Note also that insurance premiums are often negotiable.

HEALTH INSURANCE

Whether you're living in Bulgaria or just visiting, it's extremely risky not to have health insurance for yourself and your family; if you're uninsured or under-insured, you could be faced with some very high medical bills. If you're working in Bulgaria and qualify for state health benefits, you may still want to have private insurance, owing to the limitations of the state health service.

Visitors

If you have a holiday home and come to Bulgaria as a visitor (i.e. for less than 90 days at a time and less than 183 days in any year), you should check whether you qualify for free or subsidised health treatment in Bulgaria as part of a reciprocal health agreement between your home country and Bulgaria (see below). If you don't, you must choose between a private international health insurance policy (see page 208), and holiday/travel insurance (see page 207).

Reciprocal Health Agreements

Citizens of the UK are entitled to free medical, dental and hospital treatment in Bulgaria, under a reciprocal healthcare agreement between the two countries. To access healthcare, you will need a UK passport and NHS card. UK citizens must pay for medicines, however. **Most other countries don't have reciprocal health agreements**, so if you aren't covered by Bulgarian social security you must have private health insurance or a holiday/travel policy that covers you in Bulgaria.

 The UK Department of Health warns that the state healthcare sector in Bulgaria is severely limited and strongly recommends that visitors to Bulgaria have private medical insurance.

When Bulgaria joins the EU (scheduled for 2007), all EU citizens should be eligible for reduced cost or free medical treatment in Bulgaria on production of a European Health Insurance Card (EHIC). The EHIC is valid for three to five years and covers any medical treatment that becomes necessary because of either illness or an accident while outside your home country. The card gives access to state-provided medical treatment only. **An EHIC doesn't cover you for all the medical costs that you can incur or for repatriation, and so shouldn't be considered an alternative to travel or international health insurance.**

The UK Department of Health has more information on the EHIC and instructions for applying on its website (? http://www.dh.gov.uk/travellers).

Residents

If you plan to take up residence in Bulgaria and will be contributing to Bulgarian social security (called 'NOI') – e.g. if you will be working in Bulgaria – you and your family will be entitled to free or subsidised medical and dental treatment from the Bulgarian state system. Once you have a residence permit you will pay contributions through the NOI to the Bulgarian state health system, currently around 15 lev per month. This entitles you to free treatment from a GP, free referrals to a specialist, and medicines at reduced prices or free.

SURVIVAL TIP
It's recommended that you take out private health insurance while in Bulgaria, even if you're a resident, as the standard of private health care tends to be much higher than that of the state system. You should also check your entitlements under the Bulgarian state health scheme and when such cover might become effective.

Residents who don't contribute to social security (e.g. retirees) and aren't covered by a reciprocal agreement (see above) should take out a private international health insurance policy.

SURVIVAL TIP
If you're planning to take up residence in Bulgaria, you should ensure that you and your family have full health insurance during the interval between leaving your last country of residence and obtaining health insurance in Bulgaria.

One way to insure yourself for this interim period is to take out a holiday/travel insurance policy (see page 207). If you already have private health insurance, it's better to extend your present health insurance policy to provide international cover (which is usually possible) than to take out a new policy. This is particularly important if you have an existing health problem that won't be covered by a new policy.

HOLIDAY & TRAVEL INSURANCE

Holiday/travel insurance is recommended for those whose health and possessions aren't covered by an existing policy while travelling. As you're no doubt already aware, innumerable things can (and often do) go wrong with a holiday, sometimes before you even reach the airport or port, and particularly when you **don't** have insurance.

Travel insurance is available from many sources, including travel agents, insurance agents, motoring organisations, transport companies and direct from insurance companies. It isn't wise to depend on travel insurance provided by charge and credit card companies, household or car insurance policies or package holiday companies, none of which usually provide adequate cover (although you should take advantage of what they offer). For example, car insurance may include personal accident and health insurance (e.g. through Mondial Assistance) even if you don't take your car, but won't cover you for loss of belongings or cancellation of flights.

Before taking out travel insurance, carefully consider the level of cover you require and compare policies. Most policies include cover for loss of deposit or holiday cancellation, missed flights, departure, delay at both the start and end of the holiday (a common occurrence), delayed baggage, lost or stolen money, luggage and other belongings, medical expenses and accidents (including repatriation if necessary), personal liability, legal expenses and a tour operator or airline going bankrupt.

Medical expenses are an important aspect of travel insurance and you shouldn't rely on reciprocal health arrangements, where these exist (see **Reciprocal Health Arrangements** on page 205). The minimum medical insurance recommended by experts is €500,000 in Europe. If applicable, check whether pregnancy-related claims are covered and whether there are restrictions for those aged over 65 or 70. Third-party or personal liability cover should be around €1.5 to €2m in Europe. Always check any exclusion clauses in contracts by obtaining a copy of the full policy document (all the relevant information isn't always included in the insurance leaflet).

The cost of travel insurance varies considerably according to your destination and the duration of your trip. You should expect to pay around €15 to €30 for a week's insurance in Europe, around €25 to €35 for two weeks and around €60 to €70 for a month. Premiums can be higher for those aged over 65 or 70. Many insurance companies offer annual travel policies from around €75 to €100 that are good value for frequent travellers, although you should check exactly what is covered (or omitted) as these policies may not provide adequate cover. A useful website to compare travel insurance prices is Money Supermarket (🖳 http://www.moneysupermarket. com/travelinsurance).

Although travel insurance companies gladly take your money, they aren't usually so keen to honour claims and you may have to persevere before they pay up. Always be persistent and make a claim irrespective of any small print, as this may be unreasonable and therefore invalid in law. Insurance companies usually require you to report a loss (or any incident for which you intend to make a claim) to the local police (or carriers) within 24 hours and obtain a written report. Failure to do this usually means a claim won't be considered.

PRIVATE HEALTH INSURANCE

If you already have private health insurance in another country, it may be possible to extend it to cover you in Bulgaria. Bear in mind, however, that in some countries (e.g. the UK) insurance companies may automatically cancel your insurance policies without telling you if you inform them that you're moving abroad permanently!

When changing health insurance companies, make sure you inform your existing insurer and that any previous insurance claims have been settled.

 If you're planning to change your health insurance company, you should ensure that no important benefits are lost, e.g. existing medical conditions won't usually be covered by a new insurer.

If you don't have an international policy, shop around for the one that best suits your requirements. Most international insurance companies offer health policies for different areas, e.g. Europe, worldwide excluding North America, and worldwide including North America. Most companies offer different levels of cover, e.g. basic, standard and comprehensive. There's always an annual limit on medical costs and some companies also limit the charges for specific treatment or care such as specialists' fees, operations and hospital accommodation.

Most private health insurance policies don't pay family doctors' fees or pay for medicines other than those provided in a hospital, or they charge a high excess, e.g. you must pay the first €75 of a claim, which can often exceed the cost of treatment.

A medical examination isn't usually required for international health policies, although 'pre-existing' health problems are excluded for a period. Most international health policies include repatriation or evacuation, which may also cover shipment (by air) of the body of a person who dies abroad to their home country for burial. An international policy also allows you to have non-urgent medical treatment in the country of your choice.

Check whether an insurance company will settle large medical bills directly with a hospital. The major international insurers don't have 'recommended' hospitals in Bulgaria.

 If you're required to pay bills and claim reimbursement from an insurance company, it can take several months before you receive your money.

It isn't usually necessary to translate bills into English or another language, although you should check a company's policy. Most international health insurance companies provide emergency telephone assistance.

The cost of international health insurance varies considerably according to your age and the extent of cover. With most international insurance policies, you must take out a policy before a certain age, usually between 65 and 70, to be guaranteed continuous cover in your old age. When comparing policies, carefully check the extent of cover and what's included and excluded from a policy (often indicated only in **very** small print), in addition to premiums and excess charges.

Although there may be significant differences in premiums, generally you get what you pay for and can tailor premiums to your requirements. The most important questions to ask yourself are: does the policy provide the cover required and is it good value? If you're in good health and are able to pay for your own out-patient treatment, such as visits to your family doctor and prescriptions, the best value is usually a policy covering specialist and hospital treatment only.

When deciding on the type and extent of private health insurance, make sure that it covers **all** your family's present and future health requirements in Bulgaria **before** you receive a large bill. A health insurance policy should cover you for **all** essential health care whatever the reason, including accidents (e.g. sports accidents) and injuries, whether they occur in your home or while travelling.

HOUSEHOLD INSURANCE

Household insurance in Bulgaria is a fairly new concept and can be complicated to arrange, although there are a number of foreign-owned companies in the market providing insurance similar to that offered in Western countries. Building and contents insurance are normally offered separately; all-risk or multi-risk insurance isn't yet commonly available and in many cases you will need to specify exactly what you wish to insure against (e.g. fire, flood, earthquake). A basic policy might cover you only for damage caused by fire, lightning, explosions and falling objects (e.g. trees), and you may need extra or extended cover for other risks. If you're insuring with a company in another country (e.g. the UK), you will usually be able to take out a multi-risk policy, although the cost will be higher.

Building Insurance

It's wise to take out building insurance covering damage due to fire, water, explosion, storm, earthquakes or other natural catastrophes. Prices vary considerably according to where your property is located, its value and the risks covered. A small house might cost around €500 per year to insure. Building insurance is based the cost of rebuilding your home, which in turn is based on the declared value (another reason not to under-declare – see **Declared Price** on page 166). Be aware that in some areas of Bulgaria flooding is common (see **Earthquakes & Flooding** on page 29), so always read the small print of any insurance policy to make sure you're covered. Note also that most insurance companies divide Bulgaria into three zones according to earthquake risk: the highest risk area (and therefore the area with the highest insurance premiums) is in the west of the country around Sofia, the lowest risk area mostly along the Black Sea coast (see **Earthquakes & Flooding** on page 29).

SURVIVAL TIP
Make sure that you insure your property for the cost of rebuilding.

Apartments

If you're buying a new or off-plan apartment, the developer may offer building insurance as part of the sale price, but it's more common that insurance is offered as part of the maintenance contract. You should also be insured against public liability in case you cause damage to neighbouring apartments, e.g. through flooding or fire (see **Public Liability Insurance** below).

Contents

Contents are usually insured for the same risks as buildings and are insured for their replacement value. Depending on the insurance company you choose, you may have to provide an itemised list of all items of value, with serial numbers for electrical goods and receipts for items of value. Non-Bulgarian insurance companies operating in Bulgaria are usually more flexible and will often reach an agreed value for your contents, although for items of high value (e.g. jewellery and works of art) you will probably have to provide photographs and documentation such as an expert valuation.

When claiming for contents you should produce the original bills if possible (always keep receipts for expensive items) and keep in mind that replacing imported items may be much more expensive than buying them abroad. Note that contents policies usually contain security clauses (e.g. requiring a 'back-to-base' alarm, which sounds in a security company's office, or window shutters) and if you don't adhere to them a claim won't be considered.

Holiday Homes

Premiums are generally higher for holiday homes than for main residences because of their vulnerability, particularly to burglaries, and are usually based on the number of days per year a property is occupied and the intervals between periods of occupancy. Cover for theft, storm, flood and malicious damage may be suspended when a property is left empty for a long period. You may be able to negotiate with your insurance to remove any 'unoccupied' clauses if you take out a contract with a management or security company to visit and check the property regularly (e.g. every two weeks or monthly). **Some insurance companies will do their utmost to find a loophole which makes you negligent and relieves them of their liability!** Always check that the details listed on a policy are correct and read all the small print.

SURVIVAL TIP
Where applicable, it's important to ensure that a policy specifies a holiday home and not a principal home.

It's unwise to leave valuable or irreplaceable items in a holiday home or a home that will be left vacant for long periods.

Insuring Abroad

It's possible and legal to take out building and contents insurance in another country for a property in Bulgaria. The advantage is that you will have a policy you can understand and will be able to handle claims in your own language. This is often a good option for the owner of a holiday home in Bulgaria, although it can be much more expensive than insuring with a Bulgarian company, so it pays to compare premiums. It can also be much simpler to apply for contents insurance with a company outside Bulgaria, as they will usually insure for an agreed value, rather than asking you to provide receipts for all items you wish to insure (which can be difficult if you're moving into a furnished property).

Claims

If you need to make a claim on a household policy, you must usually inform your insurance company in writing (by registered letter) within two to five days of the incident (depending on the company) or within 24 hours in the case of theft. Thefts should also be reported to the local police within 24 hours, as the police statement, of which you receive a copy for your insurance company, is required when submitting your claim. If you have insurance with a non-Bulgarian company (e.g. in the UK) you will probably have to send an English-language translation of the police statement with your claim. Check whether you're covered for damage or thefts that occur while you're away from the property and are therefore unable to inform the insurance company immediately.

PUBLIC LIABILITY INSURANCE

You should take out public liability (also called third-party liability) insurance for all members of your family, either as part of your property insurance or as separate cover, particularly if you will be letting your property. This covers you for damage done or caused to third parties by you, your children, your tenants and even your pets, e.g. if your dog bites someone – although where damage is due to negligence, benefits may be reduced. You can take out public liability insurance with a non-Bulgarian insurance company, although you should always check exactly it covers you for.

If you're letting a property, make sure that you're covered for public liability in respect of your tenants, as most Bulgarian home insurance policies exclude this. If you let through an agent, he may have cover for people renting your property, but this may cover only against harm caused to a person by the property (e.g. a door shutting on someone's fingers), as opposed to any damage a tenant may cause to the property. Otherwise, your only option is to take out insurance abroad. (See also **Insurance** on page 219.)

RENTED ACCOMMODATION

If you plan to rent accommodation, it's worth taking out public liability insurance that includes damage you accidentally cause to the property and to other properties, e.g. due to floods, fire or explosion. Some travel insurance policies include this.

9.

LETTING

Many people planning to buy a holiday home in Bulgaria are interested in owning a property that will provide them with an income to cover the running costs and help with mortgage payments (or to supplement a pension). The most common method of earning money from a property is to let all or part of it (see **Types of Rental Property** below).

With prices rising fast, there's currently a good deal of speculation in the Bulgarian rental market – in both senses of the word. Many foreigners purchase properties thinking that they will be able to rent them out during the summer months and make enough money either to finance their new life in Bulgaria or at least cover their costs. However the reality is somewhat different. Rampant building of hotels in the coastal resorts has led to a glut of cheap accommodation. Most tourists come to Bulgaria on holiday packages, which include hotel accommodation. The independent travel market is small in Bulgaria and, in comparison with destinations such as Croatia or Greece, few people book their flights and accommodation separately. The situation is similar in the mountain resorts. You should certainly take any promise of 'guaranteed rental returns' with more than a pinch of salt.

 While there may be long-term potential for generating good returns from a rental property, the current prospects aren't so attractive.

Those who manage to make a modest return on property letting usually offer something special – whether it's quality, serviced accommodation for the top end of the market, an unusual or unique building (e.g. a renovated old farm house or a remote lodge in the mountains), or a stunning coastal location away from the crowds.

If you're thinking seriously about buying to let, research the market, look closely at the types of accommodation available locally and, most importantly, don't go into the deal thinking you will make your fortune!

You will also need to decide whether you're targeting short-term holiday rentals or long-term rentals, e.g. for businesspeople. If you're looking at long-term rentals, there's little market outside Sofia, although there may be some opportunities in Bourgas, Plovdiv and Varna.

The most popular destination for holidays in Bulgaria is the Black Sea Coast, followed closely by the mountain resorts. Skiing holidays in Bulgaria are increasing in popularity, as are environmental holidays in rural areas. The letting season along the Black Sea coast is the longest and generally runs from May to September, while the mountain resorts have a letting (and ski) season of around four months, from November to February. Some rural and mountain properties can be rented throughout the year, as they have a combination of snow during the winter for skiing and sun for hiking, climbing and mountain biking during the warmer months. Nevertheless, you're unlikely to achieve full occupancy anywhere, especially in the first few years, so you should budget for having occupancy for around half the season.

If you're planning to let a property, it's important not to overestimate the income, particularly if you're relying on letting income to help pay the mortgage and running costs.

 It's difficult to make a living providing holiday accommodation in most areas, as the season is short and there's too much competition.

Buyers who overstretch their financial resources often find themselves on the rental treadmill, constantly struggling to find sufficient income to cover their running costs and mortgage payments. If you've borrowed money to purchase a property in Bulgaria, you're highly unlikely to meet your mortgage payments and running costs from rental income alone. Most experts recommend that you don't purchase a home in Bulgaria (or anywhere overseas for that matter) if you need to rely on rental income to pay for it.

 Running a holiday villa or B&B is hard work and not suitable for those looking for an activity compatible with semi-retirement.

Always obtain professional advice before buying a property for letting. See also **Working** on page 40 and **Buying for Investment** on page 26. You must also notify your insurance company if a property is to be let.

TYPES OF RENTAL PROPERTY

There are essentially two types of rental property: self-catering units, which can be either outbuildings in a property you use as a principal residence or your second home let when you aren't occupying it yourself; and a permanent home in which you offer accommodation on a bed and breakfast basis (see also **Working** on page 40).

Self-catering accommodation must, of course, be self-contained (e.g. in an outhouse). It makes sense to have a number of units, reducing the running cost per unit and spreading the cost of installing amenities such as a swimming pool.

Bed and breakfast accommodation doesn't require authorisation (see below), but it's recommended that you be able to speak Bulgarian to at least a working level. If you plan to run a B&B, you will be required to register your guests with the local police (see **Registration** on page 183) as well as running and managing your business.

RULES & REGULATIONS

Self-catering Accommodation

If you let a property, it must be categorised and registered with the Ministry of Economy and Energy (⌨ http://www.mi.government.bg/eng). If you will be using an agent to let your property, he can do this for you. Even if you will be handling the letting yourself, you can pay a letting agent to categorise and register your property, which will cost around €20. Categorisation is the 'star' rating of your property, which is awarded after an inspection by local authorities. The inspection can take up to six months to occur, so you will initially receive a temporary licence as a tourist site.

It's usually recommended to apply for a star rating of two or three, as it can be more difficult to let your property to tour companies if you have a high rating (because of the higher rental cost).

As with Bulgarian hotels, star ratings for self-catering accommodation generally have more to do with the number of facilities provided (e.g. a TV in every room, ensuite bathrooms) than with the standard of those facilities or the overall quality of the accommodation. If your property is attractive and tastefully furnished (and reasonably priced), good photographs will sell it to potential customers much better than a star rating.

Bed & Breakfast Accommodation

Bed and breakfast (B&B) accommodation is slightly more complicated. If you're planning to set up a B&B you will need to do the following:

- go (with a) lawyer or a good translator to the local town hall, where you must register your property with the local council, tourist board and fire department;

- purchase, register and program a cash register (which records the details of your business); it's wise to have an English-speaking accountant to explain the process beforehand;

- obtain a service contract for the cash register (available from wherever you purchase the machine);

- obtain need a tourist registration book (from the tourist board) to record the details of your guests.

First, the tourist board will inspect your property and give it a star rating and category (e.g. hotel, guesthouse or hostel). Then the fire department will inspect it to ensure that it complies with fire safety regulations. Once theseinspections are complete, you will be issued with a certificate or licence, and you must display your star rating and status outside your property.

While the process sounds daunting, provided you have a good translator or lawyer and an accountant, it isn't complicated difficult – although it can take as long as four months.

Contracts

If you're letting through an agent, he will provide a standard rental contract. If not, you should draft a written contract or agreement for all rentals that includes a description of the property, the names of the clients, the fee paid and any deposits required (and the conditions of refund), and the dates of arrival and departure. If you do regular letting, you may wish to check with a lawyer that your agreement is legal and contains all the necessary safeguards. For example, it should specify the types of damage for which the renter is responsible. Note that if you plan to let to non-English speaking clients, you must have a letting agreement in the appropriate foreign languages.

Insurance

As yet, landlords cannot take out public liability insurance in Bulgaria. You can insure your property and contents with a Bulgarian-based insurance firm (see **Household Insurance** on page 210), but you must arrange liability insurance in your home country or another country.

If someone is injured or dies while staying at your property and you don't have public liability insurance, you can be sued for a VERY large amount of money.

LOCATION

If letting income is a priority, you should buy a property with this in mind, in which case location is paramount. Some parts of Bulgaria are better suited than others to letting (generally, the coast, mountain areas and ski resorts are the most popular). although much depends on who you think your clientele will be, e.g. people interested in hiking and mountain climbing or those looking for a beach holiday or get-away-from-it-all break. You should consider the following when deciding on the location of a rental property. For general considerations regarding location see page 77.

Climate

Properties with a pleasant year-round climate such as the Black Sea coast have the greatest letting potential, particularly outside the high season. This is also important should you wish to use the property yourself outside the high season; for example, you could let a property during the summer months, when rental rates are at their highest, and use it yourself in May or October and still enjoy fine weather. Central heating is essential if you want to let in the winter.

Proximity to an Airport

A property should be situated within easy travelling distance of a major airport, as most holidaymakers won't consider travelling for more than 45 minutes to their destination after arriving at the airport. Make sure you choose an airport with frequent flights from your home country (not just overseas charter flights – many people on charter flights have their accommodation pre-booked as part of a package) or one that is served by domestic flights.

Accessibility

It's an advantage if a property is served by public transport (e.g. local buses or trains) or is situated in a town where a car is unnecessary. If a property is located in a town or development with a maze of streets, you should provide a detailed map with directions for arrival. On the other hand, if it's in the countryside where signposts are all but non-existent, not only will you need to provide a detailed map with plenty of landmarks, but you may also need to erect signs (for which permission might be necessary). Holidaymakers who spend hours driving around trying to find a holiday home are unlikely to return or recommend it! Maps are also helpful for taxi drivers, who may be unfamiliar with the area.

Attractions

The property should be as close as possible to a major attraction (or more than one), e.g. a beach, ski resort, area of scenic beauty or tourist town, although this will again depend on the type of clientele you wish to attract. If you want to let to families, a property should be within easy distance of leisure facilities such as beaches, water parks, sports grounds (e.g. tennis, golf and watersports) and nightlife. If you're planning to let a property in a rural area, it should be somewhere with good hiking or mountain climbing possibilities or near ancient historical sites or one of Bulgaria's national parks. There are an increasing number of golf courses in Bulgaria, particularly in the north-east, which can be an advantage to many holidaymakers and is an added attraction outside the high season.

SWIMMING POOL

A swimming pool is desirable, particularly in warmer regions, as properties with pools are much easier to let than those without. It's usually necessary to have a private pool with a single-family home, but a shared pool is sufficient for an apartment or townhouse. You can also charge a higher rent for a property with a pool and you may be able to extend the season by installing a heated or indoor pool.

LETTING RATES

Letting rates vary according to the time of year, the area, and the size and quality of a property. Before deciding on a letting rate you should do as much research as possible, looking at what other properties are available in the area (if you omitted to do so before you bought the property!), what the average rent is for each type, what occupancy rates are like, if there are hotels nearby that may be in competition with your property and in what way your property differs from others on the market. Note, however, that because the rental market in Bulgaria is so new, rates have yet to 'settle' and can be unrealistic, so you may wish to disregard exceptionally high and low rates.

A house sleeping six near a beach can be let for €400 to €600 per week in high season. A luxury villa in a popular area with swimming pool and accommodation for up to 12 people can be let for between €500 and €1,000 per week in high season.

High season on the coast in Bulgaria is July and August, and sometimes the first week of September. In the mountains high season generally runs from mid-December to mid-March. Most people who let year round have low, mid- and high season rates. The mid-season usually includes June and September on the coast, when rates are around 25 to 30 per cent lower than in high season; the rest of the year is low season, when you shouldn't expect more than €200 to €250 per week for an average property. In mountain resorts, the summer may be mid-season and the autumn and spring low season.

Don't forget to factor into your charges the cost of utilities, although electricity is often charged as an extra. In particular, if your property has air-conditioning, you may want to add a service charge in summer. Air-conditioners use a lot of electricity and the cost will quickly add up if tenants run it for extended periods. It's best to provide linen (some agents provide a linen hire service), which is usually expected.

Finally, keep in mind that you must pay income tax on 80 per cent of income for property letting and, if you're a non-Bulgarian resident, a 15 per cent withholding tax is levied (see **Taxation of Property Income** on page 196).

FURNISHINGS

If you let a property, don't fill it with expensive furnishing or valuable belongings. While theft is rare, items will be damaged or broken eventually. When furnishing a property that you plan to let, you should choose durable furniture and furnishings and hard-wearing, dark carpets that won't show stains. Small properties can have a sofa-bed in the living room to accommodate two more people. Properties should be well equipped with cooking utensils, crockery and cutlery, and it's also best to provide bed linen and towels. You may also need a cot or high chair for young children. Depending on the price and rating of a property, your guests may also expect central heating, a washing machine, a dishwasher, a microwave, covered parking, a barbecue and garden furniture. Some owners provide bicycles and sports (e.g. badminton and table tennis) equipment. It isn't usual to have a telephone in rental homes, although you could install a credit card telephone or a phone that will receive incoming calls only.

KEYS

You will need several sets of spare keys, as keys will inevitably get lost at some time. If you employ a management company, its address should be on the key fob and not the address of the property. You should make every effort to get 'lost' keys returned, or you may need to change the locks (in any case, it's wise to change the locks periodically if you let a home). You don't need to provide clients with keys to all the external doors, only the front door (the others can be left in your home).

If you arrange your own lets, you can post keys to clients in your home country or they can be collected from a caretaker in Bulgaria. It's also possible to install a key-pad entry system, although small boys seem to able to crack codes quite easily!

USING AN AGENT

If you're letting a second home, the most important decision is whether to let it yourself or use a letting agent (or agents). If you don't have much spare time, you're better off using an agent, who will take care of everything and save you the time and expense of advertising and finding clients. An agent will usually charge commission of 25 per cent of gross rental income, although this can be higher depending on the level of service offered and the type of property you're letting.

Take care when selecting a letting agent, as it isn't unheard of for them to go out of business or disappear with your money. Make sure that your income is kept in an escrow account and paid regularly, or even better, choose an agent with a bonding scheme who pays you the rent **before** the arrival of guests (some do). It's absolutely essential to employ an efficient, reliable and honest company, preferably well established.

Ask an agent to substantiate rental income claims and occupancy rates by showing you examples of actual income received from other properties. Ask for the names of satisfied customers and check with them. It's also worthwhile inspecting properties managed by an agency to see if they're well looked after. Other things to ask a letting agent include the following:

- who they let to;

- where they advertise;

- what information they send to potential clients;

- whether they have contracts with holiday and travel companies;

- whether you're expected to contribute towards marketing costs;

- whether you're free to let the property yourself and use it when you wish.

The larger companies market homes via newspapers, magazines, overseas agents, colour brochures and the internet. You should also check what kind of contract you will have with the agency: whether, for example, you will receive a detailed analysis of income and expenditure and what notice you're required to give if you decide to terminate the agreement. Agency contracts usually run for a year.

Some agents offer a 'management' service, which may include some or all of the following:

- arranging routine and emergency repairs;

- reading meters (if electricity is charged extra);

- routine maintenance of house and garden, including lawn cutting and pool cleaning;

- arranging cleaning and linen changes between lets;

- advising guests on the use of equipment;

- providing guest information and advice (possibly 24-hours in the case of emergencies).

Agents should also provide someone to meet and greet clients, hand over the keys and check that everything is in order. The services provided will usually depend on whether a property is a basic rural cottage or a luxury villa. A letting agent's representative should also make periodic checks when a property is empty to ensure that it's secure and everything is in order.

SURVIVAL TIP
You may wish (or need) to make periodic checks on an agency to ensure that all bookings are being declared and that your property is being well managed and maintained.

DOING YOUR OWN LETTING

Some owners prefer to let a property to family, friends and colleagues, which allows them more control (and with luck the property will be better looked after). In fact, the best way to secure a high volume of lets is usually to do it yourself, although many owners use a local letting agency in addition to doing their own marketing in their home country.

Rental Rates & Deposits

Rental rates obviously vary considerably according to the type and size of property, its location and the season. For example, a luxury villa on the Black Sea coast or a de-luxe apartment in central Sofia may let for over €600 per week in high season, whereas a small seaside apartment might be worth only €200 per week out of season.

To get an idea of the rent you should charge, simply ring a few letting agencies and ask them what it would cost to rent a property such as yours in the same area at the time of year you plan to let. They're likely to quote the highest possible rent you can charge. You should also check advertisements in newspapers and magazines and on websites. Set a realistic rent, as there's a lot of competition.

Unless you insist on full payment with booking (which can deter clients), you should demand a booking deposit, which should be refundable only up to six weeks before the booked period. Add a returnable 'damage' deposit (e.g. €150 or a percentage of the rental charge) as security against loss (e.g. of keys) or breakages. You will need to have a simple contract or agreement form that includes details of deposit payments, etc. (see **Contracts** on page 219).

Marketing

Marketing a property doesn't mean only spending money on advertising (see below). There are many other methods, including PR and promotions, direct mail and, of course, word of mouth, some of which may be cheaper and more effective than advertising. The key to successful marketing is to know your market. Do you want to let to seaside holidaymakers, dedicated hiking or mountain climbing enthusiasts or skiers? To families, couples or groups of friends? And what about language? As well as visitors from the UK, Bulgaria is popular with German tourists – in fact, nearly half the tourists visiting Bulgaria are from Germany. Most German arrivals head for family holidays along the Black Sea coast. If you're thinking of setting up a website to advertise your property (see below) you may want to provide a German-language version (although unless your German is up to scratch you should probably specify that bookings and queries must be made in English!).

At least 4m people visit Bulgaria every year, and the top ten countries for visitor numbers to Bulgaria are Macedonia, Serbia and Montenegro (35 per cent, although this includes a lot of 'shuttle traffic' – people spending only a day or two in Bulgaria), Germany (16 per cent), Greece (15 per cent), the UK (5 per cent), Russia (3 per cent), Romania (2 per cent – also includes 'shuttle traffic'), Czech Republic, Israel, Sweden, Slovakia and Poland (less than 2 per cent each – around 70,000 visitors).

The more marketing you do, the more income you're likely to earn. It also pays to work with other local people in the same business and send surplus guests to competitors (they will be more likely to do the same for you). You should have an answerphone and a fax machine for bookings and preferably an email address, if not a website.

Advertising

You may need to do some advertising, but it need not be expensive (e.g. in specialist magazines). You can advertise among friends and colleagues, in company and club magazines (which may even be free), and on notice boards in companies, shops and public places. As well as advertising in Bulgaria and your home country, you should consider the above-mentioned countries.

Publications

There's a wide range of newspapers and magazines in which you can advertise, e.g. *Daltons Weekly* (💻 http://www.daltonsholidays.com) and newspapers such as the *Sunday Times* in the UK. Most of the English-language newspapers and magazines listed in **Appendix B** also include advertisements from property owners. You will need to experiment to find the best publications and days of the week or months to advertise.

Think about when your advertisement will appear. Most people tend to book their summer holidays in winter (and their skiing holidays in summer). Make sure you know when your advertisement will appear and how long it will run for.

 Newspaper and magazine advertising can be very expensive and yield little return.

Internet

Advertising on the internet is an increasingly popular option for property owners as it's usually free. But keep in mind that you get what you pay (or don't pay) for! 'Free' listing websites won't do any promotion or marketing, so you will be relying on people stumbling across your listing, e.g. as a result of an internet search. If you use free listing sites, put your property on as many as you can find – and then some.

Your own website will cost more in the short term to set up, but if you're serious about letting your property yourself, it's a wise investment. A website can be a comprehensive resource, with photographs, brochures, booking forms and maps of the area, as well as comprehensive information about your property and about Bulgaria in general. You can also provide information about flights, trains and buses, car rental, local attractions, sports facilities and links to other useful websites.

It may be worth paying a little extra for 'search engine optimisation', such as Google AdWords or Yahoo! Search Marketing, which raises your website's listing on search results. You pay for the number of 'clicks' on your website link, with prices ranging from €0.07 to €0.80 per ten clicks. You can specify a cost control: if your budget is, for example, €100, you will get €100 worth of clicks.

Brochures & Leaflets

It's wise to produce a coloured brochure or leaflet (or a single colour brochure with coloured photographs glued to it, although this doesn't look so professional) containing the following:

- external and internal pictures;
- important details of the property;
- the exact location and details of how to get there (with a small map);
- information about local attractions;
- the name, address and telephone number of your local caretaker or letting agent.

SURVIVAL TIP
It's necessary to make a home look as attractive as possible in a brochure without distorting the facts or misrepresentation. Advertise honestly and don't oversell.

Handling Enquiries

If you plan to let a home yourself, you will need to decide how to handle enquiries about flights and car hire. It's easier (and safer!) to let clients make their own bookings, but you should be able to offer advice and put them in touch with airlines, travel agents and car hire companies. You will also have to decide whether you want to let to smokers or accept pets or young children (some people don't let to families with children under five because of the risk of bedwetting).

Enclose a stamped, addressed envelope when sending out leaflets. **Finally, keep detailed records and ensure that you never double book!**

INFORMATION PACKS

You should provide information packs for clients who have booked: one to be sent to them before they leave home and another for them to use when they arrive.

Pre-arrival

After accepting a booking, you should provide guests with a pre-arrival information pack containing the following:

- a map of the local area and instructions on how to find the property;

- information about attractions and amenities in the local area (available free from tourist offices – usually in some sort of English!);

- emergency contact numbers for you in your home country and Bulgaria if guests have any problems or plan to arrive late;

- the keys or instructions on where to collect them on arrival.

Post-arrival

It's an advantage if you can arrange for someone to be on hand to welcome your guests when they arrive, explain how things work, and deal with any special requests or minor problems. You should also provide an information pack in your home for guests explaining the following:

- how things work, e.g. kitchen appliances, TV/video, heating and air-conditioning;

- security measures (see **Security** on page 231 and **Home Security** on page 241);

- what not to do and possible dangers (e.g. a swimming pool);

- local emergency numbers and health services such as a doctor, dentist and hospital/clinic;

- 'support services' such as a general repairman, plumber, electrician and pool maintenance person or a local caretaker who can handle any problems;

- recommended shops, restaurants and attractions.

Many people provide a visitors' book, in which guests can write their comments and recommendations regarding local restaurants and attractions.

If you really want to impress your guests, you may wish to arrange for fresh flowers, fruit, a bottle of wine and a grocery pack to greet them on their arrival. It's little touches like this that ensure repeat business and recommendations. If you go 'the extra mile', it will pay off and you may even find after the first year or two that you rarely need to advertise. Many people return to the same property each year and you should do an annual mail-shot to previous clients and send them some brochures. **Word-of-mouth advertising is the cheapest and always the best**.

MAINTENANCE

If you do your own letting, you will need to arrange for cleaning and maintenance, including pool cleaning and a gardener if applicable. You should also allow for the cost of additional equipment, such as cots and highchairs for children.

When letting a property, you should take care not to underestimate maintenance and running costs, which can be considerable.

Caretaker

If you have a second home in Bulgaria, you will find it beneficial or even essential to employ a local caretaker, irrespective of whether you let it. You can have your caretaker prepare the house for your family and guests as well as looking after it when it isn't in use. If you have a holiday home in Bulgaria, it's wise to have your caretaker check it once or twice a week and give him authority to carry out minor repairs (e.g. up to a certain cost). If you have a garden the caretaker can keep the grass down and look after the plants. Ideally, you should have someone on call seven days a week who can repair broken appliances or arrange any necessary maintenance.

 Properties are often damaged and occasionally ruined by holidaymakers, so make sure you have a good contract, take an adequate deposit and have your guests sign an inventory as well as having someone on call to repair the damage.

If you're in a rural area, you can usually arrange a caretaker through the local mayor. Expect to pay around €5 per day for a caretaker, or around €30 per month for someone to visit your property once or twice a week.

Winter

Before closing a property for the winter, you should turn off the water at the mains, drain all pipes and leave taps in the open position, remove or 'switch off' fuses, empty food cupboards and refrigerators/freezers, disconnect gas cylinders, bring in any outdoor furniture and empty dustbins. All exterior doors, large windows and shutters should of course be locked, but you should leave interior doors and a few small windows (with grilles or secure shutters), as well as wardrobes, open to provide ventilation.

If you think vermin are likely to find a way into the property, put down suitable poison (but remember where you put it so you can remove it when you return!) and put away or cover with plastic sheeting anything that can be nibbled (e.g. pillows, cushions, bedding and rugs).

If your property is in an area susceptible to flooding, move valuable and easily damaged items to an upper floor, raise the fridge, washing machine and other apparatus off the floor (e.g. on pallets) and, if necessary, fit flood boards across external doors and lay sand bags against them.

Secure anything of value against theft or leave it with a (trustworthy) neighbour. Check whether any essential work needs to be done before you leave and if necessary arrange for it to be done in your absence. Most importantly, leave a set of keys with a neighbour and have a caretaker check your home periodically (e.g. once a month). It's worth making yourself a checklist of things to be done each time you leave your property unattended.

SECURITY

Most people aren't security conscious when they go on holiday, and you should therefore provide detailed instructions for guests regarding security measures and emphasise the need to secure the property when they're out. It's also important for them to be security-conscious when in the property, particularly when in the garden or by the pool, as it isn't unusual for valuables to be stolen when guests are outside.

SURVIVAL TIP
Security is very important when buying a home in Bulgaria, particularly if it will be left empty for long periods. Take advice from neighbours and local security companies but remember that, no matter how good your security, a property is rarely impregnable, so you should never leave valuables in an unattended home unless they're kept in a safe.

When leaving a property unattended, it's important to employ all the security measures available, including the following:

● storing valuables in a safe (if applicable) – hiding them isn't a good idea, as thieves know ALL the hiding places;

● closing and locking all windows and external doors;

● locking grilles on patio and other doors;

● closing shutters and securing any bolts or locks;

● setting the alarm (if applicable) and notifying the alarm company when absent for an extended period;

- making it appear as if a property is occupied by the use of timers and leaving lights and a TV/radio on.

Keep in mind that prevention is much better than cure, as stolen property is rarely recovered. If you have a robbery, you should report it to your local police station, where you will have to make a statement. You will receive a copy, which is required by your insurance company if you make a claim (see **Household Insurance** on page 210). See also **Home Security** on page 241.

INCREASING RENTAL INCOME

It's possible to increase rental income outside the high season by offering special interest or package holidays, which can be done with other local businesses to broaden the appeal and cater for larger parties. These may include the following:

- activity holidays, such as golf, hiking, mountain climbing, kayaking or mountain biking;

- food and wine tours/tasting (Bulgarian wine is excellent but little known);

- historical or cultural tours, e.g. visiting Thracian tombs in an area.

You don't need to be an expert or conduct courses yourself but can employ someone to do it for you.

10.

MISCELLANEOUS MATTERS

This chapter contains miscellaneous information that may be helpful to homeowners in Bulgaria, including information about crime, air-conditioning, home security, postal and telephone services, shopping, television and radio, utilities and waste disposal, selling a home and wills (arranged in alphabetical order).

CRIME

Bulgaria has a relatively low 'individual' crime rate compared to other countries in Europe, but it has a high rate of organised crime and corruption. As in many post-Soviet economies, the 'law' often depends on personal favouritism and this had led to some questionable privatisation deals and allegations of judicial corruption. The EU has criticised Bulgaria repeatedly for failing to tackle high-level corruption and organised crime.

Sofia in particular has a reputation as being a centre for mafia racketeering, and parts of the city have something of a Wild West feel about them (most nightclubs have signs on the doors reading 'No Guns Allowed'). Fortunately, however, the local mafia aren't interested in foreigners, preferring to make their money from local protection rackets and smuggling and, as with most big cities, common sense is the key. Don't get into arguments or confrontations in flashy bars and restaurants and if you happen to be involved in a traffic accident (especially with a big, expensive, German car) keep your cool and apologise profusely, even if it isn't your fault.

Most reported crime in Bulgaria is petty crime such as bag or wallet snatching, pocket picking (public transport and crowded locations are favourite haunts for pickpockets), overcharging for taxis and various scams such as credit card fraud. Following the collapse of communism, there was a sharp rise in petty crime. Since 2002, when the government launched a crackdown, the petty crime rate has fallen dramatically; the only petty crime that has increased is pickpocketing, with around 3,900 arrests in 2005.

Vehicle theft is one of the most common crimes in Bulgaria, where few stolen vehicles are recovered. Thanks to its central location, Bulgaria is a transit point for vehicles stolen from western Europe where they're 'rebirthed' and sold in eastern European countries, particularly Russia. Nevertheless, 'only' around 140 vehicles per 100,000 people are stolen each year, compared with 500 per 100,000 people in France and over 600 in the UK. The most commonly stolen vehicles are four-wheel drive cars and new European saloons. Far more common, particularly in the larger cities, is theft from vehicles; a window is often smashed and valuables inside stolen. Common sense is the best prevention here: don't leave any valuables inside your car, no matter where you park.

In rural areas, the crime rate is virtually zero, although some areas have fairly high incidences of burglary and theft (usually areas where the Roma population have been forcibly settled, most often in poor-quality housing on the outskirts of towns). But in the countryside (and, in fact, in most of Bulgaria) you can safely walk almost anywhere at any time of day or night and there's no need for anxiety about crime.

Nevertheless, you should exercise the type of precautions you would in any country, such as not carrying large amounts of cash, not walking down dark streets or alleys late at night, not displaying expensive jewellery, or being drunk in public.

If you're a victim of a petty crime (particularly a scam or fraud), don't expect the Bulgarian police to respond with vigour. A lack of resources and understaffing means that the police are overworked and underpaid, so a tourist losing his wallet or passport is likely to be given a low priority. On the other hand, if you're a victim of a serious or violent crime, your complaint will be taken seriously.

Bulgarian police are surprisingly helpful and many officers speak English, although some aren't above a little 'racketeering' themselves. If you commit a traffic offence, the police may only issue you with a ticket (citation) and not an on-the-spot fine. However, if you're driving a car with foreign licence plates (particularly an expensive-looking new car), you may be stopped and 'fined' for some breach of the road rules. If you stand your ground and ask for a receipt and a written ticket, the 'fine' might inexplicably be waived! You can, however, be fined on the spot for not having a vignette (see **Bulgarian Roads** on page 93).

SURVIVAL TIP
It's compulsory for all vehicle occupants to wear seatbelts, and talking on a mobile phone while driving is illegal.

See also **Home Security** on page 241, **Security** on page 231 and **Household Insurance** on page 210.

HEATING & AIR-CONDITIONING

As a mountainous country Bulgaria has extremes of weather and even on the coast winters can be cold. Unless you plan to visit a property only in the summer, you need to consider central heating, although air-conditioning is really a luxury.

Heating

Central heating systems in Bulgaria may be powered by electricity, gas, oil, solid fuel (usually wood) or solar power. Most rural properties use wood-fired heating with an electric boiler as a back-up. Whatever form of heating you use, it's essential to have good insulation, without which up to 60 per cent of heat generated is lost through the walls and roof.

In larger towns, houses and apartments are heated by hot water pumped by the district heating company. A hangover from the communist period, the system is incredibly inefficient, although the municipal government subsidises the cost to consumers – mainly to ensure that low-income tenants (such as pensioners) can afford to keep their homes warm in winter. Since the switch to a market economy, however, electricity prices have risen substantially, and you should allow around 300 lev (€150) per month to heat an average-size two-bedroom house in winter, compared with around 100 lev (€50) using an oil-fired system or just 50 lev (€25) using a wood-fired system. As a result, many Bulgarians have recently switched to wood-fired heating systems.

If you need to install a hot water boiler, ensure that it's large enough for the size of the property, e.g. 100 litres for a one-room apartment, 150 litres for two rooms, 200 litres for three to four rooms and 300 litres for five to seven rooms.

Electric

Electricity prices rose substantially after the switch to a market-based economy and are now on a par with those in the UK at 0.17 lev (€0.08) per kilowatt hour (kWh) and forecast to double in 2007, although night-time rates are lower in most areas.

Most people living in apartments in the main towns use a combination of oil-fired heaters and electricity for heating if they aren't supplied by the district heating company (see above). Off-peak storage heaters are an economical solution for smaller, well insulated properties.

In rural areas, many Bulgarians use wood-fired stoves for heating (see **Wood** below) with a water heater attached to the back of the stove. This isn't only for reasons of economy but also because power cuts are common in some areas.

Stand-alone electric heaters (such as bar radiators) are expensive to run and are best suited to holiday homes. See also **Electricity** on page 265.

Gas

Gas central heating is common in the cities and towns where mains gas is available (see **Mains Gas** on page 270), but in rural areas wood burning heaters tend to be more popular. If you have access to mains gas, it's usually the best choice for heating, as it's clean, economical and efficient, and a gas-fired boiler is usually fairly small and can be wall mounted. In areas where there's no mains gas, you can have a gas tank installed on your property or have gas delivered in bottles. You will need space for the tank and piping will add to the already considerable cost of a gas tank. The system also requires regular maintenance and will increase your household insurance. **Having a gas tank on your property will increase your insurance premiums.**

Oil

Heating oil costs have risen with the worldwide rise in crude oil prices, making it a (relatively) expensive option. In rural areas very few people use oil to heat their homes, mainly because wood is cheaper. If you're in a remote area or your property is difficult to access, the fuel company may not be able to get a delivery truck to your house. As a rough guide, you will require around 1,000 litres of oil to heat a two-bedroom house for a year. At the current price (around 1.7 lev per litre) this works out at 1,700 lev (€850) per year.

Although more expensive, oil is much more convenient than wood, especially if you have a larger home, as you don't have to continually refill the burner and chop and stack wood. As with gas, you will need space to install the storage tank. Smaller tanks can be installed in your house, while larger tanks can either be buried in the garden or installed in an outhouse or even outdoors. Oil causes a rapid build-up of deposits, so it's essential to have your system cleaned and checked annually and to replace the jet regularly. Note also that you should wait at least two hours after an oil delivery before restarting your boiler, in order to allow any foreign bodies in the tank to settle to the bottom.

Solar Power

A solar system is, of course, the most environmentally friendly way to generate power, although solar systems must usually be combined with an electric or gas heating system as solar power cannot be relied on for heating even in the sunniest parts of Bulgaria. Solar-cell technology has advanced rapidly and a modern solar system can provide hot water even on cloudy and overcast days. The main drawback of solar power is the high cost of installation, which varies depending on how much energy you require.

In Bulgaria, solar-powered water heating is increasing in popularity and, depending on how much sunshine there is in your area, a system takes between two and five years to become cost-effective. To get an idea of costs and the type of system that might suit your property contact Apex MM, which has a showroom in Sofia (31A, Bratya Buxton Boulevard, Sofia, ☎ 02-9555 6165, 🖥 http://www.apexexperts.com).

The advantages of solar power are no maintenance or running costs and silent operation, as well as 'free' (after the installation costs have been recouped) heating and electricity. A system should last for 30 years and can be uprated to provide more power in the future. A solar power system can be used to provide electricity in a remote rural home where the cost of connecting to mains electricity is prohibitive. Improvements in solar cell and battery technology are expected to dramatically increase the efficiency and reduce the cost of solar power.

Wood

Wood in Bulgaria is cheap and readily available, and most homes, particularly in rural areas, rely on wood-burning stoves for their heating and hot water. Stoves come in a huge variety of sizes and shapes and are available almost everywhere – some models also come with a back burner, to which you can attach several radiators throughout a home. Wood for fuel is measured in cubic metres and is usually sold for around 50 lev (€25) per cubic metre. Depending on the size of your home and how warm you like it to be, five cubic metres is usually enough to get you through winter.

If you live in a village the mayor will be able to organise a delivery of wood for you, and elsewhere commercial suppliers will deliver wood to your door cut and split. Don't be tempted to collect your own firewood (i.e. chop down trees) without a licence; if you're caught by the (armed!) Bulgarian Wood Police, you will be issued with a substantial fine.

The main disadvantages of wood are the chores of chopping and stacking wood, cleaning the grate and lighting fires. Smoke can also be a problem. While an open fireplace looks pleasant, it's usually wasteful of heat and fuel. An enclosed hearth with a glass door can be had from as little as 200 lev (€100) and is more effective. It also has the advantage of less heat wastage, a reduced fire hazard, and less ash and dust.

Air-conditioning

Bulgaria's Black Sea coast has regular summer temperatures over 30°C (86°F) and, particularly if you're in an apartment block, you might want to install air-conditioning. But keep in mind that air-conditioning uses a huge amount of electricity, which is becoming increasingly expensive (see page 265), and that it can aggravate asthma or other respiratory problems.

Many new developments along the Black Sea coast have air-conditioning units installed, but they're often cheap and noisy and it's usually worth spending extra money for a better quality (usually Japanese) model, some of which have a 'silent running' mode. The most effective air-conditioners are wall-mounted units, which often have a heat pump attached for economical heating in winter. A good-quality air-conditioner costs around 1,000 to 1,500 lev (€500–750), plus 100–150 lev (€50–75) for installation. Cheaper brands, such as the Turkish-made Beko, cost around half this and can be very noisy.

Remember to have an air-conditioner serviced regularly, as the filters fill up with dust and bacteria during extended use.

Humidifiers and De-humidifiers

Central heating dries out the air in your home and can cause your family to develop coughs. If you find dry air unpleasant you can purchase a humidifier to add moisture to the air. Humidifiers that don't generate steam should be disinfected occasionally with a special liquid (to prevent colds and other nasty bugs).

If you're going to be using a holiday home only for a few weeks or months a year, it's worthwhile installing de-humidifiers, especially in the bedrooms, to prevent clothes and linen going mouldy.

HOME SECURITY

Security is obviously an important consideration for anyone buying a home in Bulgaria (or anywhere else), especially if it's a holiday home and will be unoccupied for long periods. While it's important not to underestimate security risks – even in rural areas, where crime rates are usually quite low (see **Crime** on page 236) – you shouldn't need to turn your home into a fortress, which will deter visitors as well as would-be thieves! Keep in mind your home is usually more at risk from flood or storm damage than from burglary. According to the Bulgarian Interior Ministry, burglary has fallen from around 19,000 reported break-ins in 2000 to fewer than 15,000 in 2005 (compare this with England and Wales, where in 2004/05 the number of recorded burglaries was over 40 times higher although the population is only six times greater).

Insurance premiums in Bulgaria are high and many Bulgarians don't insure their properties at all. Differing levels of security are required according to the type of cover; for example, most insurance companies won't offer contents insurance (especially against burglary) if your home doesn't have a security system installed with an alarm that alerts a security company and the police (sometimes known as a 'back-to-base alarm').

In remote areas it's suggested that owners to fit two or three locks on external doors, an alarm system (see below), grilles on doors and windows, window locks, security shutters and a safe for valuables. The advantage of grilles is that they allow you to leave windows open without inviting criminals in (unless they're **very** slim). You can fit UPVC (toughened clear plastic) security windows and doors, which can survive an attack with a sledgehammer without damage, and external steel security blinds (that can be electrically operated), although all these precautions are expensive.

When moving into a new home, it's often wise to replace the locks (or lock barrels) as soon as possible, as you have no idea how many keys are in circulation for the existing locks. This is true even for new homes, as builders often give keys to sub-contractors. In any case, it's wise to change the external locks or lock barrels periodically if you let a home. If they aren't already fitted, it's best to fit high security (double cylinder or dead bolt) locks. Some of the more expensive new properties are fitted with high security locks that are individually numbered. Extra keys for these locks can't be cut by the local locksmith and you need to obtain details from the previous owner or your landlord. Many modern apartment and villa developments have security gates and caretakers.

If you want to insure the contents of your property, you must have a security alarm fitted. It should be linked to all external doors and windows and include internal infra-red security beams; it may also include an entry keypad (whose code can be frequently changed and saves the hassle of keys if you let) and 24-hour monitoring. With a monitored system, when a sensor (e.g. smoke or forced entry) is activated or a panic button is pushed, a signal is sent automatically to a 24-hour monitoring station. The duty monitor will telephone to check whether it's a genuine alarm (a code must be given); if they cannot contact you, a response team will be sent to investigate. Such a service can cost as little as €5 per month. More sophisticated security systems using internet technology are now available, including cameras and sound recorders linked to your computer or mobile phone – although this may not be so useful if you're in another country!

You can deter thieves by ensuring that your house is well lit at night and not conspicuously unoccupied. External security 'motion detector' lights (that switch on automatically when someone approaches), random timed switches for internal lights, radios and televisions, dummy security cameras and tapes that play barking dogs (etc.) triggered by a light or heat detector may all help deter burglars. If not already present, you should have the front door of an apartment fitted with a spy-hole and chain so that you can check the identity of a visitor before opening the door. **Remember, prevention is better than cure, as stolen property is rarely recovered.**

Holiday homes are particularly vulnerable and, no matter how secure your door and window locks, a thief can usually obtain entry if he's determined enough, often by simply smashing a window or even breaking in through the roof or knocking a hole in a wall! In isolated areas, thieves can strip a house bare at their leisure and an un-monitored alarm won't be a deterrent if there's no one around to hear it.

Remember, however, that the crime rate in Bulgaria is much lower than in most Western countries, including the UK. As in any country, if you have a house full of expensive goods that is unoccupied for months at a time, you're more likely to be burgled. The best prevention against burglary is for your property to be occupied. In rural areas the best security is to get to know your neighbours and make friends with people in the village or town, so that they will keep an eye on your property when you aren't there. You can also usually pay someone to act as a caretaker or check regularly on the property and make sure the garden is maintained so that it looks as if your home is occupied.

When closing a property for an extended period, e.g. over the winter, you should ensure that everything is switched off and that it's secure (see **Winter** on page 230). Another important aspect of home security is ensuring that you have early warning of a fire, which is easily done by installing smoke detectors. Battery-operated smoke detectors can be purchased for around €10–15 and should be tested weekly to ensure that the batteries aren't exhausted. You can also fit an electric-powered gas detector that activates an alarm when a gas leak is detected.

POSTAL SERVICES

Bulgarian postal services are considered unreliable and poor by western European standards (although the British Royal Mail manages to 'lose' over 10m items per year!). The state-owned Bulgarian Posts has been partially privatised and is now a joint-stock company, operating on a for-profit basis. There are over 3,000 post offices, each serving an average of

2,600 people. The post office sign is a black horn with a lion rampant, on a yellow background.

As well as the usual post office services, a range of other services are provided. These include telephone calls, telegram and fax transmissions, domestic and international money transfers, payment of telephone and utility bills, and the sale of phone cards, newspapers and stationery. The post office (through the Post Bank) also provides financial and banking services, such as cheque and savings accounts. Post offices usually have photocopy machines and telephone booths.

The Bulgarian Posts website (🖥 http://www.bgpost.bg/eng/index.htm) has information on the services provided in post offices. Unfortunately the postcode search facility and the addresses and contact details of post offices across the country are all in Bulgarian.

The major drawback of the Bulgarian postal service is that packages often go missing, particularly international packages that contain (or look as if they contain) CDs, books, software or anything of value. It's therefore recommended to send anything important or valuable by registered post. There's no guarantee it will reach the recipient, but you may receive compensation if it disappears! The most secure (and expensive) option is to use an international courier service such as DHL, or the less expensive international 'signed for' service.

SELLING YOUR HOME

Although this book is primarily concerned with buying a home in Bulgaria, you may want to sell your Bulgarian home at some time in the future. Before offering your home for sale, you should investigate the state of the property market. For example, unless you're forced to sell, it definitely isn't recommended during a property slump, when prices are depressed. It may be wiser to let your home long term and wait until the market has recovered. It's also unwise to sell in the first few years after purchase, when you will probably make a loss unless it was an absolute bargain (and you will probably have to pay capital gains tax as well).

Having decided to sell, your first decision will be whether to sell your home yourself or use the services of an estate agent (see below). Although most properties in Bulgaria are sold through estate agents, some owners have sold their own homes. If you need to sell a property before buying a new one, this must be included as a conditional clause (see page 169) in the purchase contract for a new home.

The legal procedure is the same as for buying a property (see **Chapter 5**), but a few points are worth noting. You may be asked by an agent to sign a conditional clause in the sales contract that the sale is dependent on the buyer selling another property; you aren't obliged to do so and should be cautious if agreeing to such a clause, particularly if the buyer is selling a property in the UK, where sales can be cancelled at any stage – you won't be able to cancel your agreement even if another would-be buyer offers you cash. If a buyer wants to have the property inspected or surveyed, it's a good idea to have this done before any contracts are signed.

Price

It's important to keep in mind that (like everything) property has a market price, and the best way of ensuring a quick sale (or any sale) is to ask a realistic price. If your home is fairly standard for the area, you can find out its value by comparing the price of other homes on the market, or those that have recently been sold.

If you're marketing your property abroad, e.g. in the UK, take into account the prevailing exchange rate: if the euro is strong, this will deter foreign buyers; if it's weak, you may even be able to increase the price. Remember the Bulgarian lev is pegged to the euro, so the lev will fluctuate with the euro.

You should be prepared to drop the price slightly (e.g. 5 or 10 per cent) and should set it accordingly, but shouldn't grossly over-price a home, as this will deter buyers. Don't reject an offer out of hand unless it's ridiculously low, as you may be able to get the prospective buyer to raise his offer. When selling a second home in Bulgaria, you may want to include the furnishings and major appliances in the sale, particularly when selling a relatively inexpensive property with modest furnishings. You might add an appropriate amount to the price to cover the value of the furnishings, or alternatively you could use them as an inducement to a prospective buyer at a later stage, although this is fairly uncommon in Bulgaria.

SURVIVAL TIP

Never agree to accept part of the sale price 'under the table'; if the buyer refuses to pay the extra money, there's nothing you can do about it (at least legally!).

It can be some weeks before you receive the proceeds from the sale of a property in Bulgaria.

Presentation

The secret to selling a home quickly lies in its presentation (assuming that it's competitively priced). First impressions (exterior and interior) are vital when marketing your home and it's important to make every effort to present it in its best light and make it as attractive as possible to potential buyers. It may pay to invest in new interior decoration, new carpets, exterior paint and landscaping. A few plants and flowers can do wonders. Keep in mind that when decorating a home for resale, it's important to be conservative and not do anything radical (such as install a red or black bathroom suite); white or off-white is a good neutral colour for walls, woodwork and porcelain.

It may also pay you to do some modernisation, such as installing a new kitchen or bathroom, as these are of vital importance (particularly kitchens) when selling a home. But while modernisation might be necessary to sell an old home, you shouldn't overdo it as you can easily spend more than you will ever hope to recoup when selling. If you're using an agent, ask him what you should do (or shouldn't do) to help sell your home. If your home is in poor repair, this must be reflected in the asking price and, if major work is needed that you cannot afford, you should obtain a quotation (or two) and offer to knock this off the asking price.

Selling Your Home Yourself

While certainly not for everyone, selling your own home is a viable option for many people and is particularly recommended when you're selling an attractive home at a realistic price in a favourable market. Saving an estate agent's fees may allow you to offer the property at a more appealing price, which could be an important factor if you're looking for a quick sale.

How you market your home will depend on the type of home, the price, and the country or area where you expect your buyer to be from. For example, if your property isn't of a type and style and in an area desirable to local inhabitants, it's usually a waste of time advertising in the local press.

Advertising is the key to selling your home. The first step is to get a professional-looking 'for sale' sign made (showing your telephone number) and erect it somewhere visible. Do some research into the best publications or websites for advertising your property and place an advertisement in those that look the most promising. If you own a property in an area popular with foreign buyers, it may be worthwhile using an overseas agent (see below) or advertising in foreign newspapers and magazines, such as the

English-language publications listed in **Appendix B**. There's a growing number of websites with properties listed for sale, some charging a fee and others offering a free service. See **Appendix C** for a list of useful websites.

You could also have a leaflet printed (with pictures) extolling the virtues of your property, which you could drop into local letter boxes or have distributed with a local newspaper (many people buy a new home in the vicinity of their present home). You may also need a 'fact sheet' printed if your home's vital statistics aren't included in the leaflet and could offer a finder's fee to anyone finding you a buyer. Don't omit to market your home around local companies, schools and organisations, particularly if they have many itinerant employees.

Finally, it may help to provide information about local financing sources for potential buyers. With a bit of effort you may even make a better job of marketing your home than an agent! Unless you're in a hurry to sell, set yourself a realistic time limit for success, after which you can try an agent. When selling a home yourself, you will need to obtain legal advice about contracts and engage a notary to hold the deposit and complete the sale.

Using an Agent

Most owners prefer to use the services of an agent, either in Bulgaria or in their home country, particularly when selling a second home. You should take particular care when selecting an agent, as they vary considerably in their professionalism, expertise and experience (the best way to investigate agents is by posing as a buyer). Note that many agents cover a relatively small area, so you should take care to choose one who regularly sells properties in your area and price range. If you purchased the property through an agent, it's usually wise to use the same agent when selling, as he will be familiar with it and may still have the details on file.

Agents' Contracts

Before offering a property for sale, a Bulgarian estate agent needs a signed authorisation, called a sales mandate, from the owner. There are usually two types of mandate: a non-exclusive mandate means that you reserve the right to deal with other agents and to negotiate directly with private buyers, while an exclusive mandate gives a single agent the exclusive right to sell a property, although you can reserve the right to find a private buyer. Agents' fees are usually lower with an exclusive mandate.

Note that, if you sign a contract without reserving the right to find your own buyer, you must still pay the agent's commission even if you sell your home yourself.

Check the contract and make sure you understand exactly what you're agreeing to – you may need to hire a translator if you're unsure, as contracts are only legal if they're in Bulgarian. Make sure you don't sign two or more exclusive mandates to sell your home!

An agent with an exclusive mandate has the authority to sign a sales contract on behalf of the vendor. So before signing a contract to sell a property yourself, you need to make sure other agents to whom you've given a mandate haven't found a buyer and signed a contract on your behalf. Notify all agents with a non-exclusive mandate by registered post when a property has been sold. Contracts should state the agent's commission, what it includes, and most importantly, who must pay it.

> **SURVIVAL TIP**
> Generally, you shouldn't pay any fees unless you require extra services, and you should never pay commission until a sale is completed.

Capital Gains Tax

Capital gains tax (CGT) rules in Bulgaria are complicated and further confused by double-taxation laws. It's therefore recommended to obtain expert legal advice before deciding to sell, as there are several issues to keep in mind and the rules are constantly changing (and are likely to change significantly when Bulgaria joins the EU).

Currently, **you must pay CGT on the sale of a new home if you sell it within five years**. If you sell the property after five years, your CGT liability is zero.

If you own a house with land attached, you will have formed a limited company to own the land and will be liable for corporation tax in Bulgaria (currently 15 per cent). Any profit you take with you out of Bulgaria (e.g. if you move permanently to another country) is considered a dividend and you will be liable for CGT in your home country, minus the corporate tax you paid in Bulgaria. If you don't take any profit as a dividend, you can leave it with the company and use it to purchase another property or re-invest in an existing property, and not pay any further tax. To avoid paying CGT in your home country, you can leave the money from the sale of your property in a Bulgarian bank and withdraw it as needed. For further information, see **Capital Gains Tax** on page 198.

SHOPPING

Bulgaria isn't renowned for its shopping, although the range and quality of goods on offer is increasing as the economy gradually recovers from the crisis of the mid-'90s. The legacy of communism lingers in some establishments, where the notion of customer service is unheard of, but the arrival of major European chains is making a big impact. The larger cities now have a range of shops and you should be able to get everything you need in Sofia, with the exception of some specialist food products and luxury goods. Most of the large Western brands are available in Sofia, where there's a burgeoning market in imitation products at a much lower prices and you should beware of buying counterfeit goods.

Most towns have a supermarket and on the outskirts of towns shopping centres are starting to appear, with electronics and home appliance stores, do-it-yourself (DIY) stores and furniture retailers.

For those who aren't used to buying articles in metric measures and continental sizes, a list of comparative weights and measures is included in **Appendix D**.

Opening Hours

Shopping hours in Bulgaria are fairly standard, most shops opening from Mondays to Fridays from 09.00 to 17.30 and on Saturdays from 09.00 to 12.00 or 13.00. Shops are increasingly staying open until 20.00 on weekdays and 17.00 on Saturdays, some shops in coastal and holiday areas staying open even later and many large shops and supermarkets staying open all day Saturday and Sunday and from 07.00 to 21.00 during the week. Otherwise, few shops are open on Sundays – usually only smaller food and grocery stores – and in rural areas and small towns many shops close for lunch between 12.00 and 15.00.

Most shops close on public holidays, which are 1st January, 3rd March, Easter (which is a week later than in western Europe), 1st, 6th and 24th May, 6th and 22nd September, and 25th and 26th December.

Furniture & Furnishings

Furniture in Bulgaria ranges from cheap, mass-produced pine and chipboard items to attractive, high-quality pieces. There are plenty of skilled carpenters in Bulgaria who can make you tailor-made furniture according to your budget (within limits!). If you want 'Western' style furniture (or known brands) you will usually pay Western prices, although most large furniture retailers will deliver and install items for you.

There are a number of smaller specialist furniture makers who offer packages for furnishing new apartments and houses, ranging from furniture only to a complete fit-out, including appliances and soft furnishings. Prices for a two-bedroom home range from around €3,500 to €4,000 for furniture only to €6,000 to €7,500 for a fully-fitted package, including delivery and installation. Many estate agents offer a similar service, although (obviously) prices include a commission.

Furniture packages will save you time and hassle, but they work out expensive compared choosing furniture yourself. If you want to save money and have the time, you can pick up cheap appliances, linen and small pieces of furniture (as well as everything for the kitchen) from Metro, Technomarkt, or Technopolis. These stores are present in almost all large Bulgarian towns. For something more attractive, there are dozens of smaller furniture stores in major towns, such as Bourgas, Varna and of course Sofia, which offer individual or unusual furniture to suit all tastes. At the top end of the scale are bespoke furniture makers such as Pro Log (€ http://prolog.my.bg).

As a rough guide to the cost of pre-made furniture, you should pay around €150 for a reasonable-quality sofa bed, around €200 for a king-size bed with a mattress, around €15 for a wooden bedside table and between €50 and €100 for a large wooden dining table. Delivery charges should be around €10, although for handmade furniture you will have to wait around four to six weeks.

If you're buying a large amount of furniture from a shop, don't be reluctant to ask for a discount, as you will often receive one. Most shops also offer free home delivery, although you may have to pay a little extra if you live in an apartment that isn't on the ground floor and want items such as lounge suites carried upstairs.

When buying furniture for a home in Bulgaria, don't forget to take the climate into consideration. The kind of furniture you buy may also depend on whether it's a permanent or holiday home or whether you will be letting the property. If you intend to furnish a holiday home with antiques or expensive furniture, you will need adequate security and insurance.

Household Goods

Household goods in Bulgaria vary in quality, cheaper Bulgarian and Turkish brands generally not lasting as long as more expensive Japanese and European brands. Large retailers such as Metro and Technomarkt stock a big range of household goods and are open seven days a week, although smaller specialist retailers are often cheaper.

When importing household appliances that aren't sold in Bulgaria, you may find it difficult or impossible to get them repaired or serviced locally.

SURVIVAL TIP
If you bring appliances with you, don't forget to bring a supply of spares and refills, such as bulbs for a refrigerator or sewing machine, and spare bags for a vacuum cleaner.

If you already own small household appliances that run on a 220V/240 supply, it's worthwhile bringing them to Bulgaria, as all that's usually required is a change of plug. But if you're coming from a country with a 110V/115V electricity supply, such as the US, you will need a lot of expensive converters or transformers (see **Power Supply** on page 265) and it's better to buy new appliances in Bulgaria. Small appliances such as vacuum cleaners, grills, toasters and electric irons aren't expensive and the well known brands are of good quality. Don't bring your TV without checking its compatibility first, as TVs from many countries won't work in Bulgaria (see page 262).

If you need kitchen measuring equipment and cannot cope with decimal measures, you will need to bring your own measuring scales, jugs, cups and thermometers. (See also **Appendix D**.)

Shopping Abroad

The information in this section applies both to Bulgarian residents shopping outside Bulgaria and to foreign residents shopping in Bulgaria. Shopping abroad can save you money and, if you live in Bulgaria, can usually be combined with a weekend break or holiday for the family. However, as prices are relatively low in Bulgaria, few people shop abroad to save money but more often to pick up specialist items such as food and drink or craft products.

Some items such as consumer electronics or home appliances can be more expensive in Bulgaria than in your home country (e.g. in the UK), as the market is smaller, but you will need to factor in shipping or postage costs and any import duty you must pay on valuable items. The following table gives some price comparisons on standard appliances between Bulgaria and the UK:

Item	Price	
	Bulgaria	UK
Large fridge	€250 to 300	€250 to 300
Bar fridge	€50 to 100	€100 to 150
Television	€150 to 200	€200 to 250
Washing machine	€200 to 250	€500 to 550
Kettle	€30 to 40	€30 to 40
Clock radio	€20 to 30	€30 to 40
Small vacuum cleaner	€100 to 150	€80 to 100

If you buy goods abroad that are faulty or need repair, you may need to return them to the place of purchase. **When you buy expensive goods abroad, have them insured for their full value.**

Bulgarian customs regulations will change when Bulgaria joins the EU (scheduled for 2007) and it's worth regularly checking the Bulgarian Customs site (⌨ http://www.en.customs.bg). The regulations on importing new goods to Bulgaria are currently as follows:

● If goods have a value of less than €100, they can be imported duty free.

● If goods are worth over €100 and less than €1,500, you must pay a 5 per cent 'single customs rate' and 20 per cent VAT.

● If goods are valued at over €1,500, they're considered of a commercial nature and you will be charged a higher rate of tax.

If you don't declare goods worth over €10 and they're found by Customs 'in a normal place' (i.e. not hidden), the goods can be confiscated; if they're found 'concealed in unusual places', they will be confiscated and you will be fined.

Never attempt to import illegal goods into Bulgaria and don't agree to bring a parcel into Bulgaria or deliver a parcel in another country without knowing exactly what it contains. A well known confidence trick is to ask someone to bring a parcel into Bulgaria and post it, or to leave a parcel at a railway station or restaurant. **The parcel usually contains drugs!** Likewise, don't carry anyone else's baggage through Customs at the border or at airports.

Duty-free Allowances

Travellers aged 17 and over are entitled to import into Bulgaria the following goods purchased duty free:

● one litre of spirits (over 22 per cent proof) or two litres of sparkling or fortified wine;

● two litres of table wine;

● 200 cigarettes or 100 cigarillos or 50 cigars or 250g of tobacco;

● 500g of coffee or 200g of coffee extract and 100g of tea or 40g of tea extract;

● 50g of perfume and 250ml of eau de toilette.

Duty-free allowances apply to both outward and return journeys, even if both are made on the same day, and the combined total (i.e. double the above limits) can be imported into your 'home' country.

TELEPHONE SERVICES

Bulgaria's telecommunication system is of a reasonable standard, although reliability (and the range of services) declines the further you are from major towns. The telephone service is operated by Bulgaria Telecom (BTC, 🖥 http://www.btc.bg/en), which was privatised in 2004. Almost every house in Bulgaria has a landline connection and it's easy to get a phone connected. The mobile phone system covers the entire country, with only a few isolated mountain areas outside the network.

Broadband internet coverage is reliant on BTC's ADSL network, which currently covers 140 towns and villages (including the four largest cities, Sofia, Plovdiv, Varna and Bourgas).

The cable network is expanding, with the following cities served by CableTel (⌨ http://www.cablebulgaria.com), the largest cable operator: Burgas, Dobrich, Haskovo, Kardzhali, Lovech, Lom, Peshtera, Petrich, Plovdiv, Razgrad, Razlog, Ruse, Shumen, Sofia, Sliven, Stara Zagora, Svishtov, Targovishte, Varna and Velingrad. Cable providers offer television, telephone and internet services.

Installation & Registration

Most Bulgarian properties have a telephone line, but when you move in you will need to have it connected. It isn't possible simply to take over the telephone number of the previous occupants, who will have cancelled their subscription when they moved out.

To have a line connected, you must visit your local post office, with evidence that you're the owner or tenant of the property and proof of your identity. According to the rules, foreign residents must produce a residence permit, but this isn't always required and it's up to the official you're dealing with whether he will accept your application without a permit. If you don't have a residence permit, you should take all your limited company papers with you, including the registration papers, a copy of your certificate of tax registration and a copy of the property's title deeds or rental agreement. In any case, it's recommended that you take someone who speaks Bulgarian with you to make the process easier.

It normally takes around a month for the line to be connected. BTC will advise you within three days whether there's 'technical capacity' (i.e. if there's room on the exchange) to connect a new line. You then have 30 days to pay the connection fee (20 lev/€10) and, once BTC has received payment, they're supposed to connect your service within 20 days. Billing is monthly and can be paid by direct debit, online or at a post office.

If you are building a new property or purchase an abandoned property, you will need to have a new line installed. The process is the same as for connecting an existing line, although it can take much longer (depending on the location of the property) and the fee is 70 lev (€35).

 If you buy a property in a remote area without a telephone line, it may be expensive to have one installed, as you must pay for the line to be extended to the property. Contact BTC for an estimate.

If you already have a telephone number in Bulgaria and are moving into a different property, you can usually take your number with you if the two properties are in the same dialling code area.

If you own a property and are letting it, you can arrange to have outgoing calls limited to the local area, or to regional and national calls only, but you cannot limit the service just to incoming calls.

Broadband

Broadband internet coverage is currently available in 140 towns and villages (including the four largest cities, Sofia, Plovdiv, Varna and Bourgas). To find out if ADSL is available in your area, go to 💻 https://online.telecom.bg/adsl-report/adsl_submit-eng and enter your current telephone number (or a neighbour's).

There are two types of broadband connection available: an asymmetric digital Subscriber Line (ADSL) and an integrated services digital network (ISDN) line. The advantages of ADSL include much faster speeds than a dial-up internet connection, the ability to use your phone while on the internet and a much simpler installation process than ISDN (ADSL only requires you to plug an ADSL adaptor into a phone socket, while ISDN requires an engineer to install new plugs).

If ADSL isn't available and you aren't in a 'cabled' area, ISDN is the only option; connection costs 70 lev (€35).

Telephones

You can buy a telephone from the post office or any retailer. Cordless phones are widely available. The standard Bulgarian telephone connector has three pins. It's possible to rewire a cord from a standard RJ11 plug to the Bulgarian plug yourself, although it's safer and easier to buy an adapter plug. Adapter plugs can usually be purchased at airports and larger electronics retailers, although it's preferable to buy them before you move to Bulgaria – e.g. from Maplin (💻 http://www.maplin.co.uk), International Electrical Supplies (💻 http://www.international-electrical-supplies.com) or TeleAdapt (💻 http://www.teleadapt.com). See also **Modems** on page 261.

Using the Telephone

Bulgaria doesn't have a standard system for telephone numbers. Some areas have a four-digit dialling code (e.g. Albena, 5722) while others have only a one- or two-digit code (e.g. Sofia, 2). Subscriber numbers can range from three to seven digits. The Bulgarian telecoms regulator, CTC, has advised that four or five digit area codes are 'temporary' and will be phased out in favour of one- to three-digit codes. Numbers beginning 0898, 0899, 0887, 0888 and 0889 are mobile numbers (see **Mobile Phones** on page 259).

To make a local call (i.e. within the same dialling code area) you need to dial only the subscriber number. To call a number in a different code area, dial '0', the area code and the subscriber number. Note, however, that some areas are on analogue exchanges and require the prefix 99 instead of 0. If you cannot get a connection to a number using 0, try 99. To call Bulgaria from another country, dial your international code, the country code for Bulgaria (359), the area code, then the subscriber number.

Bulgaria now has peak and off-peak rates, the latter being at weekends and after 9pm during the week.

International Calls

It's possible to make international direct dialling (IDD) calls to most countries from both private and public telephones. To make an international call, you first need to dial 00, then the country code, the area code (the first zero) and the subscriber's number. If direct dialling isn't possible, international dialling assistance can be obtained through an operator by calling 0123. There's no international directory enquiries service, although the operator may be able to assist. If you have internet access, it's usually easier to find an online telephone directory for the country you need (for example, for the UK 💻 http://www.thephonebook.bt.com).

To obtain an operator from one of the major US telephone companies, dial ☎ 00 800 00 10 (AT&T), ☎ 00 800 10 10 (Sprint) or ☎ 00 800 00 01 (MCI Worldphone). These companies offer overseas calling cards that provide access to an English-speaking operator, and AT&T offers a 'USA Direct' service, whereby you can call an operator in any state (except Alaska).

Orbitel, a private Bulgarian telephone service provider, recently launched a service called Orbiphone 01001, allowing overseas calls at cheap rates, although the service is prepaid. You can register your telephone number on Orbitel's website (💻 http://www.orbitel.bg/en) and pay by debit card online or at a Post Bank. Alternatively, pre-paid international phone cards can be bought from kiosks and corner shops.

If you don't have a fixed or mobile phone, you can make cheap calls from internet cafés and phone kiosks, although calls are often made with an 'internet phone' and quality varies considerably according to the country you're calling.

Many people who have the internet at home are using a relatively new service called Skype (🖳 http://www.skype.com) to make international calls. Skype, which requires broadband connection, uses a technology called 'voice over internet protocol' (VoIP), allowing people with a Skype account to talk to each other free over the internet. You can use headphones plugged into your computer's sound output socket or a VoIP telephone plugged into a USB port; cordless models are available. If you want to call someone on a fixed or mobile phone, you can use a subscription service called SkypeOut. Another service called SkypeIn allows people to call you from ordinary telephones anywhere in the world.

Many Bulgarian internet companies are beginning to offer VoIP services, so if you plan to make a lot of international calls, it's worth shopping around.

Charges

Privatisation of BTC and deregulation of the telecommunications market has led to the lowering of prices for phone calls and other services, although line rental must still be paid to BTC at fixed rates. BTC offers a range of plans called 'At Home', which include up to 120 minutes of local calls and 80 minutes of international calls, starting at 20 lev (€10) per month, including the line rental charge.

Line Rental

The line rental or service charge payable to BTC varies according to the type of line and, in the case of ADSL, the length of the contract, as follows:

● **Standard line** – 10 lev (€5) per month;

● **ADSL** – There's a minimum 12-month contract for all plans but some are time-limited, instead of limited by the amount of data you download. The basic 'Tempo' plan costs 20 lev (€10) per month for a 256/64 line and 20 hours' connection; the 'Unlimited' plan costs 33 lev (€16) per month for 512/128 and has no data or time limits. There are also faster 'Biz' plans which cost more but offer extra email addresses and data hosting for web sites.

● **ISDN line** – 15 lev (€7.50) per month, private; 35 lev (€18) per month, business.

If you use an alternative telephone provider, there may be a separate monthly fee in addition to your call charges, although most providers have dropped these.

Domestic Calls

Domestic call charges are low: for example, a long-distance call between Bourgas and Sofia would cost 0.11 lev (€0.05) for the connection then 0.10 lev per minute during peak periods, or 0.045 lev per minutes off-peak (after 9pm).

International Calls

BTC has seven tariff levels for international calls, listed on its website (🖳 http://www.btc.bg/files/products/file_2_en.pdf). Calls to the UK, US, Australia, Canada and most European countries come under Tariff 1 (the cheapest) and cost either 0.3 lev (€0.15), 0.927 lev (€0.46), or 1.145 lev (€0.58) depending on your call plan.

Other telephone providers have different tariff structures for international calls. Most alternative providers also offer a variety of discount plants, such as half price on all calls to a designated 'favourite country' or to specific overseas phone numbers frequently called.

Emergency & Service Numbers

The national emergency numbers in Bulgaria are:

Number	Service
150	Ambulance
160	Fire brigade
166	Police/Traffic police

Useful telephone service numbers include the following:

Number	Service
121	Operator service for domestic calls
144	Business directory enquiries for Sofia
145	Private directory enquiries for Sofia

1286	Car breakdown service (Sofia)
146	Car breakdown service (outside Sofia)
175	Weather forecast

Fax

Fax machines can be purchased or rented from private companies and shops. Before bringing a fax machine to Bulgaria, check that it will work there or that it can be modified. For example, some British fax machines won't work, although it's possible to buy adaptors for UK phones and fax machines (see **Telephones** on page 253). Keep in mind that getting a foreign fax machine repaired may be impossible if the same model isn't sold in Bulgaria.

Public Telephones

Despite the increasing use of mobile phones (see page 259), public phone booths can be found in all towns and villages – in post offices, bus and railway stations, airports, bars, cafes, restaurants, hotels, and of course, in the streets. There are two types of public phone, using different systems and taking different types of phone card: Betkom (in blue livery) and Bulfon (orange). Bulfon phones are more widespread and usually better value for local calls, whereas Betkom phones tend to be are more reliable and better for international calls and long-distance calls within Bulgaria. Neither type of phone takes coins. Phonecards are sold at most shops and kiosks.

Mobile Phones

The mobile phone network in Bulgaria is extensive and almost the whole country has mobile phone reception. Areas with poor or no reception are usually high in mountains or in remote areas. There are three mobile phone service providers: Globul (⌨ http://www.globul.bg/eng), Mtel (⌨ http://www.mtel.bg) and Vivatel (⌨ http://www.vivatel.bg/en), owned by BTC.

As in most countries, buying a mobile phone can involve a dizzying array of choices between not only the network and the option of a contract or a 'pay-as-you-talk' system, but also a wide range of tariffs covering connection fees, monthly subscriptions, insurance and call charges.

If you want to use a foreign mobile in Bulgaria, you can buy a SIM card that will give you a Bulgarian mobile number and allow you to make and receive calls and text messages, although you may need to get your phone 'unlocked' from the network in your home country (this can be done cheaply at most mobile phone shops). The most popular SIM card is from Mtel, which is cheap and reliable for local calls (although all cards are expensive for international calls).

SURVIVAL TIP
Unless you absolutely have to, don't use your mobile phone from an overseas network to make calls in Bulgaria, as the cost will be astronomical.

The basic Mtel contract costs 9.6 lev (€4.80) per month and allows you to talk 'free' for 20 minutes. After that, calls cost 0.30 lev (€0.15) to another Mtel mobile and 0.48 lev (€0.25) to other networks (including landlines).

Internet

Internet use is quite low in Bulgaria, as the cost of buying a computer and connecting it to the internet is still beyond the means of many Bulgarians. Despite this, broadband availability is increasing and the cost of internet access is very low by western European standards. A basic, 256 kB-speed ADSL plan with BTC costs 30 lev (€15) for installation plus 20 lev (€10) per month for 20 hours. Over 20 hours, you're billed 0.01 lev (€0.005) per minute.

Dial-up is still by far the most popular way of connecting to the internet and there are over 150 companies providing dial-up internet services. A basic, 56 kB dial-up connection with BTC costs 4 lev (€2) plus 9.6 lev (€4.80) for 20 hours.

Contact details of some of the larger internet service providers (ISPs) are given below.

● BOL (🖥 http://www.bol.bg);

● BTC (🖥 http://www.btc.bg);

● Bulgaria Online (🖥 http://www.btc-net.bg);

● Digital Systems (🖥 http://www.digsys.bg);

- Euro Integra (🖳 http://www.einet.bg/en);

- Mobikom (🖳 http://www.mobikom.com/en);

- NetBG.com (🖳 http://www.netbg.com);

- Orbitel (🖳 http://www.orbitel.bg/en).

You can connect to the internet from a mobile phone, although this is expensive and slow. If you have cable TV (see page 262), you can also usually obtain internet access via the cable TV connection. Although cable internet isn't as fast as ADSL, it can work out cheaper if you already have cable connected and is more convenient than dial-up. Costs range from around 25 lev (€12) per month for dial-up access or low-speed cable connection to over 100 lev (€50) for high-speed connection. Most providers offer combined telephone and internet access packages.

For faster internet connections you can have an ADSL or ISDN line installed (see **Installation & Registration** on page 254).

 Internet speeds in Bulgaria (particularly ADSL) are noticeably slower than in many other countries (particularly the UK) as the internet 'backbone' connecting Bulgaria to the rest of the world is narrow.

Modems

Telecommunications standards in Bulgaria are the same as those in the EU, so if your modem works in Europe or has a 'CE' mark it should work in Bulgaria. If you have an ISDN line and want your computer to connect to the internet at the maximum possible speed, you will need an ISDN terminal adapter.

TELEVISION & RADIO

Before taking television (TV) sets, video cassette recorders (VCRs), DVD players and radios to Bulgaria, you should consider both transport costs and compatibility. Prices for familiar brands of TVs and other electronic equipment are about the same in Bulgaria as they are in the UK; Bulgarian brands can be purchased for much less (although they may not last as long).

TV Standards

The standards for TV sets aren't the same in Bulgaria as in some other countries, and TV sets and video recorders (see below) operating on the UK PAL system or the North American NTSC system won't function properly (or at all) in Bulgaria.

Most European countries use the PAL B/G standard, except for the UK, which uses a modified PAL-I system that is incompatible with the systems of other European countries. France uses another system entirely, called SECAM-L, which is in turn different from the SECAM standard used elsewhere in the world. If you want a TV set that will work in Bulgaria (and other European countries) you must buy a multi-standard TV. Most new television sets sold in Bulgaria contain automatic circuitry that can switch between PAL-B/G, PAL-I and SECAM-L.

VCRs

A British or US VCR won't work properly with a Bulgarian TV unless it's dual-standard. (Although you can play back a PAL-B/G video on a PAL-I VCR, there will be no sound.) Most video machines sold in Bulgaria are multi-standard PAL and may also contain an NTSC playback feature, allowing Americans to play video tapes via a PAL television. Some multi-standard TVs also have an 'NTSC-in' jack plug connection, allowing you to watch American videos.

Cable TV

The cable network in Bulgaria has been developing rapidly, although cable TV and other cable services are generally available only in cities, larger towns and holiday resorts. There are over 150 cable operators in the country, broadcasting nationally, regionally and locally. Most packages include several English-language channels, broadcasting news, sport and films. Cable TV installation costs around 50 lev (€25).

Satellite TV

Bulgaria is served by satellite TV, but depending on where you are and what channels you want to receive you may have to invest in a large satellite dish (see **Satellite Dishes** below).

The BBC's commercial subsidiary, BBC World Television, broadcasts two 24-hour channels: BBC World (24-hour news and information) and BBC Prime (general entertainment). BBC World is free-to-air, while BBC Prime is encrypted. Subscription costs for BBC Prime are £85 (€125) for an annual subscription, plus a £30 (€44) smart card administration fee. For more information and a programme guide, contact BBC World Customer Relations, PO Box 5054, London W12 0ZY, United Kingdom (🖳 http://www.bbcworld.com). BBC Prime has a programme guide listed on the internet (🖳 http://www.bbcprime.com).

Two of the larger satellite operators providing a range of channels are ITV Partner (☎ 0800-12 500, 🖳 http://www.itvpartner.com/eng) and Bulsat (🖳 http://www.bulsat.com).

Satellite Dishes

To receive programmes from any satellite, there must be no obstacles (e.g. trees, buildings or mountains) between the satellite and your dish, so check before renting or buying if being able to receive satellite broadcasts is important to you. You should also check whether you need permission from your landlord or local authorities. Dishes can be mounted in a variety of unobtrusive positions and can be painted or patterned to blend with the background.

The two main satellites covering Bulgaria are Eutelsat Hotbird 1 and Astra 2D, but whereas a 60cm dish is adequate in most areas to receive signals from the former, the latter, which carries BBC programmes, requires a much larger dish (3m or even 4.5m). In some areas you can also receive Sky TV, but you will need a digital box and a subscription from the UK.

Installation costs (including a receiver) are between around 200 and 400 lev (€100–200) depending on location and the size of dish required.

Video & DVD

Bulgarian video rental shops usually have only a few English-language titles (if any), although in the popular tourist areas along the coast the range is better. There are some specialist English-language rental shops in the main cities and the popular tourist areas. A good source of English-language films (as well as books and periodicals) is the British Council (🖳 http://www. britishcouncil.org/bulgaria), which has libraries in Sofia and Varna.

Most shops that rent or sell video tapes also offer DVDs, which are gradually superseding videos and have the advantage of providing soundtracks and subtitles in several different languages (a good way to learn Bulgarian is to have the movie dialogue in Bulgarian and the subtitles in English). English-language titles can be purchased by mail-order or via the internet (e.g. 🖳 http://www.amazon.co.uk), but make sure any post is sent via registered post or courier (see **Postal Services** on page 243).

Radio

There are a huge number of radio stations in Bulgaria broadcasting English and Bulgarian pop music. There's little English-language radio, although Bulgarian National Radio has an English-language service (🖳 http://www. bnr.bg/RadioBulgaria/Emission_English) broadcasting a range of news and information about Bulgaria. If you have an ADSL internet connection, you can receive radio broadcasts via your computer – 🖳 http://www. predavatel.com/en_index.htm has a list of all radio stations in Bulgaria broadcasting on the internet.

BBC

The BBC World Service is broadcast on short wave on several frequencies (e.g. 17640, 12095, 9410, 7320, 6195, 5875kHz) simultaneously and you can usually receive a good signal on one of them. The signal strength varies according to where you live in Bulgaria, the time of day and year, the power and positioning of your receiver, and atmospheric conditions. All BBC radio stations, including the World Service, are available on the Astra satellite (see below). BBC radio stations can also be heard live or up to seven days after broadcast via your PC using the BBC's online radio player (🖳 http://www. bbc.co.uk/radio). Schedules for BBC radio programmes on short wave and satellite are available at 🖳 http://www.bbcworldservice.com/schedules or by writing to BBC World Service, Bush House, Strand, London WC2B 4PH, UK.

Satellite Radio

If you have satellite TV, you can also receive many radio stations via satellite. For example, BBC Radio 1, 2, 3, 4 and 5, BBC World Service, Sky Radio, Virgin 1215 and many foreign-language stations are broadcast via the Astra satellites. Details are usually published in your monthly satellite subscriber newsletter. Satellite radio stations are listed in British satellite TV magazines such as *What Satellite?* and *Digital TV*.

UTILITIES

Bulgaria is a net power exporter and generates around 30 to 40 per cent of its energy requirements from nuclear power, the remainder coming mainly from coal-fired thermal power plants with a small percentage from hydro-electric power stations. The main nuclear plant is Kozloduy, which has four working reactors. Two are to be shut down in 2006 for safety reasons, and a new European-designed plant, Belene, will be operational by 2011.

As well as electricity and gas, Bulgarian homes use oil and wood for heating and hot water (see **Heating & Air-conditioning** on page 237).

Electricity

Electricity is currently supplied by the state-owned National Electricity Company (NEK), but the market will be fully liberalised by 2007 to meet EU competition requirements, allowing customers to buy electricity directly from producers. Unlike liberalisation in most Western countries, this is leading to significant price increases, as electricity has hitherto been subsidised in Bulgaria, although the government is trying to spread the price rises over an extended period. Electricity prices are currently on a par with the UK but are expected to double in 2007.

Power Supply

The electricity supply in Bulgaria is delivered to homes at 220/240 volts (V) with a frequency of 50 Hertz (Hz). If you're moving from a country with a 110V supply (e.g. the US) your electrical equipment will require a converter or a transformer to convert it to 240V, although some electrical appliances (e.g. electric razors and hair dryers) are fitted with a 110/240 volt switch. Check for the switch, which may be inside the casing, and make sure it is switched to 240V **before** connecting it to the power supply. Converters are suitable only for appliances without circuit boards or microchips that don't need to be plugged in for long periods (e.g. heaters, hair dryers, vacuum cleaners and coffee machines). Electronic appliances such as computers, fax machines, TVs and video players must be connected to the supply via a step-down transformer. Add the wattage of all the devices you intend to connect to a transformer and make sure that its power rating exceeds this sum. Converters and transformers can be bought in most DIY shops, although in most cases it's simpler (and cheaper) to buy new appliances in Bulgaria (see **Household Goods** on page 251).

An additional problem with some electrical equipment is the frequency rating, which in some countries, e.g. the US and Canada, is 60 Hertz (Hz) whereas in Bulgaria it's 50Hz. Electrical equipment without a motor is generally unaffected by the drop in frequency to 50Hz (except TVs – see page 262). Equipment with a motor may run with a 20 per cent drop in speed; however, automatic washing machines, cookers, electric clocks, record players and tape recorders are unusable in Bulgaria if not designed for 50Hz operation. To find out, look at the label on the back of the equipment. If it says 50/60Hz, it should work. If it says 60Hz, you might try it anyway, but first ensure that the voltage is correct as outlined above. Bear in mind that the transformers and motors of electrical devices designed to run at 60Hz will run hotter at 50Hz, so you should ensure that equipment has sufficient space around it for cooling.

In rural areas the power supply can often weaken or fail, sometimes for a few minutes and sometimes for several hours. Power cuts are fairly frequent in some areas, especially during thunderstorms and heavy rain. If you live in an area with an unstable power supply it's advisable to buy a power stabiliser for a computer or other vital equipment to prevent it being switched off when the power drops. If you use a computer, it's also worth fitting an uninterruptible power supply (UPS) with a battery back-up, which allows you time (up to 20 minutes) to save your work and shut down your computer after a power failure. If you're concerned about lightning strikes, you can install an 'anti-lightning' device in your fuse box. (You should also keep torches, candles and preferably a gas lamp handy!) You should also disconnect from the internet or turn off your ADSL modem during a thunderstorm, as surges from lightning strikes can be transmitted down a telephone line.

If the power keeps tripping off when you attempt to use a number of high-powered appliances simultaneously, it probably means that the rating of your power supply is too low. If this is the case, you need to ask the electricity company to uprate the power supply to your property, although your standing charge will be higher. The possible ratings are 25 amps and above 25 amps. If you have high-power appliances such as a washing machine, air-conditioning, water heater and electric heating in an average-size house, you will probably need a higher-rated supply.

Wiring Standards

Lax building standards (and consequent corner-cutting) during the communist era left many older properties in Bulgaria with dangerous wiring, especially in rural areas. For example, there may be no proper earth.

SURVIVAL TIP
One of the most important tasks after buying a property (if you haven't done so before) is to check that the electrical system is safe. The cost of having a home rewired is much lower than in western European countries.

Where possible, you should have a hot water boiler installed outside the bathroom; if this isn't possible, make sure the boiler is earthed separately or boxed in. Make sure also that you have enough power points fitted; even in new properties it's common for developers not to install enough points (although it's usually safe to run up to five or six low-wattage appliances from one socket with a multi-plug connector).

SURVIVAL TIP
It's essential to use a qualified Bulgarian electrician for electrical work. Don't be tempted to do it yourself or have an electrician from another country do the work.

Plugs, Fuses & Bulbs

Another thing to check before moving into a home in Bulgaria is whether there are any light fittings. When moving house, some people remove not only bulbs, but bulb-holders, flexes and even ceiling roses! Depending on where you've moved from, you may need new plugs or a lot of adaptors. Plug adaptors for imported lamps and other electrical apparatus may be difficult to find for some countries, so it's worth bringing some with you, as well as extension cords and multi-plug extensions that can be fitted with Bulgarian plugs.

Bulgarian plugs have two round pins for the live and neutral connections, usually with a recessed contact at 90 degrees to the pins for the earth connection. Small, low-power (under around 5 amps) electrical appliances such as table lamps, small TVs and computers don't require an earth. Plugs with an earth must be used for high-wattage appliances such as heaters, kettles, washing machines, refrigerators and cookers.

 Always make sure a plug is correctly and securely wired, as bad wiring can cause fatal injuries (and is also a fire hazard).

In modern properties, fuses are of the resetting pop-out type or earth trip system. When there's a short-circuit or the system has been overloaded, a circuit breaker is tripped and the power supply is cut. Before reconnecting the power, switch off any high-power appliances such as a washing machine or dishwasher. Make sure you know where the trip switch is located and keep a torch handy so you can find it in the dark (see **Power Supply** on page 265).

Electric light bulbs in Bulgaria are almost always of the Edison type with a screw fitting. Bayonet-fitting light bulbs are rarely used, so if you want to bring lamps or other light fitting with you that have a bayonet fitting, it's worth bringing a large supply of bulbs with you!

Converters & Transformers

Electrical equipment rated at 110V AC (e.g. from the US or Canada) requires a converter or step-down transformer to convert it to 220/240V, although some electrical appliances are fitted with a 110/240V switch. Converters can be used for heating appliances, but transformers are required for motorised appliances. Add the wattage of the devices you intend to connect to a transformer and make sure that its power rating **exceeds** this sum.

Generally, small, high-wattage electrical appliances, such as kettles, toasters, heaters and irons need large transformers. Motors in large appliances, such as cookers, refrigerators, washing machines, dryers and dishwashers, need replacing or fitting with a large transformer. In most cases it's much easier to buy new appliances in Bulgaria. Remember that the dimensions of imported cookers, microwave ovens, refrigerators, washing machines, dryers and dishwashers may be different from those in Bulgaria and so may not even fit into a Bulgarian kitchen.

Connection & Registration

You will need to apply to the local electricity distribution company to have your electricity connected and must sign a contract specifying the power supply to be installed. If it's a new property you will need to prove you're the owner by producing a copy of the title deeds or a copy of the lease if you're renting. You must usually produce your passport or residence permit. If you plan to pay by direct debit from a bank or post office account, don't forget to take along your account details.

If you're moving into an old property, you must also tell the utility company the name of the person who previously paid the bills (which will be on the title deeds). The bills are then transferred into your name, usually for a nominal fee. In many cases your estate agent can do this for you (probably over the phone); if not, it helps to take along someone who speaks Bulgarian.

Tariffs

After electricity distribution was privatised, electricity tariffs went up substantially and are now on a par with those in the UK, although they're expected to double in 2007. For an average-size house, you should expect to pay around €25 per month in summer and €75 per month in winter – more if you have electric heating (see page 238).

Meters

Meters are usually installed in a box on an outside wall of a property. However, if your meter isn't accessible from outside your property and the property isn't permanently occupied, make sure you leave the keys with a neighbour or make arrangements to have your meter read. If your meter cannot be read, you will receive an estimate based on previous bills, although it **must** be read at least once a year.

Bills

You're normally billed for your electricity each month. Bills can be paid by direct debit from a bank or in cash at the post office (Post Bank). It's also possible to pay a fixed amount each month by standing order based on your estimated usage; at the end of the year you receive a bill for the amount owing or a rebate of the amount overpaid. These methods of payment are preferable, particularly if you spend a lot of time away from your home or you're a non-resident. If you want to set up a direct debit or standing order at your bank to pay utility bills, you will need to take a copy of the deeds to your house, your limited company registration papers and someone who speaks Bulgarian.

Gas

The state-owned Bulgargaz has a monopoly on gas transmission and controls the pipeline carrying gas from Russia to southern Europe. Until 1991, it also had a monopoly on gas distribution, but this was then broken up between a number of distribution companies, which were privatised. Bulgaria imports nearly all its natural gas from Russia and most of it is currently supplied to industry, but the government has made gas a priority for the Bulgarian energy sector and residential consumption of gas is expected to double in the next five years.

Mains Gas

The gas network in Bulgaria is small, with only 500km (300mi) of pipeline, although 'gasification' is expanding. The network was originally designed to serve heavy industry, the main pipeline forming a ring around Bulgaria with small branches. Only 30 towns are currently served by the gas network: principally Bourgas, Kyustendil, Pleven, Plovdiv, Ruse, Shumen, Sliven, Stara Zagora, Varna and Vratsa. Villages close to these towns will also have mains gas. Overgas is the largest retailer of natural gas in Bulgaria, and its website (🖳 http://www.overgas.bg) includes a map of the towns connected to mains gas (click on 'Prices').

When moving into a property already connected to mains gas, you will need to contact the local distribution company to have the gas switched on and/or have the meter read and the account transferred to your name. If you want to be connected to mains gas, the cost depends on the amount of gas you expect to use (e.g. for heating or just for cooking), the average connection charge being around 300 lev (€150).

Bottled Gas

Many rural homes have cookers and some also water heaters that use bottled gas. Check when moving into a property that the gas bottle isn't empty. Keep a spare bottle or two handy and make sure you know how to change the bottles, as this can be quite a complicated procedure.

Bottles can be purchased at most petrol stations and delivery can often be arranged through your local mayor. Some houses keep their gas bottles outside, often under a lean-to. If you do this you must buy propane gas rather than butane, as it can withstand a greater range of temperatures than butane, which is for internal use only (in fact, propane gas bottles **must** be kept outside a house). For information about gas tanks, see page 239.

 If you're planning to buy or rent an apartment, check whether gas bottles are permitted, as they're prohibited in many new apartments.

Water

The water supply in Bulgaria, like other areas of infrastructure, suffered from years of underdevelopment. The cities suffer from massive water leaks due to ageing pipes, while in the countryside over a third of rural properties aren't connected to mains water and only one in ten towns has a sewerage system. Nevertheless, mains water is safe to drink in the cities, although many people in rural areas drink bottled water and only use tap water for washing up and watering the garden.

The old municipal Water and Sewage Departments have been privatised into regional water companies and a number of private companies have begun investing in water supply and waste water management in joint ventures with the regional companies, bringing much needed improvements to Bulgaria's water and sewage systems.

Most properties that are connected to mains water are metered, so that you pay only for the water you use and are charged per cubic metre (1,000 litres). When moving into a new house, ask the local water company to read your meter and transfer the account to your name.

Water shortages are rare in the towns and cities (although they do occur in summer) but are common in some rural areas. It's possible to have a storage tank installed for emergencies and you should also keep a back-up supply for watering the garden or alternately recycle your house water.

Supply & Connection

If you buy a property in or near a town or village that has mains water, it will probably already be connected. However, some older properties and brand new properties need a connection, which can be expensive as you must pay for digging the trenches required for the pipes. The connection cost can vary considerably according to the type of terrain and soil (or rock!) that must be dug to lay pipes.

SURVIVAL TIP
If you're thinking of buying a property and installing a mains water supply, obtain an estimate before signing the purchase contract.

If you rely on a well or spring for your water, be aware that in most villages well water is contaminated with sewage, as they aren't sunk very deep into the ground. Wells and springs can also dry up, particularly in summer in mountainous areas. One option is to have a bore sunk, which is an expensive but more reliable source of fresh water.

 Always confirm that a rural property has a reliable water source and check it or have it checked by an expert (see Inspections & Surveys on page 126).

If the water source is on a neighbour's land, make sure there's no dispute about the ownership of the water and your right to use it, e.g. that it cannot be stopped or drained away by your neighbours.

Cost

Mains water costs depend on where you live, although they aren't usually more than 25 to 35 lev (€12–17) per month. You don't pay water charges for well water or water from a stream or river running through your property.

Sewerage

Properties in urban areas are usually connected to mains drainage, whereas those in rural areas usually have individual sewage systems (see **Septic Tanks** on page 131). If you have a septic tank, you should use enzyme bio-digesters and employ bleach and drain unblockers sparingly, as they kill the friendly bacteria that prevent nasty smells, and don't use cleaning agents such as ammonia, as they will destroy the tank. Septic tanks should be emptied every three to five years.

> **SURVIVAL TIP**
> Before buying a property with its own sewage system, you should have it checked by an expert. Before buying a property or plot without a system, you should obtain expert advice as to whether such a system can be installed and what the cost will be (see Septic Tanks on page 131).

APPENDICES

Appendix A: USEFUL ADDRESSES

Embassies & Consulates

Foreign embassies and consulates are located in the capital, Sofia (those of selected countries are listed below).

Australia: 37 Trakia Street, 1504 (☎ 02-946 1334).

Canada: 9 Moskovska Street (☎ 02-969 9710).

France: 21A Oborishte Street, 1504 (☎ 02-946 1040).

Germany: 25 Jolio Curie Street, 1113 (☎ 02-963 4101).

Netherlands: 15 Oborishte Street, 1504 (☎ 02-816 0300).

South Africa: 26 Bacho Kiro Street, 2nd Floor, 1000 (☎ 02-981 6682).

United Kingdom: 9 Moskovska Street, 1000 (☎ 02-933 9222).

United States of America: 16 Kozyak Street (☎ 02-937 5100).

Some countries also have consulates in other cities; Britain has an honorary consulate at 40 Graf Igantiev Street, PO Box 229, Varna (☎ 05-2665 5555). Note that honorary consulates aren't permanently staffed and should be contacted in emergencies only (e.g. for urgent passport renewals or replacements).

Property Exhibition Organisers

Below is a list of the main exhibition organisers in the UK and Ireland. You may be charged an admission fee to some of their exhibitions.

Homes Overseas (☎ UK 0870-906 3763, 🖳 http://events.home overseas.co.uk). One of the largest organisers of international property exhibitions, who stage over 30 exhibitions each year at a range of venues in the UK and Ireland.

International Property Show (☎ 01962-736712, 💻 http://www. internationalpropertyshow.com). Takes place several times a year in London and Manchester.

Invest in Property Show (☎ 0870-906 3766, 💻 http://www. investinpropertyshow.com). Takes place in April at Earls Court in London.

World Class Homes (☎ 0800-731 4713, 💻 http://www. worldclasshomes.co.uk). Exhibitions are held in small venues around the UK and include mainly British property developers.

World of Property (☎ 01323-726 040, 💻 http://www.outbound publishing.com). The *World of Property* magazine publishers (see **Appendix B**) organise three large property exhibitions a year, two in southern Britain and one in the north.

Other Organisations

British Association of Removers (BAR), Tangent House 62 Exchange Road Watford Hertfordshire WD18 0TG, UK (☎ 01923 699480, 💻 http://www.removers.org.uk).

British Council (Sofia), 7 Krakra Street, Sofia 1504 (☎ 02-942 4344).

British Council (Varna), 1 Drin Street, Varna 9000 (☎ 05-260 5880).

British Bulgarian Chamber of Commerce, PO Box 123, Bromley BR1 4ZX, UK (☎ 020-8464 5007, 💻 http://www.bbcc.bg).

Bulgaria Telecom (BTC), 6 Stefan Karadzha Street, Sofia 1000 (☎ 02-949 6456, 💻 http://www.btc.bg/en).

Bulgarian Embassy (London), 186-188 Queen's Gate, London SW7 5HL, UK (☎ 0870-060 2350, 💻 http://www.bulgarian embassy.org.uk).

Bulgarian Embassy (Washington), 1621 22nd Street, NW, Washington DC 20008, USA (☎ 202-387 0174, 💻 http://www. bulgaria-embassy.org).

Bulgarian Post (GPO), 120 A Rakovski Street, Sofia 1000 (☎ 02-832 0095, 💻 http://www.bgpost.bg).

Bulgarian Tourist Authority, 1 Sveta Nedelia Square, 1000 Sofia (☎ 02-987 9778, 💻 http://www.bulgariatravel.org).

Department for Environment, Food and Rural Affairs (DEFRA), Nobel House, 17 Smith Square, London, SW1P 3JR, UK (☎ 0845-933 5577, 💻 http://www.defra.gov.uk).

Federation of Overseas Property Developers, Agents and Consultants (FOPDAC), First Floor, 618 Newmarket Road, Cambridge CB5 8LP, UK (☎ 0870-350 1223, 💻 http://www.fopdac.com).

Invest Bulgaria, 5 Hristo Kovachev Street, Sofia 1527 (☎ 02-843 0416, 💻 http://www.investbulgaria.com).

Ministry of the Interior (MVR), 29 Shesti Septemvri Street, Sofia 1000 (☎ 02-982 5000, 💻 http://www.mvr.bg/en).

Natsionalna Elektricheska Kompania (NEK), 5 Veslets Street, 1040 Sofia (☎ 02-926 3636, 💻 http://www.nek.bg).

Appendix B: FURTHER READING

English-language Newspapers & Magazines

Homes Worldwide, Merricks Media Ltd, Units 3 & 4, Riverside Court, Lower Bristol Road, Bath BA2 3DZ, UK (☎ 01225-786800, 🖳 http://www.homesworldwide.co.uk). Quarterly magazine covering property worldwide, with a Central & Eastern Europe section including Bulgaria.

Quest Bulgaria Magazine, 17 Raceys Close, Emneth, Norfolk PE14 8BT, UK (🖳 http://www.questbg.com). Monthly magazine about buying and investing in property in Bulgaria.

Sofia Echo, 23 Shipka Street, Sofia 1504 (☎ 02-943 1115, 🖳 http://www.sofiaecho.com). Weekly newspaper.

Tema News, 19 Vistosha Boulevard, Sofia 1000 (☎ 02-933 0910, 🖳 http://www.temanews.com). Weekly news magazine.

APPENDIX C: USEFUL WEBSITES

Below is a list of general websites that might be of interest and aren't included elsewhere in this book; websites relevant to specific aspects of buying a home in Bulgaria are given in the appropriate section. Websites usually offer free access, although some require a subscription or payment for services. Relocation and other companies specialising in expatriate services often have websites, although these may provide only information that a company is prepared to offer free of charge, which may be rather biased. However, there are plenty of volunteer sites run by expatriates providing practical information and tips.

A particularly useful section found on most expatriate sites is the 'message board' or 'forum', where expatriates answer questions based on their experience and knowledge and offer an insight into what living and working in Bulgaria is really like; these are offered by some magazine websites (see **Appendix B**).

Websites are listed under headings in alphabetical order and the list is by no means definitive.

Bulgarian Property

Every estate agent selling property to foreigners in Bulgaria has a website. To find those most relevant to you, search the web for the name of the area you're interested in with key words such as 'real estate' or 'property'. The following is a selection of property websites offering property in Bulgaria – there are literally hundreds of others.

Anglo Bulgarian Properties (💻 http://www.anglobulgarianproperties.co.uk). Properties for sale in coastal areas and in the mountains near Borovets.

Barrasford and Bird (💻 http://www.barrasfordandbird.co.uk). Well-established company with offices in the UK and Sofia, Pamporovo, Sveti Vlas and Sunny Beach.

Best Bulgarian Properties (💻 http://www.thebestbulgarianproperties.com). Based in Bourgas and Elhovo. Property in most areas.

BG Balkan Estate (🖳 http://www.bgbalkanestate.com). Specialises in properties in central Bulgaria, with offices in the UK, Germany, Nova Zagora and Sunny Beach.

BG Home Services (🖳 http://www.bghomeservices.com). Based in the UK, with property all over Bulgaria.

BG Properties (🖳 http://www.bg-properties.com). Specialises in properties under €50,000.

BK Real Estate (🖳 http://www.bkrealestate-bg.com). Site under construction.

Bulgaria Revealed (🖳 http://www.bulgariarevealed.com). Property in most areas. The website requires registration to view a property list.

Bulgarian Address (🖳 http://www.bulgarianaddressltd.com). Coastal, mountain and rural properties, as well as property in Sofia.

Bulgarian Black Sea Properties (🖳 http://www.bul properties.com). Property on the Black Sea coast.

Bulgarian Dreams (🖳 http://www.bulgariandreams.com). Coastal, mountain and city properties.

Bulgarian Estates (🖳 http://www.bulgarianestates.org). Property in most areas.

Bulgarian Property Consultants (🖳 http://www.topbulgarianproperties.com). Residential property in most areas, as well as commercial and industrial property.

Experience BG (🖳 http://www.experiencebg.co.uk). Coastal and mountain properties.

Helis (🖳 http://www.helis.bg). Properties on the southern Black Sea coast.

Homefinders Bulgaria (🖳 http://www.homefinders-bg.co.uk). Houses and land in most areas.

INS Properties (🖳 http://www.insproperties.com). Property in most areas. Based in Plovdiv.

Kirov Real Estate (🖳 http://www.kirov.bg). New and off-plan apartments in coastal areas.

MacAnthony Realty International (🖳 http://www.macanthony realty.com). Property in most areas, plus property in other countries.

My Bulgaria (🖳 http://www.mybulgaria.info).Property in most areas, plus an interesting forum.

New Skys (🖳 http://www.newskys.co.uk).Property in most areas, plus property in numerous other countries.

Property.BG (🖳 http://www.property.bg). Property in most areas.

Rila Properties (🖳 http://www.zojan.com). Property in most areas.

Rock Arch Estates (🖳 http://www.rockarch.co.uk). Property in most areas.

Bulgarian Lawyers

Many Bulgarian lawyers speak English (and often German and Russian). The British Embassy in Sofia (🖳 http://www.british-embassy.bg) has a list of English-speaking lawyers on its website (click on 'Services' in the top left, then 'Consular').

Lex.bg (🖳 http://www.lex.bg) is an online directory of legal services in Bulgaria, including lawyers, notaries and legal firms. The site is in English and lists practicing lawyers in each of Bulgaria's regions.

Some English-speaking law firms specialising in property and tax law are listed below.

Legacon (🖳 http://www.legaconsult.com). Tax, commercial and property law.

Georgiev, Todorov and Co. (🖳 http://www.georg-tod.com). All areas of Bulgarian law.

Borislav Boyanov and Co. (🖳 http://www.boyanov.com). All areas of Bulgaria law, with a focus on business and commercial law.

Overseas Lawyers

Grace and Co. (🖳 http://www.graceandco.co.uk). Commercial, personal and overseas property law.

International Property Law Centre (🖳 http://www.international-propertylaw.co.uk). Specialists in property law in several countries, including Bulgaria.

General Information

Beach Bulgaria (🖳 http://www.beachbulgaria.com). Information on the Black Sea coast.

Bulgaria Ski (🖳 http://www.bulgariski.com). Information on all of Bulgaria's ski resorts.

Bulgaria Travel (🖳 http://www.bulgariatravel.org). Official tourist information site.

Bulgarian State Railways (🖳 http://www.bdz.bg). Includes an online train timetable.

Discover Bulgaria (🖳 http://www.discover-bulgaria.com). Sightseeing and travel information.

ETAP Group (🖳 http://etapgroup.com/etap/en). One of Bulgaria's largest bus companies, with ticket pricing and times.

Euro Portal (🖳 http://www.evroportal.bg). News and information on Bulgaria's accession to the EU.

Government.BG (🖳 http://www.government.bg). Links to and information on all Bulgarian government ministries.

My Bulgaria (🖳 http://www.mybulgaria.info). Comprehensive source of information for living and buying in Bulgaria, with vibrant and useful forums.

National Statistical Institute (🖳 http://www.nsi.bg). Everything you need to know about Bulgaria, in numbers!

Sofia (🖳 http://www.sofia.com). Tourist and general information about the capital.

Sofia News Agency (Novinite) (🖳 http://www.novinite.com). Daily online news service.

Tourism Bulgaria (🖳 http://www.tourism-bulgaria.com). General information.

Travel Bulgaria (🖳 http://www.travel-bulgaria.com). General tourist information.

Expatriate Sites

An American Abroad (🖳 http://www.anamericanabroad.com). This website offers advice, information and services to Americans abroad.

Australians Abroad (🖳 http://www.australiansabroad.com). Information for Australians with a large and busy forum to exchange information and advice.

British Expatriates (🖳 http://www.britishexpat.com). This website keeps British expatriates in touch with events and information about the UK.

Escape Artist (🖳 http://www.escapeartist.com). An excellent website and probably the most comprehensive, packed with resources, links and directories covering most expatriate destinations. You can also subscribe to the monthly online expatriate magazines, *Escape from America* and *Offshore Real Estate Quarterly*.

Expat Exchange (🖳 http://www.expatexchange.com). Reportedly the largest online community for English-speaking expatriates, provides a series of articles on relocation and also a question and answer facility through its expatriate network.

Expat World (🖳 http://www.expatworld.net). 'The newsletter of international living.' Contains a wealth of information for American and British expatriates, including a subscription newsletter.

Expatriate Expert (🖳 http://www.expatexpert.com). A website run by expatriate Robin Pascoe, providing invaluable advice and support.

Expatriates.com (🖳 http://www.expatriates.com). Online community for expatriates in most cities and countries of the world, with a big section on housing available and wanted.

Export.gov (🖳 http://www.export.gov). A huge website providing a wealth of information principally for Americans planning to trade and invest abroad but useful for anyone planning a move abroad.

Family Life Abroad (🖳 http://www.familylifeabroad.com). A wealth of information and articles on coping with family life abroad.

Foreign Wives Club (🖳 http://www.foreignwivesclub.com). An online community for women in bicultural marriages.

Real Post Reports (🖳 http://www.realpostreports.com). Provides relocation services, recommended reading lists and plenty of 'real-life' stories containing anecdotes and impressions written by expatriates in just about every city of the world.

Southern Cross Group (🖳 http://www.southern-cross-group.org). 'The voice for Australians overseas.' Advocacy group providing support and information for expatriate Australians.

Third Culture Kids (🖳 http://www.tckworld.com). A website designed for expatriate children living abroad.

UK Trade and Investment (🖳 http://www.uktradeinvest.gov.uk). A government website that aims to provide trade and investment information on just about every country in the world. Even if you aren't planning to do business abroad, the information is comprehensive and up to date.

Women of the World (🖳 http://www.wow-net.org). A website designed for female expatriates anywhere in the world.

World Travel Guide (🖳 http://www.wtgonline.com). A general website for world travellers and expatriates.

Worldwise Directory (🖳 http://www.suzylamplugh.org/worldwise). This website, run by the Suzy Lamplugh charity for personal safety, provides a useful directory of countries with practical information and special emphasis on safety, particularly for women.

Travel Information & Warnings

The websites listed below provide daily-updated information about the political situation and natural disasters around the world, plus general travel and health advice and embassy addresses.

Australian Department of Foreign Affairs and Trade (🖥 http://www.smartraveller.gov.au).

British Foreign and Commonwealth Office (🖥 http://www. fco.gov.uk/travel).

Canadian Department of Foreign Affairs (🖥 http://www.fac-aec.gc.ca). Also publishes a series of useful free booklets for Canadians moving abroad.

New Zealand Ministry of Foreign Affairs and Trade (🖥 http://www.mft.govt.nz).

SaveWealth Travel (🖥 http://www.savewealth.com/travel/warnings).

The Travel Doctor (🖥 http://www.tmvc.com.au). Contains a country-by-country vaccination guide.

Travel Documents (🖥 http://www.traveldocs.com). Useful information about travel, specific countries and documents needed to travel.

Travel for Kids (🖥 http://www.travelforkids.com). Advice on travelling with children around the world.

US State Department (🖥 http://www.state.gov/travel).

World Health Organization (🖥 http://www.who.int).

Appendix D: WEIGHTS & MEASURES

Bulgaria uses the metric system of measurement. Those who are more familiar with the imperial system will find the tables on the following pages useful. Some comparisons are approximate but are close enough for most everyday uses. In addition to the variety of measurement systems used, clothes sizes often vary considerably with the manufacturer (as we all know only too well!). Try all clothes on before buying and don't be afraid to return something if, when you try it on at home, you decide it doesn't fit (most shops will exchange goods or give a refund).

Women's Clothes

Continental	34	36	38	40	42	44	46	48	50	52
UK	8	10	12	14	16	18	20	22	24	26
US	6	8	10	12	14	16	18	20	22	24

Pullovers

	Women's						Men's					
Continental	40	42	44	46	48	50	44	46	48	50	52	54
UK	34	36	38	40	42	44	34	36	38	40	42	44
US	34	36	38	40	42	44	sm	med	lar	xl		

Men's Shirts

Continental	36	37	38	39	40	41	42	43	44	46
UK/US	14	14	15	15	16	16	17	17	18	-

Men's Underwear

Continental	5	6	7	8	9	10
UK	34	36	38	40	42	44
US	sm	med		lar	xl	

Note: sm = small, med = medium, lar = large, xl = extra large

Children's Clothes

Continental	92	104	116	128	140	152
UK	16/18	20/22	24/26	28/30	32/34	36/38
US	2	4	6	8	10	12

Children's Shoes

Continental	18	19	20	21	22	23	24	25	26	27	28	29	30	31	32
UK/US	2	3	4	4	5	6	7	7	8	9	10	11	11	12	13

Continental	33	34	35	36	37	38
UK/US	1	2	2	3	4	5

Shoes (Women's and Men's)

Continental	35	36	37	37	38	39	40	41	42	42	43	44
UK	2	3	3	4	4	5	6	7	7	8	9	9
US	4	5	5	6	6	7	8	9	9	10	10	11

Weight

Imperial	Metric	Metric	Imperial
1oz	28.35g	1g	0.035oz
1lb*	454g	100g	3.5oz
1cwt	50.8kg	250g	9oz
1 ton	1,016kg	500g	18oz
2,205lb	1 tonne	1kg	2.2lb

Length

Imperial	Metric	Metric	Imperial
1in	2.54cm	1cm	0.39in
1ft	30.48cm	1m	3ft 3.25in
1yd	91.44cm	1km	0.62mi
1mi	1.6km	8km	5mi

Capacity

Imperial	Metric	Metric	Imperial
1 UK pint	0.57 litre	1 litre	1.75 UK pints
1 US pint	0.47 litre	1 litre	2.13 US pints
1 UK gallon	4.54 litres	1 litre	0.22 UK gallon
1 US gallon	3.78 litres	1 litre	0.26 US gallon

Note: An American 'cup' = around 250ml or 0.25 litre.

Area

Imperial	Metric	Metric	Imperial
1 sq. in	0.45 sq. cm	1 sq. cm	0.15 sq. in
1 sq. ft	0.09 sq. m	1 sq. m	10.76 sq. ft
1 sq. yd	0.84 sq. m	1 sq. m	1.2 sq. yds
1 acre	0.4 hectares	1 hectare	2.47 acres
1 sq. mile	2.56 sq. km	1 sq. km	0.39 sq. mile

Note: An *are* is one-hundredth of a hectare or 100m^2.

Temperature

°Celsius	°Fahrenheit	
0	32	(freezing point of water)
5	41	
10	50	
15	59	
20	68	
25	77	
30	86	
35	95	
40	104	
50	122	

Notes: The boiling point of water is 100°C / 212°F.

Normal body temperature (if you're alive and well) is 37°C / 98.4°F.

Temperature Conversion

Celsius to Fahrenheit: multiply by 9, divide by 5 and add 32. (For a quick and approximate conversion, double the Celsius temperature and add 30.)

Fahrenheit to Celsius: subtract 32, multiply by 5 and divide by 9. (For a quick and approximate conversion, subtract 30 from the Fahrenheit temperature and divide by 2.)

Oven Temperatures

Gas	Electric	
	°F	°C
-	225–250	110–120
1	275	140
2	300	150
3	325	160
4	350	180
5	375	190
6	400	200
7	425	220
8	450	230
9	475	240

Air Pressure

PSI	Bar
10	0.5
20	1.4
30	2
40	2.8

APPENDIX E: MAP

The map of Bulgaria opposite shows the regions of Bulgaria (listed below), whose capital cities have the same name. A map showing major towns and geographical features is on page 6.

Blagoevgrad

Bourgas

Dobrich

Gabrovo

Haskovo

Kardzhali

Kyustendil

Lovech

Montana

Pazardzhik

Pernik

Pleven

Plovdiv

Razgrad

Ruse

Shumen

Silistra

Sliven

Smolyan

Sofia

Sofia District

Stara Zagora

Targovishte

Varna

Veliko Tarnovo

Vidin

Vratsa

Yambol

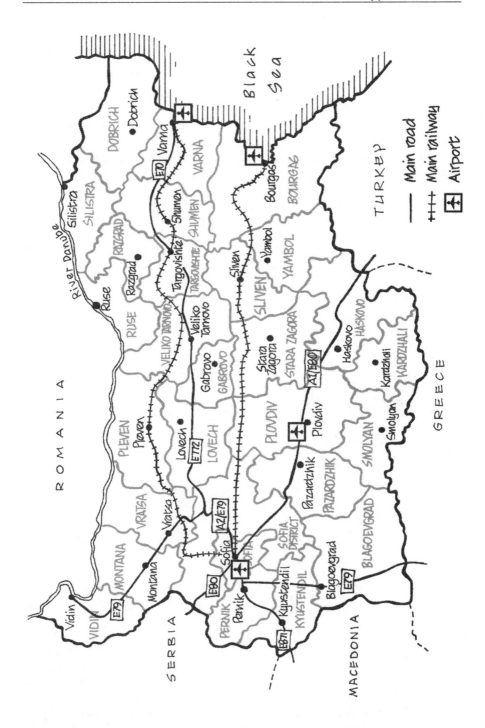

Appendix F: AIRLINE SERVICES

Scheduled Flights

Currently only British Airways and Bulgaria Air fly direct to Bulgaria from the UK throughout the year. Other airlines with connections to Bulgaria (usually via an airport in the airline's home country) are also listed below. Information was correct in January 2006.

Direct Flights

Flight	Origin	Destination
British Airways (BA890)	London Heathrow	Sofia
British Airways (BA2860)	London Gatwick	Varna (March to September)
Bulgaria Air (FB496)	London Gatwick	Sofia
Bulgaria Air (FB498)	London Gatwick	Varna
Bulgaria Air (FB502)	London Heathrow	Bourgas
Hemus Air (DU852)	London Heathrow	Sofia

Airlines

Code	Airline	UK Tel. No.	Website
AF	Air France	0870-142 4343	http://www.airfrance.co.uk
AT	Alitalia	020-8745 8297	http://www.alitalia.co.uk
AA	Austrian	0870-124 2625	http://www.aua.com
BA	British Airways	0870-850 9850	http://www.britishairways.com
BG	Bulgaria Air	020-7637 7637	http://www.bulgaria-air.co.uk
CZ	Czech (CSA)	0870-444 3747	http://www.czechairlines.co.uk
KL	KLM	0870-507 4074	http://www.klmuk.com

LT	Lufthansa	0845-773 7747	http://www.lufthansa.com
LO	LOT	0845-601 0949	http://www.lot.com
MH	Malev	0870-909 0577	http://www.malev.hu
SW	Swiss	0845-601 0956	http://www.swiss.com

Charter Flights

The main charter airlines flying to Bulgaria from the UK are listed below. It's sometimes possible to get a 'flight only' package with a charter airline, which can be cheaper than a scheduled flight (although the dates are less flexible).

Code	Airline	Telephone	Website
AV	Avro	0870-458 2841	http://www.avro.co.uk
BH	Balkan Holidays	0845-130 1114	http://www.balkanholidays.co.uk
EX	Excel	0870-169 0169	http://www.xl.com
FC	First Choice	0870-850 3999	http://www.firstchoice.co.uk
FL	Fly-4-Less	0800-011 1185	http://www.fly-4-less.com
TF	Thomson Fly	0870-190 0737	http://www.thomsonfly.com

INDEX

R

LIVING AND WORKING SERIES

Living and Working books are essential reading for anyone planning to spend time abroad, including holiday-home owners, retirees, visitors, business people, migrants, students and even extra-terrestrials! They're packed with important and useful information designed to help you **avoid costly mistakes and save both time and money.** Topics covered include how to:

- Find a job with a good salary & conditions
- Obtain a residence permit
- Avoid and overcome problems
- Find your dream home
- Get the best education for your family
- Make the best use of public transport
- Endure local motoring habits
- Obtain the best health treatment
- Stretch your money further
- Make the most of your leisure time
- Enjoy the local sporting life
- Find the best shopping bargains
- Insure yourself against most eventualities
- Use post office and telephone services
- Do numerous other things not listed above

Living and Working books are the most comprehensive and up-to-date source of practical information available about everyday life abroad. They aren't, however, boring text books, but interesting and entertaining guides written in a highly readable style.

Discover what it's really like to live and work abroad!

Order your copies today by phone, fax, post or email from: Survival Books, PO Box 3780, YEOVIL, BA21 5WX, United Kingdom (☎/🖨 +44 (0)1935-700060, ✉ sales@survivalbooks.net, 💻 www.survivalbooks.net).

BUYING A HOME SERIES

Buying a Home books, including *Buying, Selling & Letting Property*, are essential reading for anyone planning to purchase property abroad. They're packed with vital information to guide you through the property purchase jungle and help you **avoid the sort of disasters that can turn your dream home into a nightmare!** Topics covered include:

- Avoiding problems
- Choosing the region
- Finding the right home and location
- Estate agents
- Finance, mortgages and taxes
- Home security
- Utilities, heating and air-conditioning
- Moving house and settling in
- Renting and letting
- Permits and visas
- Travelling and communications
- Health and insurance
- Renting a car and driving
- Retirement and starting a business
- And much, much more!

Buying a Home books are the most comprehensive and up-to-date source of information available about buying property abroad. Whether you want a detached house, townhouse or apartment, a holiday or a permanent home, these books will help make your dreams come true.

Save yourself time, trouble and money!

Order your copies today by phone, fax, post or email from: Survival Books, PO Box 3780, YEOVIL, BA21 5WX, United Kingdom (☎/▤ +44 (0)1935-700060, ✉ sales@survivalbooks.net, 🖥 www.survivalbooks.net).

OTHER SURVIVAL BOOKS

The Alien's Guides: *The Alien's Guides to Britain* and *France* will help you to appreciate the peculiarities (in both senses) of the British and French.

The Best Places to Buy a Home in France/Spain: The most comprehensive homebuying guides to France and Spain, containing detailed regional profiles.

Buying, Selling and Letting Property: The most comprehensive and up-to-date source of information on buying, selling and letting property in the UK.

Earning Money From Your Home: Essential guides to earning income from property in France and Spain, including short- and long-term letting.

Foreigners in France/Spain: Triumphs & Disasters: Real-life experiences of people who have emigrated to France and Spain, recounted in their own words.

Lifelines: Essential guides to life in specific regions of France and Spain. See order form for a list of current titles in the series.

Making a Living: Essential guides to self-employment and starting a business in France and Spain.

Renovating & Maintaining Your French Home: The ultimate guide to renovating and maintaining your dream home in France.

Retiring: Retiring Abroad is the most comprehensive source of practical information available about retiring to a foreign country. Retiring Abroad in Spain and Retiring Abroad in France provide up-to-date information on the two most popular retirement destinations.

Rural Living in France: The most comprehensive source of practical information available about life in rural France.

Shooting Caterpillars in Spain: The hilarious but compelling story of two innocents abroad in the depths of Andalusia in the late '80s.

Surprised by France: Even after living there for ten years, Donald Carroll finds plenty of surprises in the Hexagon.

Broaden your horizons with Survival Books!

Order your copies today by phone, fax, post or email from: Survival Books, PO Box 3780, YEOVIL, BA21 5WX, United Kingdom (☎/▤ +44 (0)1935-700060, ✉ sales@survivalbooks.net, 💻 www.survivalbooks.net).

Qty.	Title	Price (incl. p&p)			Total
		UK	Europe	World	
	The Alien's Guide to Britain	£7.45	£9.45	£12.95	
	The Alien's Guide to France	£7.45	£9.45	£12.95	
	The Best Places to Buy a Home in France	£14.45	£16.45	£19.95	
	The Best Places to Buy a Home in Spain	£14.45	£16.45	£19.95	
	Buying a Home Abroad	£14.45	£16.45	£19.95	
	Buying a Home in Australia & NZ	£14.45	£16.45	£19.95	
	Buying a Home in Cyprus	£14.45	£16.45	£19.95	
	Buying a Home in Florida	£14.45	£16.45	£19.95	
	Buying a Home in France	£14.45	£16.45	£19.95	
	Buying a Home in Greece	£14.45	£16.45	£19.95	
	Buying a Home in Ireland	£12.45	£14.45	£17.95	
	Buying a Home in Italy	£14.45	£16.45	£19.95	
	Buying a Home in Portugal	£14.45	£16.45	£19.95	
	Buying a Home in South Africa	£14.45	£16.45	£19.95	
	Buying a Home in Spain	£14.45	£16.45	£19.95	
	Buying, Letting & Selling Property	£12.45	£14.45	£17.95	
	Buying or Renting a Home in London	£14.45	£16.45	£19.95	
	Buying or Renting a Home in New York	£14.45	£16.45	£19.95	
	Earning Money From Your French Home	£14.45	£16.45	£19.95	
	Earning Money From Your Spanish Home	£14.45	£16.45	£19.95	
	Foreigners in France: Triumphs & Disasters	£12.45	£14.45	£17.95	
	Foreigners in Spain: Triumphs & Disasters	£12.45	£14.45	£17.95	
	Costa Blanca Lifeline	£12.45	£14.45	£17.95	
	Costa del Sol Lifeline	£12.45	£14.45	£17.95	
	Dordogne/Lot Lifeline	£12.45	£14.45	£17.95	
	Normandy Lifeline	£12.45	£14.45	£17.95	
	Poitou-Charentes Lifeline	£11.95	£14.45	£17.95	
	Provence-Côte d'Azur Lifeline	£12.45	£14.45	£17.95	
	Living & Working Abroad	£15.45	£17.45	£20.95	
	Living & Working in America	£17.45	£19.45	£22.95	
	Living & Working in Australia	£17.45	£19.45	£22.95	
	Living & Working in Britain	£17.45	£19.45	£22.95	
	Living & Working in Canada	£17.45	£19.45	£22.95	
	Living & Working in the European Union	£17.45	£19.45	£22.95	
	Total carried forward (see over)				

ORDER FORM

Qty.	Title	UK	Europe	World	Total
			Total brought forward		
		UK	Europe	World	
	Living & Working in the Far East	£17.45	£19.45	£22.95	
	Living & Working in France	£17.45	£19.45	£22.95	
	Living & Working in Germany	£17.45	£19.45	£22.95	
	L&W in the Gulf States & Saudi Arabia	£17.45	£19.45	£22.95	
	L&W in Holland, Belgium & Luxembourg	£15.45	£17.45	£20.95	
	Living & Working in Ireland	£15.45	£17.45	£20.95	
	Living & Working in Italy	£17.45	£19.45	£22.95	
	Living & Working in London	£14.45	£16.45	£19.95	
	Living & Working in New Zealand	£17.45	£19.45	£22.95	
	Living & Working in Spain	£17.45	£19.45	£22.95	
	Living & Working in Switzerland	£17.45	£19.45	£22.95	
	Making a Living in France	£14.45	£16.45	£19.95	
	Making a Living in Spain	£14.45	£16.45	£19.95	
	Renovating Your French Home	£17.45	£19.45	£22.95	
	Retiring Abroad	£15.45	£17.45	£20.95	
	Retiring in France	£14.45	£16.45	£19.95	
	Retiring in Spain	£14.45	£16.45	£19.95	
	Rural Living in France	£14.45	£16.45	£19.95	
	Shooting Caterpillars in Spain	£10.45	£12.45	£15.95	
	Surprised by France	£12.45	£14.45	£17.95	
				Grand Total	

Order your copies today by phone, fax, post or email from: Survival Books, PO Box 3780, YEOVIL, BA21 5WX, United Kingdom (☎/▤ +44 (0)1935-700060, ✉ sales@survivalbooks.net, ▣ www.survivalbooks.net). If you aren't entirely satisfied, simply return them to us within 14 days for a full and unconditional refund.

I enclose a cheque for the grand total/Please charge my Amex/Delta/Maestro (Switch)/MasterCard/Visa card as follows. (delete as applicable)

Card No. _ _ _ _   _ _ _ _   _ _ _ _   _ _ _ _   Security Code* _ _ _

Expiry date _____   Issue number (Maestro/Switch only) _____

Signature _____   Tel. No. _____

NAME _____

ADDRESS _____

_____

* The security code is the last three digits on the signature strip.